TEACHING FOR JUSTICE: IMPLEMENTING SOCIAL JUSTICE IN THE LIS CLASSROOM

This book is number one in the
Series on Critical Race Studies and Multiculturalism in LIS,
Rose L. Chou and Annie Pho, series editors.

TEACHING FOR JUSTICE: IMPLEMENTING SOCIAL JUSTICE IN THE LIS CLASSROOM

Edited by
Nicole A. Cooke and Miriam E. Sweeney

LIBRARY JUICE PRESS
SACRAMENTO, CA

Published in 2017 by Library Juice Press

Library Juice Press
PO Box 188784
Sacramento, CA 95822

http://libraryjuicepress.com/

This book is printed on acid-free, sustainably-sourced paper.

Library of Congress Cataloging-in-Publication Data

Names: Cooke, Nicole A., editor. | Sweeney, Miriam E., editor.
Title: Teaching for justice : implementing social justice in the LIS classroom / edited By Nicole A. Cooke and Miriam E. Sweeney.
Description: Sacramento, CA : Library Juice Press, 2017. | Series: Series on critical race studies and multiculturalism in LIS ; 1 | Includes bibliographical references and index.
Identifiers: LCCN 2016017740 | ISBN 9781634000178
Subjects: LCSH: Library education--Social aspects. | Library education--Social aspects--United States. | Social justice--Study and teaching (Graduate) | Social justice--Study and teaching (Graduate)--United States. | Library schools--Curricula. | Library schools--Curricula--United States.
Classification: LCC Z668 .T375 2017 | DDC 020.71/1--dc23
LC record available at https://lccn.loc.gov/2016017740

Contents

INTRODUCTION

Nicole A. Cooke and Miriam E. Sweeney

This book is a response to the rising awareness among Library and Information Science (LIS) educators of the need to actively integrate social justice frameworks, values, and strategies into LIS teaching practices and curricula as a foundation for training the next generation of just and critically-minded library and information professionals. "Teaching for justice" is a timely topic, as internal conversations about professional identity, status, scope of the field, and the role of LIS education are playing out against a panoply of complex external forces that include: decreased public funding for education and social services, increased state spending on mass incarceration and defense, widening wealth gaps, and the privatization of information. These are just some of the forces that are held in tension with LIS core professional values that emphasize access, democracy, public good, intellectual freedom, diversity, and social responsibility.[1] These tensions are felt in the lived experiences of members of our communities, and most keenly impact the opportunities and well-being of those belonging to oppressed and marginalized groups.

For instance, the #blacklivesmatter movement's protest of racialized state violence, police brutality and a discriminatory criminal justice

---

1. American Library Association, "Core Values of Librarianship," June 29, 2004, http://www.ala.org/advocacy/intfreedom/statementspols/corevalues.

system, along with the broader sustained call for racial justice in this nation, underscores the high-stakes implications of these tensions for people of color. Similarly, the continued violence levied against LGBTQ people in the midst of seeming gains for civil rights, such as the Supreme Court ruling on same-sex marriage, highlights the complex and uneven ways in which inequality and oppression are expressed. Those at the margins—the poor, the young, people of color, trans and gender non-conforming persons—remain vulnerable to violence and have less access to economic resources, social support, and safety nets. The recent mass shooting at Pulse, a gay nightclub in Orlando with many Latinx and non-white patrons, was a tragic reminder of the intersectional dimensions that shape this violence and fear. Lastly, the climate for immigrants and Muslims has turned increasingly hostile during the last presidential campaign cycle, with candidates on each side of the aisle calling for more surveillance initiatives and an increased reach of data gathering in the name of combating "terrorism." These examples demonstrate what is at stake for our user communities, and underscore the importance of training LIS professionals to make connections between the field's core values and their professional practice. It is the responsibility of LIS educators to actively engage these tensions in their courses as part and parcel of preparing students to responsibly attend to the complexities of professional practice in this landscape.

Libraries and librarians have the potential to serve as the frontlines of advocacy and information provision in their communities. Research demonstrates the critical community-building and informational roles that libraries take on in times of economic downturn,[2] natural disasters,[3] and social crises.[4] For example, recently, the Ferguson, Missouri and

2. Kathryn Sigler et al., "The Role of Public Libraries, the Internet, and Economic Uncertainty," in *Librarianship in Times of Crisis*, ed. Anne Woodworth, Advances in Librarianship 34 (Bingley, UK: Emerald, 2011), 19-35.

3. John Carlo Bertot et al., "Public Access Computing and Internet Access in Public Libraries: The Role of Public Libraries in E-Government and Emergency Situations," *First Monday* 11, no. 9 (September 4, 2006), http://uncommonculture.org/ojs/index.php/fm/article/view/1392

4. Timothy Inklebarger, "Ferguson's Safe Haven." *American Libraries Magazine*,

Baltimore, Maryland public libraries made headlines when they stayed resolutely open amidst school closings during the protests in their cities over the respective deaths of Michael Brown and Freddie Gray.[5] The subsequent responses from the library community in light of these (and other) tragic events resulted in interventions such as the creation and sharing of resources, libguides, and curricular guides to support learning and teaching about race, racism, and racial justice from librarians and LIS educators.[6] More recently, in the wake of the killings of Alton Sterling and Philandro Castile, a collective of youth librarians calling themselves "Storytime Underground" took to Twitter in support of the #blacklivesmatter movement, using social media to engage the public and profession in conversations about the library's role as an advocate for justice.[7] These examples are encouraging, demonstrating the ways that librarians can be change agents in their communities, working beyond the normative frameworks of their institutions in support of social justice goals.

Yet these examples also raise questions for LIS educators; are we, in fact, preparing students to engage in justice oriented professional practice? Do they have the appropriate knowledge and tools available to them to name, and interrogate, structures of power and inequality as they impact information professions and user communities? We cannot

---

(November 10, 2014), http://americanlibrariesmagazine.org/2014/11/10/fergusons-safe-haven/.

5. Megan Cottrell, "Libraries Respond to Community Needs in Times of Crisis," *American Libraries Magazine*, (May 15, 2015), http://americanlibrariesmagazine.org/2015/05/15/libraries-respond-to-community-needs-in-times-of-crisis/.

6. Nicole Pagowsky and Niamh Wallace, "Black Lives Matter! Shedding Library Neutrality Rhetoric for Social Justice," *College & Research Libraries* News 76, no. 4 (2015): 196–214. For examples of such resources, see: San Francisco Public Schools http://sfusd.libguides.com/blacklivesmatter; The Oakland Public Library http://oaklandlibrary.org/blogs/from-main-library/listen-learn-participate-blacklivesmatter-resource-series; and Hennepin County Library http://www.slj.com/2016/07/books-media/librarian-creates-blacklivesmatter-booklist-for-teens/#.

7. Clarissa-Jan Lim, "Librarians Respond on Twitter to the Idea That They Shouldn't Have Opinions," *A Plus* (July 15, 2016), http://aplus.com/a/black-lives-matter-storytime-underground.

expect that students will somehow magically be prepared to take part in conversations about power and privilege, or be automatically culturally competent and self-reflective in their practice. These are skill sets that have to be intentionally developed, refined, and practiced as part of a life-long education process. Additionally, many LIS students come to their graduate education without prior exposure to cultural studies, gender and feminist studies, or ethnic and race studies courses. Initiating conversations about power reflected in systems of race, gender, class, and sexuality at this late stage provides a challenge for LIS educators who are effectually tasked with teaching students proficiency in these areas along with discipline-specific knowledge. Thus, spreading social justice education across the LIS curriculum is crucial for sharing the burden among educators, as well as for normalizing these values to our students.

Lastly, it is crucial that students come to think of justice-oriented professional practice as part and parcel of everyday LIS work, not just as a component to exceptional moments such as those illustrated in the examples at Ferguson and Baltimore. The real stakes are in keeping justice anchored as a foundational and persistent feature of LIS professional norms and status quo. Social justice as an ethical framework can guide daily activities such as policy development, collection building, interpersonal interactions, reference work, information literacy, programming, outreach activities, and cataloging. Our role as LIS educators is to make these connections explicit for our students and provide them with the tools and strategies they can use as they go forward. This book is a contribution to gathering the voices of LIS educators who employ social justice frameworks in their courses, with the purpose of sharing ideas and strategies for teaching. It is our hope that the chapters in this book spark conversations, creativity, and solidarity among LIS educators towards teaching for justice.

The ALISE Conference Workshop

In January of 2015 the editors of this volume, along with Kevin Rioux, co-organized a workshop at the annual Association of Library and Information Science Educators' (ALISE) conference. Entitled Social Justice in the LIS Classroom: Making it Happen, it was a half-day pre-conference professional development opportunity that addressed issues of social justice and their potential application in the library and information science classroom. Fifty faculty members, adjunct instructors, doctoral students, and other library and information scholars gathered together to learn how to better incorporate social justice into their course content. The workshop was made possible by the overall conference theme of "Mirrors & Windows: Reflections on Social Justice and Re-Imagining LIS Education" (http://www.alise.org/alise-2015-conference). It was an uncommon, if not overdue, opportunity to specifically focus on the issue of social justice and its relationship to all facets of LIS education.

The workshop had a three-part structure that provided the pedagogical foundation and motivation for teaching social justice as a full course or as a theme within topic courses that seemingly "have no relationship" to such issues. The first portion presented social justice as a theory for pedagogy; the second portion featured a series of lightning talks from LIS classroom instructors; and the third portion gave participants the opportunity to brainstorm together, share experiences, and develop a plan of action for innovating in their classrooms.

As the workshop organizers, who are also full time classroom instructors who teach through a lens of social justice and critical information practice, our goal was to impart the importance and history of social justice theory and practice within the information professions; articulate reasons for explicitly incorporating social justice thinking into the LIS curriculum; provide examples of LIS faculty and information professionals who use social justice theory to drive their teaching and practice; and help participants develop individualized goals and strategies for the inclusion of social justice elements in their teaching / curriculum / institution. Participants left prepared with strong arguments for inclusion of social justice in their LIS classroom, curriculum, and school policies; an array of practical techniques intended to secure such inclusion; and—as a result of discussion and hands-on application—a sense of renewed confidence in advocating for incorporation of social justice as a mainstay of LIS education.

As the workshop came to a close, the organizers and participants wanted to keep the conversation going, share it with a wider audience, and encourage collaboration among educators in the service of infusing social justice across the LIS curriculum. This volume highlights the commitment and efforts of LIS faculty and instructors, many of whom spoke at the January workshop, who feature social justice theory and strategies in their courses and classroom practices. This book is geared towards LIS instructors who have begun to incorporate social justice into their course content, as well as those who are interested in learning more about how to better or further address social justice in their classrooms. This text also serves as a lasting document of the workshop, and will hopefully serve as an ongoing source of pedagogical inspiration for social justice educators in LIS and beyond.

Social Justice in LIS

Social justice is certainly related to diversity, but they are not exactly the same. While a recognition and commitment to diversity is about including and incorporating different cultures and perspectives, social justice asks that we go beyond including and incorporating. Social justice implies action, it challenges us to work towards the betterment, equality, and respect for those we want to include. Given that the societal landscape is increasingly complex and often contentious, and the communities served by libraries are increasingly diverse and intersectional, it becomes imperative that information professionals be equipped to recognize, celebrate, and advocate for diverse communities. It therefore becomes imperative that LIS classrooms be proactive in preparing our graduates for such work.

Conversations about social justice and diversity in LIS have been going on for decades, but it seems these conversations were cyclical and often died down before lasting change had the opportunity to occur. Surely there are many wonderful initiatives related to diversity that are evident (e.g., diversity recruitment initiatives and scholarships), but where are the social justice initiatives? In the last few years the conversation has begun again, this time with more focus on social justice. In addition to the aforementioned 2015 ALISE conference, the LIS literature is taking more notice of social justice. The publisher of this volume, Library Juice Press, has demonstrated a commitment to publishing in this area, and important professional journals have published special issues dedicated to thoughts, ideas, and research that center issues of social justice and how they relates to and influence LIS research, pedagogy, and curriculum development (e.g., the Fall 2015 issue of *Library Trends* and the January 2016 issue of *Library Quarterly*).[8]

There are many explicit definitions of social justice, some that lean more towards issues of diversity, others that emphasize human rights, and still others that promote radical action. The common thread through the definitions is the desire to disrupt the status quo. "Social justice is about giving voice to communities who have been forced into silence; social justice is about equity and equal access."[9] In their work *Public Libraries and Social Justice*, Vincent and Pateman[10] suggest that libraries and information professionals should not only embrace issues of equality and diversity, but should foster an active and collaborative relationship with the communities being served in an effort to truly uncover and serve their needs.

How can this complexity, which is a combination of awareness and action, best be taught in the classroom? In part, teaching and imparting social justice sensibilities involves working with students on the development of critical consciousness and cultural competence, and helping students reflect upon the role they might want to play in the

---

8. Bharat Bharat Mehra, ed., "Social Justice in Library and Information Science and Services," special issue, *Library Trends* 64, no. 2 (2015); Paul Jaeger, ed., "Information, Community, Policy," special issue, *Library Quarterly* 86, no. 2 (2016).

9. Humboldt State University, "Social Justice Summit," 2015, http://www2.humboldt.edu.summit/.

10. John Pateman and John Vincent, *Public Libraries and Social Justice* (Farnham, UK: Ashgate, 2012).

movement. This can be a tall order, and it may require a more intense and risky approach to the teaching and learning process, but it can be done. The chapters you will read in this volume are examples of the variety of ways social justice is being taught in LIS classrooms around the United States. These authors/educators offer their personal reflections and strategies, and detail the energy, creativity, and struggles that manifest in their social justice classrooms.

Hopefully, this book will make visible viable pedagogical models, validate the experiences of those currently trying to do this work in their classrooms, spur more conversations, conference presentations, and research; and engender a larger community that allows social justice educators a space and opportunity to create, collect, and share resources that support social justice teaching and learning.

Teaching for Justice

The following chapters are reflections from library and information science educators about strategies for supporting a justice-oriented LIS curriculum. All of the contributors have experience teaching either a stand-alone course related to social justice, or otherwise infuse social justice principles and frameworks across the LIS curriculum in their courses. These reflections are conceived as conversations among LIS educators about teaching, and they cover theoretical, personal, and analytic takes on teaching practice. Coming out of the ALISE workshop, we realized that not only did the educators want practical takeaways and strategies to carry over into their classrooms, but they also wanted to discuss their fears, mistakes, and the challenges associated with teaching contested subjects such as race, gender, and sexuality in their classes. The contributions in this volume, therefore, represent the range of these desires from multiple perspectives and subject positions. The book is structured thematically, beginning with potential theoretical frameworks for further developing LIS-specific conceptions of social justice in LIS curricula. The next set of chapters explore various challenges associated with teaching social justice topics in the classroom including implementing critical pedagogy in the classroom, exploring power and privilege in classroom dynamics, and adapting social justice activities to the online course environment. The final chapters explore justice-oriented approaches for learning opportunities and service initiatives outside the traditional classroom.

Kevin Rioux articulates a "unified social justice stance for LIS curricula" to help bridge potentially disparate conceptual understandings of social justice within the field. He begins by tracing the ways that social justice values have been integrated into core services and professional values over the history of the profession, acknowledging the "blind spots" of power and privilege that have shaped these same initiatives. Rioux suggests that the diffuse understandings and meanings of social justice within the field create barriers for LIS educators in terms of advancing common objectives and forming an "LIS-specific framework of social justice." He observes that the neo-liberal context of higher education and conservative institutional environments present additional hurdles for educators attempting to advance social justice education in the LIS classroom. Rioux argues that a unified social justice stance for the profession has the potential to provide justification and support for educators in mitigating these barriers by linking together diffuse efforts of social action across LIS, while at the same time promoting the theoretical deepening of social justice engagement in the field.

John Burgess suggests sustainability theory as a potential framework for social justice in LIS that is compatible with extant professional values, such as fair and equitable access to information and the public good. Burgess argues that the benefit of sustainability theory for LIS is the emphasis on long-term thinking and the development of ethical practices that contribute to the flourishing of all humans, not just in the present but well into the future. This "long game" approach requires LIS professionals to rethink the creation, management, preservation, and protection of information in terms of broader environmental and social impacts across time, for all of humanity. Burgess identifies the strengths of sustainability as a justice advocacy framework in terms of the interconnectedness of global environmental and human interests.

By mapping sustainability ethics to the American Library Association (ALA) accreditation standards and student learning outcomes for degree granting LIS graduate programs, he provides strategies for integrating sustainability theory into course modules, stand alone courses, and across curricula.

Robin Kurz offers a candid personal reflection of her own awakening to critical and feminist pedagogy as a doctoral student in LIS, and her resultant journey as an LIS faculty member transforming this theory into praxis through the development and teaching of her own courses. Kurz describes reflection and reflexivity as both a feminist practice and the foundational elements of engaged pedagogy. She describes the "first tentative steps" of making transgressive changes to her courses through the centering of social justice topics, including issues of race and racism and critiques of power. In the spirit of transparency and sharing, Kurz showcases her struggles, strategies, and fears as she works to dislodge prevailing paradigms and assumptions about the profession from the curriculum by explicitly turning the classroom conversation to questions of power, privilege, and (in)equalities. She shares specific readings, lesson planning tips, and classroom activities that have been successful (and unsuccessful) in her courses. Through her reflections, Kurz reminds us that the process of teaching social justice requires a parallel journey of learning and reflecting.

Julie Winklestein asks, "In my work as a librarian, what would I have wanted to know about social justice? What information or training would have made a difference in the way I practiced my librarianship?" In answering these questions, she identifies the concept of "cultural humility" as a potential starting place for social justice librarianship. Winklestein adopts cultural humility as a concept that goes beyond popular notions of "cultural sensitivity," which focuses on respect and tolerance, and "cultural competence," which focuses on knowledge-building. Instead, she defines cultural humility as a practice that calls for self-evaluation and self-critique, particularly from members of the dominant culture, with the purpose of recognizing larger patterns of inequity and redressing power imbalances. Winklestein identifies cultural humility as a tool to address dominant "cultural scripts" that perpetuate stereotypes and contain messages about the superiority and inferiority of cultural and racial groups. Using examples from three different children's literature courses that she has taught, Winklestein provides examples of how she has used children's literature as a vehicle to enable discussions of cultural scripts in the classroom. Using cultural humility as the lens and framework for these discussions, she encourages the self-reflection of her students as they locate themselves as active participants in systems of power and privilege and consider justice-oriented interventions for professional practice.

Sandra Hughes-Hassell and **Katy Vance** introduce their master's level LIS course "Youth and Children's Services in a Diverse Society," which draws on critical race theory (CRT) and other cross-disciplinary frameworks to prepare students to work with diverse user communities. They discuss five key themes of CRT and demonstrate how they have embodied these themes in their course design. Hughes-Hassell and Vance center their course around tenets of CRT as a way to help youth services librarians "recognize the racist legacies of LIS structures, how racism and privilege still impact youth and libraries today, and, then, to devise ways to transform libraries into equitable institutions." The authors offer in-depth descriptions of their learning outcomes, the management and cultivation of the classroom environment to promote productive discussions, major assignments in the course, and challenges associated with teaching social justice in the LIS classroom.

Kafi Kumasi describes the challenges of translating courses that have a multicultural focus to the online learning environment. She notes that multicultural courses, more than others, tend to necessitate that students "bring their personal backgrounds and cultural experiences into the course activities." She points out that this can be more difficult in online course environments where students may feel, paradoxically, more free to speak and share due to a perceived anonymity in terms of their physical identity. Kumasi details how she mitigates these challenges while translating a class exercise that depends on physio-spatial movement, "The Privilege Walk," from a face-to-face to an online course exercise ("The Virtual Privilege Walk"). This chapter provides insight into the creative instructional design techniques that may be employed to support multicultural courses and justice-oriented pedagogies in online learning environments.

Sarah Park Dahlen notes that justice-oriented education needs to take place *before* graduate school and would ideally be integrated into the undergraduate curriculum. This training would better prepare LIS students entering their graduate programs for conversations about power and privilege in the field, and set up the expectation of these topics as part and parcel of their education. In this chapter, Dahlen describes the challenges and rewards associated with teaching her course, "Dismantling Racism: Social Justice and Children's Literature," to non-LIS undergraduate students. Dahlen uses the framework of the ALISE diversity statement's "ABCs," or the Affective, Behavioral, and Cognitive dimensions "that impact what we know, how we think, and how we behave in terms of diversity" as a lens to analyze her course structure and experience. Importantly, her reflection points to the challenges that women of color have in the classroom in terms of claiming authority, particularly when they ask their (mostly white) students to critique racist structures and ideologies of whiteness. Dahlen positions student feedback and reactions to the course in terms of both challenges and rewards, each side validating the need for integration of social justice education into earlier phases of the educational system.

Jenny Bossaller evaluates the intentions and outcomes of three graduate level LIS study abroad programs that she designed and taught at the University of Missouri. She argues that study abroad programs and other experiential education initiatives have the potential to be transformative for students in ways that can supplement a justice-oriented curriculum. Bossaller provides descriptions of the structure and student experiences for three separate courses, taking place in the United Kingdom, Ireland, and South Africa, respectively. She describes the intention of these trips as "broadening students' understanding of social justice issues in libraries and archives, and of exploring the responsibilities of libraries and archives with regard to national heritage and political viewpoints." Using student feedback as evidence, Bossaller finds that the study abroad experiences afforded her students the opportunities to consider contested viewpoints and counter-narratives of political events, step outside their zones of comfort and familiarity, develop greater senses of empathy, and form expanded views of the role of libraries and archives in society within varied cultural and political contexts.

Bharat Mehra and **Vandana Singh** discuss the integration of social justice agendas in the teaching of library management courses that were formed as a part of two grant projects associated with the "Information Technology Rural Library Master's Scholarship Program." These programs targeted library paraprofessionals in the Southern and Central Appalachian (SCA) region who were working part-time on their master's degrees in LIS at the University of Tennessee in a synchronous distance education program. In their chapter, Mehra and Singh extend the concept of "embedded librarian" beyond the institutional context (as in the academic library), towards a much broader regional and community-driven understanding. Students in this program belong to the communities they seek to transform; therefore they are uniquely positioned as change agents empowered to "transform their own situations and circumstances" through the embedded model. Mehra and Singh provide an overview of the program and associated courses, detailing the rural context of the communities, the library leadership-in-training cohorts, and the integration of social justice themes and frameworks that shape the program. They make a case for the power of embedded learning as a model that fosters empowerment and provides the professional skills needed for students to become change agents in their own communities.

The chapters in this book share similar themes beyond the common value and objective of implementing justice-oriented pedagogy in LIS. For example, multiple authors in this volume identify critical self-reflection as an important facet of social justice pedagogy that promotes reflexive action and interventions. Another theme is the importance of innovation and experimentation for rethinking course content, activities, and sites of learning in support of social justice objectives. Many of our authors identify children's literature and youth services as ideal topics and services in the field for teaching justice advocacy approaches. Finally, several of our authors address the affective and emotional dimensions associated with the labor of teaching social justice topics, including the particular challenges faculty of color may experience when mobilizing conversations about justice and power in their institutions. These themes point to the challenges associated with transforming the normative space of higher education that go beyond updating content modules in a given course. A social justice curriculum, by definition, critiques and disrupts the normative environment, exposing asymmetrical power relations within the classroom and discipline, for the purpose of formulating interventions and actions to redress inequalities associated with the status quo. It is our hope that the conversations in this book will inspire, validate, and support other LIS educators as they contribute to more broadly dislodging LIS from the power-blind narratives that continue to shape curricula, research, and professional practice in the field. To this end, we present the following chapters, along with resources that were shared as part of the ALISE workshop for instructors in the appendices of the book.

Bibliography

American Library Association. "Core Values of Libraianship." June 29, 2004. http://www.ala.org/advocacy/intfreedom/statementspols/corevalues.

Bertot, John Carlo, Paul T. Jaeger, Lesley A. Langa, and Charles R. McClure. "Public Access Computing and Internet Access in Public Libraries: The Role of Public Libraries in E-Government and Emergency Situations." *First Monday* 11, no. 9 (September 4, 2006). http://uncommonculture.org/ojs/index.php/fm/article/view/1392.

Cottrell, Megan. "Libraries Respond to Community Needs in Times of Crisis." *American Libraries*, May 15, 2015. http://americanlibrariesmagazine.org/2015/05/15/libraries-respond-to-community-needs-in-times-of-crisis/.

Humboldt State University. "Social Justice Summit." 2015. http://www2.humboldt.edu.summit/.

Inklebarger, Timothy. "Ferguson's Safe Haven." *American Libraries*, November 10, 2014. http://americanlibrariesmagazine.org/2014/11/10/fergusons-safe-haven/.

Jaeger, Paul, ed. "Information, Community, Policy." Special issue, *Library Quarterly* 86, no. 2 (2016).

Mehra, Bharat, ed. "Social Justice in Library and Information Science and Services." Special issue, *Library Trends* 64, no. 2 (2015).

Pagowsky, Nicole, and Niamh Wallace. "Black Lives Matter! Shedding Library Neutrality Rhetoric for Social Justice." *College & Research Libraries News* 76, no. 4 (2015): 196-214.

Pateman, John, and John Vincent. *Public Libraries and Social Justice.* Farnham, UK: Ashgate, 2012.

Sigler, Kathryn, Paul T. Jaeger, John Carlo Bertot, Abigail J. McDermott, Elizabeth J. DeCoster, and Lesley A. Langa. "The Role of Public Libraries, the Internet, and Economic Uncertainty." In *Librarianship in Times of Crisis*, edited by Anne Woodworth, 19-35. Advances in Librarianship 34. Bingley, UK: Emerald, 2011.

SECTION ONE:
THEORETICAL FRAMEWORKS FOR SOCIAL JUSTICE IN LIS CURRICULA

Chapter 1

Toward a Unified Social Justice Stance for Library and Information Science Curricula

Kevin Rioux

Introduction

Marginalization, discrimination, lack of economic opportunity, and unequal access to information resources are all among the fairness issues that continue to affect communities served by libraries and other information organizations. Professional mandates urge library and information science (LIS) workers to find renewed energy and better tools to be part of solutions to these and other social problems, and to find a sense of purpose in effecting positive social change.[1] Accordingly, *social justice* has become an increasingly popular term to describe the varied discussions and activities that engage LIS researchers and practitioners as they create agendas to address inequities.[2] Because they teach the

1. Paul T. Jaeger, Natalie Greene Taylor, and Ursula Gorham, *Libraries, Human Rights, and Social Justice: Enabling Access and Promoting Inclusion* (Lanham, MD: Rowman & Littlefield, 2015).

2. Johannes J. Britz and Shana Ponelis, "Social Justice and the International Flow of Knowledge with Specific Reference to African Scholars," *Aslib Proceedings* 64, no. 5 (2012): 462-77; Paul T. Jaeger et al., "Library Research and What Libraries Actually Do Now: Education, Inclusion, Social Services, Public Spaces, Digital Literacy, Social Justice, Human Rights, and Other Community Needs," *Library Quarterly* 84, no. 4 (October 1, 2014): 491-93, doi:10.1086/677785; Bharat Mehra, Kendra S. Albright, and Kevin Rioux, "A

theories and the nuts-and-bolts practice of LIS to new members of the profession, LIS educators also address these concerns by conveying real-world practice contexts in which future LIS professionals can make contributions to societal challenges.[3] To facilitate these pedagogical goals, LIS educators actively exchange understandings, opinions, and practices regarding social justice.[4] Given these undertakings, I offer this essay in which I share ideas, teaching strategies, literature resources, and conceptual frameworks collected and developed over the years as I've discussed social justice with LIS graduate students and colleagues.

I begin with a concise historical overview of social justice activity carried out by American public librarians. I demonstrate how LIS professionals have long been engaged in social justice activity, and I show how this history can be used as a preliminary context for discussing social justice in LIS education. I then suggest that efforts to create new, theoretically-robust social justice frameworks specific to LIS can facilitate social action by linking together diffuse terms and constructs that are currently used in social agendas pursued by LIS faculty and other information professionals. I conclude the essay with tips for using social

---

Practical Framework for Social Justice Research in the Information Professions," *Proceedings of the American Society for Information Science and Technology* 43, no. 1 (January 1, 2006): 1-10, doi:10.1002/meet.14504301275; Bharat Mehra, Kendra S. Albright, and Kevin Rioux, "A Practical Framework for Social Justice Research in the Information Professions," *Proceedings of the American Society for Information Science and Technology* 43, no. 1 (January 1, 2006): 1-10, doi:10.1002/meet.14504301275; Paul T. Jaeger et al., "The Virtuous Circle Revisited: Injecting Diversity, Inclusion, Rights, Justice, and Equity into LIS from Education to Advocacy," *Library Quarterly* 85, no. 2 (April 1, 2015): 150-71, doi:10.1086/680154; Suzie Allard, Bharat Mehra, and M. Asim Qayym, "Intercultural Leadership Toolkit for Librarians: Building Awareness to Effectively Serve Diverse Multicultural Populations.," *Education Libraries* 30, no. 1 (2007): 5–12.

3. Maria T. Accardi, Emily Drabinski, and Alana Kumbier, eds., *Critical Library Instruction: Theories and Methods* (Duluth, MN: Library Juice Press, 2010); Jeff Katz, "Addressing Special Needs and At-Risk Populations in Library Education Programs," *Public Libraries* 48, no. 6 (December 11, 2009): 34–37.

4. "ALISE 2015 Conference," accessed August 17, 2015, http://www.alise.org/2015-conference-2; "ALISE2015: ALISE Academy," accessed August 17, 2015, http://alise2015.sched.org/event/e1cc79c6188d269ec0faee1d146ffe5a.

justice metatheory as a tool for building the foundations of a unified social justice stance for LIS curricula, and for facilitating increasingly focused and effective theory-building and discourse for social justice in the field.

Social Justice: A Longstanding Characteristic of Librarianship

As emphasized throughout this essay, the term social justice is multifaceted and complex. It's not easy to settle upon a point of departure for introducing the topic of social justice in LIS to a classroom of students or to fellow LIS teachers. Whenever I engage with this topic, I've found it helpful to begin by underscoring the long track record that information professionals have with social justice agendas. Of course, the exact origin of social justice thinking in LIS is elusive. But given that public libraries in particular have positively enhanced the lives of millions of people over many years, a brief review of the emergence of public librarianship in the United States and the related social justice features of this emergence provides a logical and useful beginning point for discussing social justice work in LIS education contexts. This is not to suggest that social justice work is only performed in public libraries; that's certainly not the case. But the public in "public libraries" indicates that they are, indeed, social phenomena, and that they are surely expressions of an egalitarian impulse that values fairness.[5]

Kathleen de la Peña McCook has been a prolific observer of public libraries, and she characterizes them thusly: "The public library is simultaneously a tangible representation of humanity's ideals and a place where library services are delivered. The library can be a public space that inspires, sustains, and anchors a community's education and cultural

5. John Pateman and John Vincent, *Public Libraries and Social Justice* (Farnham, UK: Ashgate, 2010); John Mark Tucker and Edward A. Goedeken, "History of Libraries," in *Encyclopedia of Library and Information Sciences*, 3rd ed. (Taylor & Francis, 2009), 2080-95.

self-perception."[6] Certainly, this is a strong statement illustrating intrinsic links between the public library and the elements and ideals of fairness and equity. Keeping this statement in mind, in this section I summarize historic social justice actions within public librarianship and share ideas and sources that I have found to be useful for initially setting the context in class lectures and collegial discussions regarding social justice in LIS education.

Origins in valuing the common good

As I speak about early public librarianship with students and colleagues, I take the opportunity to emphasize how public librarianship from its beginnings has been driven by ideals that center on the common good. The Boston Public Library, which opened in 1854 during the Industrial Revolution, was the first large city public library established in the United States.[7] At the time, Boston was a growing, cosmopolitan, well-connected city, with a number of extant public infrastructures and educational institutions. Its civic attitudes were generally forward-looking. Given these outlooks and advantages, Boston's leaders were motivated to establish libraries for the benefit of the general public, with goals of promoting literacy and reading (especially among newly-arrived young factory workers), expanding informal education, and for general personal development.[8] Boston's example of positioning its public library as a common good quickly spread, and by the turn of the century, nearly one thousand public libraries had been established across the U.S.[9]

---

6. Kathleen de la Peña McCook, "Community Anchors for Lifelong Learning," in *Information Services Today: An Introduction*, ed. Sandra Hirsh (Lanham, MD: Rowan & Littlefield, 2015), 70–81.

7. Richard Rubin, *Foundations of Library and Information Science*, 3rd ed. (New York: Neal-Schuman Publishers, 2010).

8. Jesse H. Shera, *Foundations Of The Public Library The Origins Of The Public Library Movement In New England 1629-1855* (Chicago: University Of Chicago Press, 1949), http://archive.org/details/foundationsofthe012037mbp.

9. Kathleen de la Peña McCook, *Introduction to Public Librarianship*, 2nd ed. (New York: Neal-Schuman Publishers, 2011).

Service to new Americans

This growth of public libraries was contemporaneous with large waves of mostly European immigrants who were seeking to escape political instability, persecution, and poverty by moving to the United States.[10] Upon arrival, however, many of these new Americans struggled with the English language and with discrimination, and were often forced to take employment in dangerous and/or exploitative circumstances (e.g., mines, piecework factories, stockyards). Many remained poor.

Newly professionalized public librarians were eager to make a contribution to society by working with these new Americans. Dedicating themselves to understanding the needs of assimilating immigrant communities in the first decades of the twentieth century, public librarians developed "programming for the foreign born" services that included English language courses, literacy courses, native culture and language events, and civic information guides for new city residents.[11] By the 1920s, the concept of the public library being an agency for lifelong learning and a resource for all Americans was firmly established, particularly in urban areas.

The People's University

These and other programs led to the emergence of the "People's University" ideal in the 1930s. In public libraries, i.e., the "People's University," the working class (under particular duress during the Great Depression) could find entertainment, improve work skills, and seek

10. Kathleen de la Peña McCook and Katharine J. Phenix, "Public Librarianship," in *Encyclopedia of Library and Information Sciences*, 3rd ed. (Taylor & Francis, 2009), 4340-46.

11. Deanna B. Marcum and Elizabeth W. Stone, "Literacy: The Library Legacy; in Helping Immigrants Access America, Turn-of-the-Century Librarians Were Pioneers of Literacy Training," *American Libraries* 22 (March 1991): 202-5.

personal development—all of which fostered engaged citizenship, promoted economic opportunities, and enhanced democracy.[12]

Buttressing democracy

Buttressing democracy was also the motivation for public librarians to extend service to military personnel during World War II through collaborations with the American Red Cross and the YMCA.[13] Fascism and Communism were perceived to be truly threatening ideologies at the time. Reading fostered by public libraries was seen as having important social, cultural, and recreational value, and many believed democracy was dependent on citizens' lifelong learning and expanded literacy.[14] Based on this thinking, official plans to make public library services available to all Americans became part of post-war strategies to improve society.[15]

Expanding service outside of large cities

A focus on expanding the nation's intellectual strength remained a government priority after World War II, particularly in light of the subsequent Cold War and the successful Soviet launch of the Sputnik satellite in 1957.[16] Reading, knowledge creation, and libraries were a national agenda, and with the passage of the 1956 Library Services Act (LSA), federal funds were made available to establish public libraries in unserved rural areas.[17]

---

12. Alvin Saunders Johnson, *The Public Library: A People's University*, (New York: American Association for Adult Education, 1938), http://hdl.handle.net/2027/uc1.b3389062.

13. Tucker and Goedeken, "History of Libraries."

14. Molly Guptill Manning, *When Books Went to War: The Stories That Helped Us Win World War II*, First Printing edition (Boston: Houghton Mifflin Harcourt, 2014).

15. McCook, "Community Anchors for Lifelong Learning."

16. Virginia H. Mathews, "Public Library Rebirth," *American Libraries* 37, no. 9 (October 2006): 48-53.

17. McCook, *Introduction to Public Librarianship.*

Meager responses to racial segregation

Even though public libraries expanded throughout the first half of the twentieth century, service was not equally distributed to all Americans. In the 1950s, racial segregation remained the norm for public libraries in many American communities, particularly in the South.[18] The few segregated public libraries for black Americans that did exist were severely underfunded and underdeveloped, although black librarians did develop an ethos of community, literacy, exploration, and education in these facilities.[19] LIS education for blacks was also truncated and segregated. Several state library associations were segregated, and professional meetings and conferences were not necessarily open to black librarians.[20]

Although public librarians had created a notable social justice track record in other areas by mid-century, the response to these racial inequities was relatively meager and slow. Contemporary library historians offer evidence showing that at the time, the majority of the LIS profession was not willing to work against status quo segregation in public libraries, or lacked the skills to do so.[21] Integrated public libraries (and a fully integrated LIS profession) would have to wait a few more years.[22]

---

18. Rosemary Ruhig Du Mont, "Race in American Librarianship: Attitudes of the Library Profession," *Journal of Library History* 21, no. 3 (1986): 488-509.

19. Michael Fultz, "Black Public Libraries in the South in the Era of De Jure Segregation," *Libraries & the Cultural Record* 41, no. 3 (2006): 337-59; Alma Dawson, "Celebrating African-American Librarians and Librarianship," *Library Trends* 49, no. 1 (2000): 49–87.

20. Du Mont, "Race in American Librarianship: Attitudes of the Library Profession."

21. Ibid.; Cheryl Knott Malone, "Toward a Multicultural American Public Library History," *Libraries & Culture* 35, no. 1 (2000): 77-87; Donnarae MacCann, "Libraries for Immigrants and Minorities: A Study in Contrasts," in *Social Responsibility in Librarianship: Essays on Equality*, ed. Donnarae MacCann (Jefferson, NC: McFarland & Co, 1989), 97-116.

22. Stephen Cresswell, "The Last Days of Jim Crow in Southern Libraries," *Libraries & Culture* 31, no. 3/4 (July 1, 1996): 557-73.

Service for diverse populations

By the 1960s, the civil rights movement, attitudes about gender, public demonstrations, Vietnam War protests, and President Johnson's War on Poverty had radically changed the cultural contexts in which information professionals worked, and had given them additional social justice factors to consider.[23] Of particular relevance was the 1966 Library Services Construction Act (LSCA), which required library programming to be locally-driven rather than driven at the national level. This encouraged public librarians to develop a number of programs for underserved local populations, including outreach to the elderly and homebound, literacy programs for adults, and tailored services for children and young adults.[24]

During these years, segregation in libraries was also discontinued, and public library services created especially for (and by) African Americans, Latino Americans, and other groups expanded in the 1970s and 1980s. By then, the American Library Association's (ALA) Social Responsibilities Roundtable and ALA affiliates REFORMA (the National Association to Promote Library and Information Services to Latinos and the Spanish Speaking), the Black Caucus, the American Indian Library Association, the Asian-Pacific American Librarians Association, and the Chinese American Librarians Association were raising awareness of diversity and equal access issues for members of the ALA and the profession at large. Other groups were also established during this time within the ALA to prioritize public library service to non-readers, new readers, sexual minorities, incarcerated persons and ex-offenders, older adults, people with disabilities, the poor, and the homeless.[25]

---

23. Mathews, "Public Library Rebirth."

24. McCook, "Community Anchors for Lifelong Learning."

25. American Library Association, "Round Tables," accessed August 24, 2015, http://www.ala.org/groups/rts.

Internet access for all

With the advent of the Mosaic web browser in 1993, Internet usage increased exponentially, and public libraries were among the first organizations to offer digital literacy workshops and access to this paradigm-shifting information technology. Millions of people experienced the exciting potential of the World Wide Web for the first time at public libraries—a continuation of the democratic information access and education philosophy begun by public librarians decades before.[26]

However, a by-product of the Internet was the digital divide, an economic and social inequality that refers to disparities in Internet use and quality of access. The digital divide is concentrated among older, less educated, less affluent populations as well as in rural areas that have fewer Internet provider choices and slower connections.[27] In response to the digital divide and other concurrent social issues, groups such as the Progressive Librarians' Guild,[28] the "Revolting Librarians,"[29] various ALA committees, task forces, interest groups, and others concerned with diversity and inclusion began to ask critical questions about the relationships between public libraries and centers of power in society, including large information and technology companies. Asking questions about whether public libraries were extensions of people or of big corporations and political interests was uncomfortable for many librarians, but these issues needed to be explored if LIS was going to mature, expand, and be able to withstand the challenges that come with change.

---

26. John Carlo Bertot, Paul T. Jaeger, and Charles R. McClure, eds., *Public Libraries and the Internet: Roles, Perspectives, and Implications* (Santa Barbara, CA: Libraries Unlimited, 2011).

27. Council of Economic Advisers, "Issue Brief: Mapping the Digital Divide," July 2015, https://www.whitehouse.gov/sites/default/files/wh_digital_divide_issue_brief.pdf.

28. "Progressive Librarians Guild," accessed August 24, 2015, http://www.progressivelibrariansguild.org/.

29. Katia Roberto and Jessamyn West, eds., *Revolting Librarians Redux: Radical Librarians Speak Out* (Jefferson, NC: McFarland & Co, 2003).

Continuing work for the common good

In the tradition of their predecessors, today's public librarians continue to work toward a society in which all citizens can thrive. They build diverse cultural awareness, help support small businesses, provide career development workshops and materials, and offer programs and resources for numerous social groups and special interests. They also provide important access to the larger world for millions of people who don't have internet access at their homes.[30] Scott Bonner, director of the Ferguson (MO) Public Library, is a contemporary exemplar of a public librarian driven by a social justice orientation. After Ferguson schools were shut down in August, 2014 amidst public demonstrations in the aftermath of the police shooting death of Michael Brown, an unarmed local teenager, Bonner coordinated with area teachers and volunteers to tutor more than 200 schoolchildren at his public library facility, as well as arranged meals for the kids.[31] Bonner modestly brushed aside media commentary calling him a local hero, saying his actions were simply rooted in the Ferguson Public Library Mission.[32]

Likewise, in Baltimore, a series of violent protests followed the April 2015 death of Freddie Gray in police custody. Yet Enoch Pratt Free Library manager Melanie Townsend Diggs kept her branch near the center of the rioting open. She said her decision was based on her library's mission to provide the best service for the public. Diggs and her staff maintained a safe haven and a physical community space for neighborhood residents where they could access regular programming and services, as well as information on the unfolding events. Diggs and her staff also worked to provide meals for kids and to help area residents

30. McCook and Phenix, "Public Librarianship."

31. Willie Miller, "Connecting Libraries and Social Justice," *American Libraries*, accessed August 23, 2015, http://americanlibrariesmagazine.org/blogs/the-scoop/connecting-libraries-and-social-justice/.

32. "Scott Bonner Gives a 'Warts and All' Recap of the Events in Ferguson," I Love Libraries, accessed August 23, 2015, http://www.ilovelibraries.org/article/scott-bonner-gives-%E2%80%9Cwarts-and-all%E2%80%9D-recap-events-ferguson.

get diapers and other necessary items because area stores were closed during the emergency. These actions further underscore the "libraries as place" values that make public libraries de facto community hubs. Like Scott Bonner, Melanie Townsend Diggs says that she and her staff did not perform acts of heroism—they performed acts of people-centered librarianship.[33]

This brief overview shows that public librarians have long worked for positive change in their communities, and that a social justice ethos is an intrinsic part of library and information science practice. This is just a small sample; there are certainly many other historical highlights of social justice history in librarianship (see Mehra, Rioux, and Albright[34] for further examples). To the extent that professional training prepared these public librarians to do the work demonstrated here suggests that LIS education was also a factor in these efforts.

Developing Awareness of Blind Spots

As with all service professions and academic disciplines, LIS is continuously evolving. It has retained its traditional roots, but it is also adopting more actively self-reflective and reflexive practices and assessment processes in order to develop a sharper awareness of social inequities and related "blind spots" within LIS discourse and practice. For example, some LIS observers seek to increase awareness of power relationships that exist in the information landscape among LIS educators, researchers, and practitioners. Related questions are also being raised about notions of librarians "helping people," a traditional idea about LIS service that,

33. "ALA 2015: Pelosi Honors Baltimore Librarians for 'Heroic' Work During Unrest," PublishersWeekly.com, accessed November 23, 2015, http://www.publishersweekly.com/pw/by-topic/digital/conferences/article/67339-ala-2015-pelosi-honors-baltimore-librarians-for-heroic-work-during-unrest.html; "Libraries Respond to Community Needs in Times of Crisis," *American Libraries,* accessed November 23, 2015, http://americanlibrariesmagazine.org/2015/05/15/libraries-respond-to-community-needs-in-times-of-crisis/.

34. Bharat Mehra, Kevin S. Rioux, and Kendra S. Albright, "Social Justice in Library and Information Science," in *Encyclopedia of Library and Information Sciences*, 3rd ed. (Taylor & Francis, 2009), 4820-36.

in fact, places librarians in positions of power over users. As a result, partnering with users as equals is becoming a more accepted means of characterizing information service.[35]

Members of the field are also being urged to ask critical questions such as: For whom do given information services end up benefitting? Are there implicit biases and social control factors associated with those traditional "public good" services that have, in fact, buttressed an unfair status quo?[36] There are also calls for LIS professionals and educators to engage in more explicit and focused explorations about race, to better discern the nature of institutional whiteness in information organizations, and to test and critique current models of multiculturalism.[37]

Diffuse Characterizations of Social Justice: Implications for LIS Curricula

These discussions about LIS history are quite inspirational for my students (as they are for me and my teaching colleagues). Our conversation usually segues into spirited talk about values and attitudes associated with these activities, all the while using a number of different terms, vocabularies, and perspectives. As we talk, we casually bat around the

35. Mehra, Albright, and Rioux, "A Practical Framework for Social Justice Research in the Information Professions;" Bharat Mehra, "Integrating Socially-Relevant Projects and Achieving Meaningful Community Outcomes in Required Library and Information Science Courses: From a Service Model to Community Engagement," in *The Service Connection: Library and Information Science Education and Service to Communities*, ed. Loriene Roy (Chicago: ALA Editions, 2009).

36. Malone, "Toward a Multicultural American Public Library History;" MacCann, "Libraries for Immigrants and Minorities: A Study in Contrasts;" Wayne A. Wiegand, "Tunnel Vision and Blind Spots: What the Past Tells Us about the Present; Reflections on the Twentieth-Century History of American Librarianship," *Library Quarterly* 69, no. 1 (1999): 1–32.

37. Christine Pawley, "Unequal Legacies: Race and Multiculturalism in the LIS Curriculum," *Library Quarterly* 76, no. 2 (2006): 149–68, doi:10.1086/506955; Todd Honma, "Trippin' Over the Color Line: The Invisibility of Race in Library and Information Studies," *InterActions: UCLA Journal of Education and Information Studies* 1, no. 2 (June 21, 2005), http://escholarship.org/uc/item/4nj0w1mp.

term *social justice*, but it's not long before a semantic challenge presents itself, usually by someone asking, *"What exactly do we mean by social justice?"* Relevant to this essay and this edited volume, a similar question is *"What does social justice mean in the context of LIS education?"*

To begin exploring these two questions, I follow up my review of social justice history in American public libraries by informing my audience that the term *social justice* as an integrated construct is not particularly old. One of the earliest articulations of it comes from an encyclical called *Rerum Novarum: On Capital and Labor* published by Pope Leo XIII in 1891. This document focused on labor unions' efforts to secure the rights of workers.[38] The term was subsequently adopted in secular discourse in various domains such as law, political science, and philosophy. However, a universally-accepted definition of social justice in LIS remains elusive.[39] Again, what do LIS educators, practitioners, and researchers mean when they use the term social justice? At this point, the answer is not clear, but the question is quite compelling. I use this state of affairs to drive further exploratory discussions in my classes, typically asking the following questions:

- What does the term *social justice* mean to you?
- Why do we humans deserve social justice?
- Is social justice culturally determined, or are there universal principles of social justice?
- Do we learn the principles of social justice? Or do we have an innate sense about social justice matters?
- What is the source of social justice? Secular law? God? Humanism? Rationalism? Other?

---

38. "Rerum Novarum: Encyclical of Pope Leo XIII on Capital and Labor," The Vatican, accessed August 27, 2015, http://w2.vatican.va/content/leo-xiii/en/encyclicals/documents/hf_l-xiii_enc_15051891_rerum-novarum.html.

39. Mehra, Rioux, and Albright, "Social Justice in Library and Information Science."

- Why and how is *social justice* a useful framework for the work we do as information professionals?

After my students discuss these questions in class or on a Blackboard forum, I ask them to write a short reflection paper about these areas of inquiry. I encourage them to ask themselves: what does your gender, class, race, ethnicity, socioeconomic status, religion, age, education level, sexual orientation, etc., have to do with how you answer these questions? I've used this class exercise many times, and I've found that it inspires curiosity, introspection, and deep reflection.

Responses are mixed, but most of the time, they all suggest that raising the profile of social justice in the LIS classroom is in order. Typically, initial student comments generally characterize social justice as a scenario in which people are free to live as equals with equal rights. Interestingly, students often imply that social justice somehow originates in legal documents such as the U. S. Constitution or the Bill of Rights.

As they speak about how their gender, class, race, and other demographic variables relate to social justice, some students speak of instances in which they believe they themselves were denied justice as a member of a minority group. When these comments occur, I take the opportunity to teach about the concepts of individual dignity and diversity as elements of social justice thinking.

A vague sense of efficient duty and obligation to the public to abstain from prejudice or rudeness in the workplace is a common reason students cite for using social justice as a guide for library practice. Questions about the universality of social justice, and why humans deserve social justice, are seemingly the toughest questions for students to address.

These student responses indicate that ideas about social justice among LIS students are underdeveloped and under-articulated. This points to areas of opportunity for interested LIS educators to raise awareness and knowledge of the social justice concept. I have found that this exercise also uncovers students' motivations for wanting to join the LIS profession. Many students indicate in their essays that they want to be information professionals because they want to reach out to their fellow humans and do something positive with their careers. They are indeed eager to learn a vocabulary that helps them express and understand how their own LIS interests and career plans relate to social justice.

But, as will be shown, the language of social justice, particularly as it is treated in LIS, is diffuse and complex within the scholarly literature. Although not all LIS efforts toward positive social change are characterized as *social justice*, these actions are certainly a subject for LIS commentators, whether they be educators, researchers, practitioners, or students. Many LIS teachers and scholars who write about social justice in LIS chose other umbrella terms. For example, some writers primarily position their work within a *human rights* framework,[40] which is often based on the United Nations Universal Declaration of Human Rights.[41] Others take an *ethics* position, which considers the moral aspects of information, its provision, and the individuals who seek and use it.[42] *Inclusion* and *diversity* positions are concerned with acknowledging the differences between individual humans and how these differences are related to inclusive library service; these are particularly rich areas of discourse within LIS education.[43] Still others relate social justice to looking at LIS practice and education through critical theory or progressive

---

40. Toni Samek, *Librarianship and Human Rights: A Twenty-First Century Guide* (Oxford: Chandos, 2007); McCook, *Introduction to Public Librarianship.*

41. "The Universal Declaration of Human Rights," accessed August 28, 2015, http://www.un.org/en/documents/udhr/.

42. Toni Carbo, "Ethics Education for Information Professionals," *Journal of Library Administration* 47, no. 3/4 (May 2008): 5–25, doi:10.1080/01930820802186324; Mark D. Winston, "Ethical Leadership and Ethical Decision Making: A Meta-Analysis of Research Related to Ethics Education," *Library & Information Science Research* 29, no. 2 (June 2007): 230–51, doi:10.1016/j.lisr.2007.04.002.

43. Shari A. Lee et al., "Igniting Diversity: Actionable Methods and Ideas for Advancing Diversity in LIS Education in the US.," *Journal of Education for Library & Information Science* 56 (March 2, 2015): S47–60; Denice Adkins, Christina Virden, and Charles Yier, "Learning about Diversity: The Roles of LIS Education, LIS Associations, and Lived Experience," *Library Quarterly* 85, no. 2 (April 1, 2015): 139–49, doi:10.1086/680153.

lenses that expose hidden power imbalances.[44] Information policy and standards are also related to social justice.[45] And then there are LIS educators, researchers, and practitioners who simply characterize their work as supporting a type of positive community engagement and development.[46]

Regardless of stated position, there is still much mixing and conflation of terms. **Figure 1** shows these as a set of relationships with the term social justice in the center. However, in actual contemporary LIS discourse, any of the featured terms could be the central term, depending on one's perspective – a complex and dynamic model, as it were.

Other characterizations of social justice in LIS are even more finely granulated than the terms in **Figure 1**. While I was preparing this essay, I took a cursory sweep through several venues in which the LIS profession communicates with itself and the larger world. I looked at LIS scholarly literature in proprietary databases, scholarly books about librarianship, public library websites, library/information organization websites, LIS practitioner journals, and blogs about libraries and library service. I was quickly able to list nearly thirty disparate topics and terms relatable to social justice that had been taken up by LIS educators, practitioners, researchers and students (see **Table 1**).

---

44. Robert Schroeder and Christopher V. Hollister, "Librarians' Views on Critical Theories and Critical Practices," *Behavioral & Social Sciences Librarian* 33, no. 2 (April 3, 2014): 91–119, doi:10.1080/01639269.2014.912104; Gloria J. Leckie, Lisa M. Given, and John Buschman, eds., *Critical Theory for Library and Information Science: Exploring the Social from Across the Disciplines* (Santa Barbara, CA: Libraries Unlimited, 2010).

45. Lisa P. Nathan, Alice MacGougan, and Elizabeth Shaffer, "If Not Us, Who? Social Media Policy and the iSchool Classroom," *Journal of Education for Library & Information Science* 55, no. 2 (2014): 112–32; Paul T. Jaeger and John Carlo Bertot, "Responsibility Rolls Down: Public Libraries and the Social and Policy Obligations of Ensuring Access to E-Government and Government Information," *Public Library Quarterly* 30, no. 2 (June 4, 2011): 91–116..

46. Sandra Hughes-Hassell and Julie Stivers, "Examining Youth Services Librarians' Perceptions of Cultural Knowledge as an Integral Part of Their Professional Practice," *School Libraries Worldwide* 21, no. 1 (January 2015): 121–36, doi:10.14265.21.1.008; Marjatta Asu and Leanne Clendening, "It Takes a Library to Raise a Community," Partnership: *Canadian Journal of Library & Information Practice & Research* 2, no. 2 (July 2007): 1–16.

Figure 1. The term social justice related to similar terms used in LIS

The sheer variety of projects and diversity of terms demonstrated by the simple review summarized in **Figure 1** and **Table 1** confirms that working toward positive social change is very much part of LIS ethos and practice. There are even more social justice characterizations that one can easily find, as this is certainly a very dynamic subject in LIS. Yet this rich-but-diffuse discourse presents some practical challenges to LIS instructors who wish to incorporate notions of social justice in their classrooms.

Human Migration	Rural Library Services	Privacy
e-Citizenship	Special Needs Patrons	Environmental Sustainability
Intellectual Freedom	Serving LGBTQ Communities	Occupy Movement
Healthcare/ Disease Prevention	Refugee Services	Black Lives Matter Movement
Climate Change	Advocacy	Prison Libraries
Poverty	Social Media/ Big Data	Faith/Religion
Employment Training	Information Behavior	Sustainable Development
ICTs in the Developing World	Libraries Without Borders	Free and Open Software
Truth Commissions, Archives	Memory Projects for Local Culture	Community Building

Table 1. Disparate social justice topics and terms examined in LIS

For example, as mentioned earlier in this essay, it's difficult to choose an entry point for incorporating social justice thinking in LIS courses. The multi-faceted nature of social justice in LIS, with its array of terms and labels, may leave instructors wondering how to logically choose a perspective for their lessons without privileging or biasing any given topic or confusing students. The words *activist* or *advocate*, which are commonly used in LIS discourse about social justice, may cause uneasiness, as they touch on one's personal politics and perhaps trigger unwanted introspection. This may be particularly true if one's LIS teaching colleagues hold the traditional opinion that explicitly and actively advocating for social change is not within the purview of LIS education—i.e., the perennial library neutrality debate.[47]

47. Alison M. Lewis, ed., *Questioning Library Neutrality: Essays from Progressive Librarian* (Duluth, MN: Library Juice Press, 2008); Randall C. Jimerson, "Archives for All: Professional Responsibility and Social Justice," *American Archivist* 70, no. 2 (October 1, 2007): 252–81.

It is also sometimes difficult to counter criticism or convince skeptical colleagues and stakeholders that *social justice* is in fact a meaningful term in the LIS academic environment. Disparate or conceptually isolated social justice voices in LIS may be easy for critics to dismiss with comments like, "oh, he's just got an axe to grind," or "she's overly sensitive," or "he's obsessive about this one pie-in-the-sky thing." Additional conceptual integration may provide leverage against the facile and common view that social justice is just a naïve, vague, "it's nice to be nice to the nice" concept.

Although it is gratifying and pedagogically enriching for both instructors and students to consciously apply social justice frameworks in the LIS classroom, it can also be a bit of a "hot potato." In some universities, LIS educators may get the impression that it would be better organizational politics to position their teaching within other frameworks. This is particularly true in parts of the country where the term *social justice* is not generally well regarded, and is often identified solely as a function of the political left, or is considered a form of mere political correctness and/or elitism.

Also, LIS educators need to remember that in this time of neoliberal economics, fiscal austerity, and the decline of unions, the language of social struggle that is often associated with LIS social justice projects may be perceived as being old-fashioned and more rooted in early-to-mid twentieth century Marxian texts rather than being in sync with today's realities. This could be especially true among some younger teaching colleagues and students who may believe it impractical to adhere to values that appear to be reduced, defeated, or made irrelevant by rapid change and shifting power balances.

Furthermore, because social justice focuses on complex human dynamics, it takes time to think deeply about ways to bring it into the LIS classroom. In this era of increased demands for accountability on university campuses, LIS faculty may be distracted or discouraged by administrative assessment demands. As a mostly qualitative concept, social justice may not easily lend itself to the mix of typically quantitative outcomes and goals that drive program assessment activities.

These and other challenges suggest that, at this stage, social justice education in LIS is in need of an explicit, unified, and clarifying intellectual position or attitude—that is, a *stance.* Thus far, I've noted that LIS is indeed a profession deeply concerned with ideals for a better world. I've also shown that social justice, in its various instantiations, motivates students, practitioners, researchers, and educators to encourage positive community action within LIS contexts. In order to even begin addressing the question, *"What does the term social justice mean in the context of LIS education?"* LIS educators must work towards explicit conceptual frameworks for their discourse about LIS professional preparation and social justice. This would reduce confusion among students, provide an organization scheme for lessons, and would help integrate the discourse about LIS and social justice. This would also contribute to LIS-specific social justice theory-building, allowing it to stand as a dynamic, strong, and meaningful idea in the profession.

Toward a Unified Social Justice Stance for LIS Curricula

Developing an explicit, unified, and clarifying social justice stance for LIS curricula will take time, effort, engagement, and commitment on the parts of many individuals, and the field is at the early stages of this task. Thus the query *"What does social justice mean in LIS education?"* will necessarily remain a guiding question for now.

In the meantime, my own modest contribution toward a unified social justice stance for LIS curricula is sharing my experiences in finding traction and leverage for social justice in my teaching by using a framework that I call a social justice metatheory for LIS education.[48] Essentially, a metatheory is an integrative conceptual tool consisting of a set of assumptions that orients and directs action.[49] Metatheories

48. Kevin Rioux, "Metatheory in Library and Information Science: A Nascent Social Justice Approach.," *Journal of Education for Library & Information Science* 51, no. 1 (2010): 9–17.

49. E. J. Lawler and R. Ford, "Metatheory and Friendly Competition in Theory Growth: The Case of Power Processes in Bargaining," in *Theoretical*

can add clarity and guide discourse and professional practice, including those in LIS education.[50]

The elements of this social justice metatheory for LIS education are listed below. Within each assumption, I arrange examples of activities that I typically use and topics that I typically cover in my classes that are guided by this approach.

Assumption 1: All humans have an inherent worth and deserve information services that help address their needs. To address this assumption in my LIS classes, I often lead with the United Nations' Universal Declaration of Human Rights (UDHR).[51] The foundational premise of this document, spearheaded by Eleanor Roosevelt and proclaimed by the United Nations General Assembly in 1948, is that all humans do indeed have inherent worth. Article 19, in particular, addresses information services: "Everyone has the right to freedom of opinion and expression; this right includes freedom to hold opinions without interference and to seek, receive and impart information and ideas through any media and regardless of frontiers." While discussing this document, I also ask my students to consider other articles of the UDHR, and how they too could apply to the goal of providing information services to everyone. I also ask them to seek out and report on the scholarly commentary about the UDHR from LIS researchers (e.g., Edwards and Edwards).[52] This is also a part of my courses in which I discuss relationships between universal information access and human migration and diversity.

Research Programs: Studies in the Growth of Theory, ed. J. Berger and M. Zelditch (Stanford, CA: Stanford University Press, 1993), 172–210.

50. J. C. Alexander, *Theoretical Logic in Sociology: Positivism, Presuppositions, and Current Controversies*, vol. 1 (Berkeley, CA: University of California Press, 1982); D. G. Wagner and J. Berger, "Do Sociological Theories Grow?" *American Journal of Sociology* 90, no. 4 (1985): 697–728.

51. "The Universal Declaration of Human Rights," accessed August 28, 2015, http://www.un.org/en/documents/udhr/.

52. Julie Biando Edwards and Stephan P. Edwards, eds., *Beyond Article 19: Libraries and Social and Cultural Rights* (Duluth, MN: Library Juice Press, 2010).

Assumption 2: People perceive reality and information in different ways, and in different contexts. This needs to be acknowledged. I have found this assumption to be a useful bridge for introducing class discussions about user demographics and the social justice issues related to varied human information behaviors. I ask students to research how people seek out, share, and use information in their everyday life contexts (e.g., Savolainen[53]) and present reports (either in person or in a Blackboard group) on how the LIS scholarly and practitioner literature treats variables such as income, education, age, ethnicity, sexual orientation, gender, etc., with regard to information services. I also cover here issues related to information literacy, non-users of traditional library services, diversity, and the importance of patron-librarian partnerships.

Assumption 3: There are many different types of information and knowledge, and these are societal resources. As I discuss this area with students, I position library services as common goods that make available diverse and vital societal resources that exist in many formats. I create class exercises that have them consider their own assumptions about what constitutes "useful" or "proper" or "good" information. I also challenge them to see how non-traditional library formats such as maker movements, oral histories, art, music, religious artifacts, handicrafts, etc., are indeed sources of information and knowledge exchange, and that individuals' lived experiences also constitute information and knowledge. Discussions about equitable access, patron-librarian partnerships, diversity, subsidiarity, intellectual freedom, and libraries-as-place enhance the lessons covered.

Assumption 4: LIS theory, practice, research, and professional preparation are pursued with the ultimate goal of bringing positive change to service constituencies. I give my students evidence for this assumption in the form of the various mission statements of the American Library Association (ALA), the Association for Information

53. Reijo Savolainen, "Everyday Life Information Seeking: Approaching Information Seeking in the Context of 'Way of Life,'" *Library & Information Science Research* 17, no. 3 (1995): 259–94, doi:10.1016/0740-8188(95)90048-9.

Science & Technology (ASIS&T), the International Federation of Library Associations and Institutions (IFLA), the New York Library Association (NYLA), and other information service-related organizations and advocacy groups. As they read these statements, I ask them to keep in mind the notion of eudaimonia (i.e., human flourishing and well-being) and its relationship to the goals of the LIS professions. Other relevant topics that I cover are integrated human development models, the humanist aspects of the history of Western librarianship, and current theories of information service.

Assumption 5: The provision of information is an inherently powerful activity. Distributing information is, in itself, a political act. In all of my LIS courses, I tell my students that facilitating people's information needs as an information professional is, in itself, a political act. Most students are very stimulated by this idea, which encourages much discussion about information work and poverty, access to quality education, diversity, citizenship, democratic values, media politics, the cost of information products, privacy, globalization, healthcare, family structures, prejudice, privilege, distribution of wealth, etc.

As indicated, this metatheoretical framework, used as an integrative tool, has helped me tie semantic and pedagogical loose ends together. Use of it has provided clarity and structure to the lessons about social justice topics covered in my LIS courses. This social justice metatheory has also been used by LIS researchers and practitioners to discuss social justice issues in school libraries,[54] archives,[55] diversity in LIS education,[56]

54. Deborah Lang Froggatt, "The Informationally Underserved: Not Always Diverse, but Always a Social Justice Advocacy Model," *School Libraries Worldwide* 21, no. 1 (January 2015): 54–72; Punit Dadlani and Ross Todd, "Information Technology Services and School Libraries: A Coninuum of Social Justice," in *Qualitative and Quantitative Methods in Libraries (QQML) Special Issue Social Justice, Social Inclusion*, 2014, 39–48.

55. Stacy Wood et al., "Mobilizing Records: Re-Framing Archival Description to Support Human Rights," *Archival Science* 14 (2014): 397–419.

56. Laurie J. Bonnici et al., "Physiological Access as a Social Justice Type in LIS Curricula," *Journal of Education for Library & Information Science* 53, no. 2 (Spring 2012): 115–29.

and LIS theory-building.[57] As it stands now, this framework currently includes five assumptions or elements, but because by nature metatheories are flexible, it certainly can be expanded by other LIS educators in both number of assumptions or elements, and contexts for application.

Conclusion

LIS educators are motivated to exchange ideas about social justice in LIS curricula because they realize these orientations truly distinguish and enrich students' experiences in professional preparation programs. Social justice concepts are indeed didactic and popular. Aspiring information workers are drawn to LIS education and careers because they instinctively understand that social justice is an intrinsic part of the profession. These students want to be an active, positive part of the solution to a variety of societal challenges. No matter what a student's LIS interest, it's likely that he or she can connect those interests with social justice concepts. The job of LIS teachers is to act on our professional mandates and to nurture and develop these student motivations and instincts.

LIS educators must find the best ways to convey the capacity of social justice ideas, showing them to be a powerful foundation for a career of service and community engagement in any library setting. To be sure, they must work towards a common set of social justice terms and language for LIS curricula via theory building. As all academics know, true and robust knowledge creation and sharing in any discipline is driven by theory, supplemented by continued discourse and research. I put forth the ideas, strategies, and frameworks presented in this essay for consideration, in hope that they will contribute to these goals and to enhancing the implementation of social justice in the LIS classroom.

---

57. Kafi D. Kumasi, Deborah H. Charbonneau, and Dian Walster, "Theory Talk in the Library Science Literature: An Exploratory Analysis," *Library & Information Science Research* 35 (2013): 175–80.

Paul Jaeger and his colleagues describe the current stage of social justice thinking in LIS as "becoming what we already are."[58] Driven by social justice ideals carried on from the discipline's past and its current dynamism, LIS educators can take that to heart as they work together to develop a unified social justice stance for Library and Information Science curricula.

Bibliography

Accardi, Maria T., Emily Drabinski, and Alana Kumbier, eds. *Critical Library Instruction: Theories and Methods*. Duluth, MN: Library Juice Press, 2010.

Adkins, Denice, Christina Virden, and Charles Yier. "Learning about Diversity: The Roles of LIS Education, LIS Associations, and Lived Experience." *Library Quarterly* 85, no. 2 (April 1, 2015): 139-49. doi:10.1086/680153.

"ALA 2015: Pelosi Honors Baltimore Librarians for 'Heroic' Work During Unrest." *PublishersWeekly.com*. Accessed November 23, 2015. http://www.publishersweekly.com/pw/by-topic/digital/conferences/article/67339-ala-2015-pelosi-honors-baltimore-librarians-for-heroic-work-during-unrest.html.

Alexander, J. C. *Theoretical Logic in Sociology: Positivism, Presuppositions, and Current Controversies*. Vol. 1. Berkeley, CA: University of California Press, 1982.

"ALISE2015: ALISE Academy." Accessed August 17, 2015. http://alise2015.sched.org/event/e1cc79c6188d269ec-0faee1d146ffe5a.

58. Paul T. Jaeger, Natalie Greene Taylor, and Ursula Gorham, *Libraries, Human Rights, and Social Justice: Enabling Access and Promoting Inclusion* (Lanham, MD: Rowman & Littlefield Publishers, 2015).

"ALISE 2015 Conference." Accessed August 17, 2015. http://www.alise.org/2015-conference-2.

Allard, Suzie, Bharat Mehra, and M. Asim Qayym. "Intercultural Leadership Toolkit for Librarians: Building Awareness to Effectively Serve Diverse Multicultural Populations." *Education Libraries* 30, no. 1 (2007): 5-12.

American Library Association. "Round Tables." Accessed August 24, 2015. http://www.ala.org/groups/rts.

Asu, Marjatta, and Leanne Clendening. "It Takes a Library to Raise a Community." *Partnership: The Canadian Journal of Library & Information Practice & Research* 2, no. 2 (July 2007): 1-16.

Bertot, John Carlo, Paul T. Jaeger, and Charles R. McClure, eds. *Public Libraries and the Internet: Roles, Perspectives, and Implications*. Santa Barbara, CA: Libraries Unlimited, 2011.

Bonnici, Laurie J., Stephanie L. Maatta, Muriel K. Wells, Jackie Brodsky, and III Meadows Charles W. "Physiological Access as a Social Justice Type in LIS Curricula." *Journal of Education for Library & Information Science* 53, no. 2 (Spring 2012): 115-29.

Britz, Johannes J., and Shana Ponelis. "Social Justice and the International Flow of Knowledge with Specific Reference to African Scholars." *Aslib Proceedings* 64, no. 5 (2012): 462-77. doi:http://dx.doi.org.jerome.stjohns.edu:81/10.1108/00012531211263094.

Carbo, Toni. "Ethics Education for Information Professionals." *Journal of Library Administration* 47, no. 3/4 (May 2008): 5-25. doi:10.1080/01930820802186324.

Council of Economic Advisers. "Issue Brief: Mapping the Digital Divide," July 2015. https://www.whitehouse.gov/sites/default/files/wh_digital_divide_issue_brief.pdf.

Cresswell, Stephen. "The Last Days of Jim Crow in Southern Libraries." *Libraries & Culture* 31, no. 3/4 (July 1, 1996): 557-73.

Dadlani, Punit, and Ross Todd. "Information Technology Services and School Libraries: A Coninuum of Social Justice." In *Qualitative and Quantitative Methods in Libraries (QQML) Special Issue Social Justice, Social Inclusion*, 39-48, 2014.

Dawson, Alma. "Celebrating African-American Librarians and Librarianship." *Library Trends* 49, no. 1 (2000): 49–87.

Du Mont, Rosemary Ruhig. "Race in American Librarianship: Attitudes of the Library Profession." *Journal of Library History (1974-1987)* 21, no. 3 (1986): 488–509.

Edward A. Goedeken, and John Mark Tucker. "History of Libraries." In *Encyclopedia of Library and Information Sciences*, 2080–95. 3rd ed. Taylor & Francis, 2009.

Edwards, Julie Biando, and Stephan P. Edwards, eds. *Beyond Article 19: Libraries and Social and Cultural Rights*. Duluth, MN: Library Juice Press, 2010.

Fultz, Michael. "Black Public Libraries in the South in the Era of De Jure Segregation." *Libraries & the Cultural Record* 41, no. 3 (2006): 337–59.

Honma, Todd. "Trippin' Over the Color Line: The Invisibility of Race in Library and Information Studies." *InterActions: UCLA Journal of Education and Information Studies* 1, no. 2 (June 21, 2005). http://escholarship.org/uc/item/4nj0w1mp.

Hughes-Hassell, Sandra, and Julie Stivers. "Examining Youth Services Librarians' Perceptions of Cultural Knowledge as an Integral Part of Their Professional Practice." *School Libraries Worldwide* 21, no. 1 (January 2015): 121–36. doi:10.14265.21.1.008.

Jaeger, Paul T., and John Carlo Bertot. "Responsibility Rolls Down: Public Libraries and the Social and Policy Obligations of Ensuring Access to E-Government and Government Information." *Public Library Quarterly* 30, no. 2 (June 4, 2011): 91–116.

Jaeger, Paul T., Nicole A. Cooke, Cecilia Feltis, Michelle Hamiel, Fiona Jardine, and Katie Shilton. "The Virtuous Circle Revisited: Injecting Diversity, Inclusion, Rights, Justice, and Equity into LIS from Education to Advocacy." *Library Quarterly* 85, no. 2 (April 1, 2015): 150–71. doi:10.1086/680154.

Jaeger, Paul T., Ursula Gorham, Natalie Greene Taylor, Karen Kettnich, Lindsay C. Sarin, and Kaitlin J. Peterson. "Library Research and What Libraries Actually Do Now: Education, Inclusion, Social Services, Public Spaces, Digital Literacy, Social Justice, Human Rights, and Other Community Needs." *Library Quarterly* 84, no. 4 (October 1, 2014): 491–93. doi:10.1086/677785.

Jaeger, Paul T., Natalie Greene Taylor, and Ursula Gorham. *Libraries, Human Rights, and Social Justice: Enabling Access and Promoting Inclusion*. Lanham, MD: Rowman & Littlefield, 2015.

Jesse H. Shera. *Foundations of the Public Library: The Origins of the Public Library Movement in New England 1629-1855*. Chicago: University Of Chicago Press, 1949. http://archive.org/details/foundationsofthe012037mbp.

Jimerson, Randall C. "Archives for All: Professional Responsibility and Social Justice." *American Archivist* 70, no. 2 (October 1, 2007): 252–81.

Johnson, Alvin Saunders. *The Public Library: A People's University*. New York: American Association for Adult Education, 1938. http://hdl.handle.net/2027/uc1.b3389062.

Katz, Jeff. "Addressing Special Needs and At-Risk Populations in Library Education Programs." *Public Libraries* 48, no. 6 (December 11, 2009): 34–37.

Kumasi, Kafi D., Deborah H. Charbonneau, and Dian Walster. "Theory Talk in the Library Science Literature: An Exploratory Analysis." *Library & Information Science Research* 35 (2013): 175–80.

Lang Froggatt, Deborah. "The Informationally Underserved: Not Always Diverse, but Always a Social Justice Advocacy Model." *School Libraries Worldwide* 21, no. 1 (January 2015): 54–72.

Lawler, E. J., and R. Ford. "Metatheory and Friendly Competition in Theory Growth: The Case of Power Processes in Bargaining." In *Theoretical Research Programs: Studies in the Growth of Theory*, 172–210. Edited by J. Berger and M. Zelditch, Stanford, CA: Stanford University Press, 1993.

Leckie, Gloria J., Lisa M. Given, and John Buschman, eds. *Critical Theory for Library and Information Science: Exploring the Social from across the Disciplines*. Santa Barbara, CA: Libraries Unlimited, 2010.

Lee, Shari A., Renate Chancellor, Clara M. Chu, Howard Rodriguez-Mori, and Loriene Roy. "Igniting Diversity: Actionable Methods and Ideas for Advancing Diversity in LIS Education in the US." *Journal of Education for Library & Information Science* 56 (March 2, 2015): S47–60.

Lewis, Alison M., ed. *Questioning Library Neutrality: Essays from Progressive Librarian*. Duluth, MN: Library Juice Press, 2008.

"Libraries Respond to Community Needs in Times of Crisis." *American Libraries*. Accessed November 23, 2015. http://americanlibrariesmagazine.org/2015/05/15/libraries-respond-to-community-needs-in-times-of-crisis/.

MacCann, Donnarae. "Libraries for Immigrants and Minorities: A Study in Contrasts." In *Social Responsibility in Librarianship: Essays on Equality*, 97–116. Edited by Donnarae MacCann, Jefferson, NC: McFarland & Co, 1989.

Malone, Cheryl Knott. "Toward a Multicultural American Public Library History." *Libraries & Culture* 35, no. 1 (2000): 77–87.

Manning, Molly Guptill. *When Books Went to War: The Stories That Helped Us Win World War II*. First Printing ed. Boston: Houghton Mifflin Harcourt, 2014.

Marcum, Deanna B., and Elizabeth W. Stone. "Literacy: The Library Legacy; in Helping Immigrants Access America, Turn-of-the-Century Librarians Were Pioneers of Literacy Training." *American Libraries* 22 (March 1991): 202–5.

Mathews, Virginia H. "Public Library Rebirth." *American Libraries* 37, no. 9 (October 2006): 48–53.

McCook, Kathleen de la Peña. "Community Anchors for Lifelong Learning." *In Information Services Today: An Introduction*, 70–81. Edited by Sandra Hirsh. Lanham, MD: Rowan & Littlefield, 2015.

McCook, Kathleen de la Peña. *Introduction to Public Librarianship*. 2nd ed. New York: Neal-Schuman Publishers, 2011.

McCook, Kathleen de la Peña, and Katharine J. Phenix. "Public Librarianship." In *Encyclopedia of Library and Information Sciences*, 4340–46. 3rd ed. Taylor & Francis, 2009.

Mehra, Bharat. "Integrating Socially-Relevant Projects and Achieving Meaningful Community Outcomes in Required Library and Information Science Courses: From a Service Model to Community Engagement." In *The Service Connection: Library and Information Science Education and Service to Communities*. Edited by Loriene Roy, Chicago: ALA Editions, 2009.

Mehra, Bharat, Kendra S. Albright, and Kevin Rioux. "A Practical Framework for Social Justice Research in the Information Professions." *Proceedings of the American Society for Information Science and Technology* 43, no. 1 (January 1, 2006): 1–10. doi:10.1002/meet.14504301275.

Mehra, Bharat, Kevin S. Rioux, and Kendra S. Albright. "Social Justice in Library and Information Science." In *Encyclopedia of Library and Information Sciences*, 4820–36. 3rd ed. Taylor & Francis, 2009.

Miller, Willie. "Connecting Libraries and Social Justice." *American Libraries*. Accessed August 23, 2015. http://americanlibrariesmagazine.org/blogs/the-scoop/connecting-libraries-and-social-justice/.

Nathan, Lisa P., Alice MacGougan, and Elizabeth Shaffer. "If Not Us, Who? Social Media Policy and the iSchool Classroom." *Journal of Education for Library & Information Science* 55, no. 2 (2014): 112–32.

Pateman, John, and John Vincent. *Public Libraries and Social Justice.* Farnham, England ; Burlington, VT: Ashgate, 2010.

Pawley, Christine. "Unequal Legacies: Race and Multiculturalism in the LIS Curriculum." *Library Quarterly* 76, no. 2 (2006): 149–68. doi:10.1086/506955.

"Progressive Librarians Guild" Accessed August 24, 2015. http://www.progressivelibrariansguild.org/.

Rawls, John. *A Theory of Justice.* Cambridge, MA: Belknap Press of Harvard University Press, 1971.

"Rerum Novarum: Encyclical of Pope Leo XIII on Capital and Labor." The Vatican. Accessed August 27, 2015. http://w2.vatican.va/content/leo-xiii/en/encyclicals/documents/hf_l-xiii_enc_15051891_rerum-novarum.html.

Rioux, Kevin. "Metatheory in Library and Information Science: A Nascent Social Justice Approach." *Journal of Education for Library & Information Science* 51, no. 1 (Winter 2010): 9–17.

Roberto, Katia, and Jessamyn West, eds. *Revolting Librarians Redux: Radical Librarians Speak out.* Jefferson, N.C: McFarland & Co, 2003.

Rubin, Richard. *Foundations of Library and Information Science.* 3rd ed. New York: Neal-Schuman Publishers, 2010.

Samek, Toni. *Librarianship and Human Rights: A Twenty-First Century Guide.* Oxford: Chandos, 2007.

Savolainen, Reijo. "Everyday Life Information Seeking: Approaching Information Seeking in the Context of 'Way of Life.'" *Library & Information Science Research* 17, no. 3 (1995): 259–94. doi:10.1016/0740-8188(95)90048-9.

Schroeder, Robert, and Christopher V. Hollister. "Librarians' Views on Critical Theories and Critical Practices." *Behavioral & Social Sciences Librarian* 33, no. 2 (April 3, 2014): 91–119. doi:10.1080/01639269.2014.912104.

"Scott Bonner Gives a 'Warts and All' Recap of the Events in Ferguson." I Love Libraries. Accessed August 23, 2015. http://www.ilovelibraries.org/article/scott-bonner-gives-%E2%80%9Cwarts-and-all%E2%80%9D-recap-events-ferguson.

"The Universal Declaration of Human Rights." Accessed August 28, 2015. http://www.un.org/en/documents/udhr/.

Wagner, D. G., and J. Berger. "Do Sociological Theories Grow?" *American Journal of Sociology* 90, no. 4 (1985): 697–728.

Wiegand, Wayne A. "Tunnel Vision and Blind Spots: What the Past Tells Us about the Present; Reflections on the Twentieth-Century History of American Librarianship." *Library Quarterly* 69, no. 1 (1999): 1–32.

Winston, Mark D. "Ethical Leadership and Ethical Decision Making: A Meta-Analysis of Research Related to Ethics Education." *Library & Information Science Research* 29, no. 2 (June 2007): 230–51. doi:10.1016/j.lisr.2007.04.002.

Wood, Stacy, Kathy Carbone, Cifor Marika, Anne Gilliland, and Ricardo Punzalan. "Mobilizing Records: Re-Framing Archival Description to Support Human Rights." *Archival Science* 14 (2014): 397–419.

Chapter 2

Teaching for the Long Game: Sustainability as a Framework for LIS Education

John T. F. Burgess

Considering Sustainability for LIS Practice

This essay is designed to provide faculty members who are teaching in the area of Library and Information Science (LIS) with a framework for introducing sustainability theory into their program's curriculum. The first task of this essay then is to make a case that incorporating sustainability theory into the LIS curriculum is beneficial to both the learning experience of future LIS practitioners and to the long-term health and viability of the communities they will serve. The second task is to demonstrate that the two are compatible in a way that it is possible to teach one without diluting the mission of the other. This is a practical essay in that regard, but also a persuasive one, conveying the message that sustainability theory is not supplemental to LIS practice but rather is essential to the success of the profession's larger mission in the long run. Presented here are three main sections: a summary of the moral imperatives associated with sustainability theory and how they connect with existing LIS professional ethics; a discussion of why teaching sustainability should be considered a justice issue; and suggestions on how to introduce sustainability into the LIS curriculum as modules in core courses and as special topics elective courses.

Collectively, what is presented here should be considered a framework for LIS education because it provides a moral imperative for action, meshes well with existing social justice efforts, provides a new and important sense of purpose to existing subjects and objectives, and teaches a new skill that otherwise would not be part of the curriculum. The objective of the sustainability framework is as simple as it is daunting: to help LIS practitioners reframe what it means to serve the information needs of a society. Instead of serving only to satisfy the information need of the individual, or only serving the society in an institutional capacity, *LIS professionals are called upon to act in ways that will promote and sustain an environment where humans are more likely to flourish and thus are capable of having information needs.*[1] Conversely, LIS professionals would be prompted to oppose actions that would make the continued flourishing of the human species less likely. In light of sustainability theory, any prudent activity pertaining to the capacity of a society to use knowledge to promote human flourishing should be considered a legitimate domain of research or practice for the LIS profession. In addition to existing skills and ethics related to satisfying the information need, and to skills and ethics of fair and equitable use of information in society, a third set of skills and ethics emerge. These require one to consider the LIS professional expertise regarding the creation, use, and protection of knowledge as an instrument with the potential to help maximize the collective longevity of the human species, potentially deep into the future.

In a profession that is consistently struggling with material and ethical crises in unjust societies as well as the realities of operating decision and budget constraints, adding further obligations to the human deep future might seem naïve or idealistic, particularly in a volume on teaching for

1. Flourishing here is consistent with the Greek ethical concept of Eudaimonia, the prudent growth towards life goals or objectives one has decided are virtuous. Just as a human being cannot be said to flourish as the result of any given decision, but only flourishes over the fullness of a lifetime, no single policy can ensure that a species flourishes. In the cases of both the individual and the species it is the decision to seek flourishing instead of other more immediate opportunities that is virtuous.

justice. However, sustainability is not a futurist theory or an ideology. It is a school of thought that is meant to guide policy and decision making in the present and brings with it strong justice imperatives. If done effectively, teaching for sustainability will help students to be more fully cognizant of how injustices done today hurt not only the living, but also our descendants for generations to come, and in extreme cases may negatively impact even the existence of those future generations. In this way, sustainability is a form of social justice.

Sustainability is compatible with social justice, because both have their moral authority anchored in the idea of distributive justice. Distributive justice is the belief that the burdens and benefits of a society should be evenly distributed throughout the population.[2] When viewed from the perspective of sustainability theory one would see that a culture of consumerism, where one's sense of self worth is tied to owning the latest technological innovations in an endless upgrade cycle, creates twin burdens that must be corrected. The first burden is placed on those who labor without fair compensation to serve the needs of the wealthy global minority. The second burden is placed on those future generations who will inherit a world denuded of many of natural resources available today and most likely will be denied the benefit of a stable and predicable climate, which had proven so hospitable to cultural and technological growth. The former burden is visible to us, and thus is already in the sights of social justice activists. It is the second burden that is addressed by sustainability. How is it possible to advocate for the rights of people who do not yet exist?

Much of the work of creating a just society is to identify burdens that are being ignored, raising those burdens above the threshold of awareness, and moving the public to collectively act on behalf of the burdened population. This collective action may take many forms, including solidarity movements, the equitable redistribution of wealth and capital, and reforms of exploitative social institutions. In all cases, the

2. Loretta Capeheart and Dragan Milovanovic, "Distributive Justice," in *Social Justice: Theories, Issues & Movements* (New Brunswick, N.J.: Rutgers University Press, 2007), 29.

aim of the action is to make changes in the present that will benefit people in the present. That the action will also benefit people in the future is important, but not an immediate goal. Sustainability action is no different. Thus, the explicit belief communicated in this essay is that being better equipped to think about sustainability, and the long term flourishing of the species, will lead to making decisions that will remove a burden for those in the here and now, and as a consequence of changes made today will have benefits for those in the future. Consider this belief to be analogous to a position that attending to the health care, education, and security needs of a child today both improves the quality of life for that child in the present, and increases their chances of a healthy life in the future for themselves and their descendants.

Defining Sustainability Theory

Sustainability theory is an applied philosophy.[3] Being a philosophy means that it offers an internally consistent way of interpreting the world, while being applied means that it is focused on real-world problems and solutions instead of theory for theory's sake. Application is also the approach taken in this essay: to provide an internally consistent argument for why it is appropriate and beneficial to teach sustainability in LIS programs while emphasizing practical considerations over exploring in excessive detail the philosophical discourse on the subject.[4] Instead, the main theme of this essay is that LIS students will benefit personally and professionally from being taught the mindset of long-term thinking, defined here as a way of considering the world that emphasizes the importance of evaluating decisions in the present with an eye towards

3. Here the term "sustainability" is used to emphasize the practices one undertakes to sustain a viable biosphere, while "sustainability theory" is used to refer to the philosophy and ethics that guide and inform sustainability practices.

4. While a philosophical quest for clarity on what are the bases of our obligations to future generations is laudable and important work, the intricacies of current argumentation on the subject are beyond the scope of an introductory chapter on teaching the concepts in a professional program.

the long-term significance of our actions. When embraced, long-term thinking yields the ability to resist innate and external pressures that lead us without merit to privilege immediate rewards over a potentially greater good in the long term. This way of thinking will be demonstrated to offer clear benefits to autonomy and adaptability, two desired traits in a professional. These benefits extend to students as individual practitioners, to the communities they serve, to their profession in general, and (most importantly as part of collective action) to the overall health of the human species. While developing long-term thinking skills is the goal, sustainability is more than just a useful context in which to develop that skill. Instead, it is an issue of justice not only for the current generation but also for future ones as well. Before considering why sustainability should be taught in the LIS curriculum it is important to define sustainability, understand the moral questions it poses, and consider its implications for justice advocacy.

Sustainability theory is a field of thought concerned with the best way for human beings to fulfill our obligations as members of an interconnected, immensely complex biosphere, while still honoring the human desire to flourish. This emphasis on obligations makes sustainability a theory of ethical practice. Sustainability theory is only one line of thought within a larger tradition of environmental philosophy, which is a systematic consideration of the nature of the relationship between humanity and the so-called "natural" world.[5] So-called because the idea of nature being a category that is fundamentally distinct from the category of humans may be seen as reductive, both of the radically dependent nature of humanity on the environment with which we co-evolved and in terms of the character of the biosphere, the complexity of which is not subject to the limitations of human language or imagination. Feminist ecologists such as Karen Warren advocate resisting the

5. In this essay the terms "nature" and "natural world" are used synonymously with the technical term "biosphere," or sum of life on Earth, and do not convey a notion of nature as something that is categorically distinct from humanity; rather, humanity is that part of an interconnected continuity that is capable of and thus obliged to engage in rational discourse about its relationship with the remainder of the continuity.

"othering" of nature, likening it to the objectification of women and members of minority populations.[6] Other concerns of environmental philosophy include climate ethics, the study of obligations specific to the consequences of anthropogenic climate change and other human geoengineering experiments; ethics of speciation, the ethical obligations that members of a species have to other members of the same species, compared to a different species; population ethics, the duties of living persons to future or past generations; and environmental economic justice, which deals with matters of equitable allocation and scarcity of non-renewable resources, including human labor. Of these, sustainability theory is the best fit as a potential partner with the objectives of LIS professional education, both because sustainability theory takes into accounts the human desire for flourishing and because its practical orientation lines up well with the pragmatic nature of many LIS ethical principles. The next step in defining sustainability is to understand what it means to fulfill obligations to the natural world.

Moral Obligations to Nature and Their Significance for LIS Practices

A belief may be called "moral" when it is easily understood, guides behavior unambiguously towards a model of the good, and is broadly accepted by a society to the exclusion of alternative propositions.[7] One key moral question is whether nature should be considered an instrumental good, a *means* for facilitating human accomplishments, or an intrinsic good, an *end*, regardless of the needs of humans? Another moral question is, are our duties to the natural world primarily anthropocentric, meaning primarily to our fellow humans, or are they non-anthropocentric, where

6. Karen Warren, *Ecofeminist Philosophy: A Western Perspective on What It Is and Why It Matters* (Lanham, MD: Rowman & Littlefield, 2000), 1.

7. As an example of morality in LIS professional ethics, consider the unambiguous moral authority given to those who act to oppose censorship. "Banned Book Week" not only communicates an ethic, it establishes a norm of the good for practitioners both to follow and to celebrate following. In this way, morals are a key part of identity formation.

other concerns are given equal or greater consideration? These possible concerns may include theological or spiritual obligations or they may be purely secular concepts, for example deep ecology, the belief that no one species in more important than any other. Determining where the LIS profession lies on the axis of the goodness of the natural world and the appropriate degree of anthropocentrism will go a long way toward clarifying how sustainability should be taught. Given that this essay is a practical guide and not a work of moral philosophy, the objective here is not to declare one position morally correct and the other suspect. Instead, this essay has the practical aim of guiding action in a logically consistent way within the relevant LIS context. Therefore, what matters is that a choice be made in order to limit and focus the range of ethical obligations that must be considered, and that the choice make sense given the requirements of the context in which they are employed.

In order for an argument on the goodness of fit between sustainability theory and LIS ethics to be received as worthwhile, an effort must be made to align the values of both disciplines. As will be demonstrated in more detail in the section below on specific ways of adding sustainability theory to the LIS curriculum, LIS professional ethics emerged primarily from dealing with ethical crises that arose within the communities in which they practice.[8] If the good provided by LIS institutions is instrumental, and the purpose for those institutions is to satisfy anthropomorphic needs, then it seems likely that one could characterize LIS practice as leaning towards an instrumental and anthropocentric understanding of the good brought by the profession. While LIS professional ethics such as social responsibility, intellectual freedom, neutrality, and the common good do find traction, regardless of how loftily those ideas are expressed, they only make sense in service of a human population. Therefore, in the context of this essay and with the stated aim of the practical incorporation of sustainability theory into the LIS curriculum, the most appropriate take on the obligations of

8. Jean L. Preer, *Library Ethics* (Westport, CT: Libraries Unlimited, 2008), 83.

sustainability to put forward is an anthropocentric and instrumentalist approach.[9]

The Three Es of Sustainability

Having established which moral obligations are at play in bringing sustainability theory into LIS education, it is appropriate to consider what activities are involved in sustainability practice to see if those activities are also compatible. Anthropocentric, instrumentalist sustainability practices are those activities that are believed, in aggregate, more likely to promote human flourishing. Even though, as stated before, any action by information professions which might lead to flourishing is fit for LIS research and practice, realistically speaking there needs to be some limit to the scope of activities to give LIS practitioners a chance to specialize in sustainability practice. In keeping with Mandy Henk's formulation of sustainability, the approach to sustainability practice discussed in this essay has three main applications: ecology, economy, and equity, which together comprise what are called the "Three Es" of sustainability.[10]

Ecology is the application that is already most strongly associated with the idea of sustainability. An ecology is a process of mutual interdependence taking place over a span of time. Ecologies may be disrupted, and when they are, that disruption is often disastrous. Thinking ecologically means being aware of the importance of systems and of process, not just causes and effects, and certainly not a simple competition between winners and losers. Ecology practices represent the stewardship of renewable and non-renewable natural resources, to maximize their useful availability over the duration of human existence.[11] Advocating

9. Just as LIS professional ethics do not have authority over the personal ethics of individual practitioners, this assertion that the best fit for sustainability and LIS education is anthropocentric and instrumental does nothing to preclude individual LIS practitioners from holding intrinsic, non-anthropocentric beliefs about sustainability, up to and including religious animism.

10. Mandy Henk, *Ecology, Economy, Equity: The Path to a Carbon-Neutral Library* (Chicago: American Library Association Editions, 2014), 5.

11. This is what is known as shallow ecology, or minimizing the impacts of human activity on the ecosystem.

for ecological thinking is a social justice practice because it is another foundation for the principle of distribution. Here, distribution is not valued only because of its association with fairness, but also with mutual survival. Any organism, including humans, that hoards resources to the extent that nothing else can compete, destroys the viability of the ecosystem not just for itself, but also for all species. It is an act of social justice then to identify where human misuse of resources is leading to current suffering and may lead to ecological collapse in the future. Within the context of LIS ecological practice, the most obvious and immediate are those associated with the "greening libraries" movement: actions librarians can take to lessen the environmental impacts created by their institutions.[12] An application of ecological practice that is one step beyond internal policies is advocacy for policies that minimize environmental impact within local communities. Libraries come in many different types: public, academic, school, and special. Similarly many kinds of institutions have archives, and museums may represent interests as diverse as corporations, communities, or single families. Since LIS institutions have an uncommonly broad footprint from being distributed throughout so many domains in a society, giving LIS students the skills they will need as professionals to inform, educate, and advocate for environmental policy reforms will increase their ability to affect positive change across these domains.

More proactively in terms of applications of sustainability for ecology, LIS professionals can participate in open access and open data movements. This will allow their expertise in the organization of knowledge to contribute to areas of scientific and technological innovations that slow the pace of environmental degradation due to our consumption economy. Slowing the pace gives more time for everyone to develop ways of being in the world that are more compatible with the realities of finite amounts of non-renewable resources. These ways of being may also be more rewarding than satisfying hedonism alone. Finally,

12. Monika Antonelli and Mark McCullough, eds., *Greening Libraries* (Los Angeles: Library Juice Press, 2012), 1.

even adopting a shallow ecological stance means that it is important to look to the long-term consequences of actions today. In order for us to expect our leaders in business and government to think of long-term consequences, we have to make it possible to do so. That means that as administrators of institutions of memory, LIS professionals are charged with recording what those decisions were and making them available to as wide an audience as possible. Without awareness of decisions made, opportunities to hold leaders accountable are limited. Likewise, as administrators of institutions of discovery, LIS professionals gather together the latest research and increasingly the data used in research as well. This research is often the best source of the kind of information that separates useful policy from fatuous policy. Institutions of discovery also provide expertise in how to locate this information, making it more likely to be available in a "just in time" context.

The second area of practical application is the *economy*. The global economy is another complex network of mutual interdependence, analogous to the biosphere. Fair distribution of economic opportunity is to the global economy what maximizing evolutionary diversity is to an ecology: a way of increasing the overall potential for adaptation. Advocating for the fair division of labor is a well-establish good that has been sought by social justice reform movements inspired by diverse thinkers such as Jean-Jacques Rousseau, Peter Kropotkin, and Karl Marx and Frederick Engels. Fair economic opportunity would mean that access to capital (the best precursor tool to innovation that we currently have available) would not be limited only to those who through no merit of their own were born into wealthy nations, but that it instead be as broadly distributed as possible. This could be done in a system that is still driven by ideas of competition and the validity of market economies, until such time as better systems may be devised. In addition to this kind of base calculation that it is valuable to maximize adaptability as a form of species health, there is also a far less remote reason to advocate for more economic mobility. Poverty leads to physical and psychological suffering, often in the form of hunger or limited access to affordable healthcare or creative opportunities. Experiencing suffering makes it difficult or even impossible to flourish.[13] This holds true for individuals and for societies. Worse even than suffering is tolerance of suffering. Sustainability practices for economics draw on the same kinds of awareness that come from understanding sustainability practices for ecologies: that we are interdependent and, while fragile as individuals, we are capable of globally transformative feats collectively.

LIS professionals' contributions to economic sustainability practices unfold similarly to their contributions to ecological sustainability. The first sphere of influence is with libraries, archives, and museums. Fair economic practices begin with fair labor practices within LIS institutions. It also means that the funds entrusted in these institutions should be spent in ways that are mindful of the needs of the poor and disadvantaged whenever possible. When purchasing resources, practitioners should be mindful of the economic goals and policies of the companies they are doing business with. Those resources should also be purchased with an eye for the longevity and availability of access to the resource. Resources that have the fewest restrictions on their use, either technologically or through policy, are preferred. Beyond that, recall again that LIS institutions are present in many different contexts within society. Building partnerships and good relationships with boards of directors, university administrations, or division heads may provide a degree of persuasive influence on immediate economic policy decisions. Next, LIS professionals may work collectively to influence economic systems within the knowledge creation industries by continuing to advocate for reforms to the practices of scholarly publishing. Working to further the aims of the open access movement and to develop institutional repositories of publications and data is one way to provide the broadest access possible to useful knowledge, with the hope that access to knowledge will lead to a variety of educational opportunities. While education is certainly

13. Lisa Tessman, *Burdened Virtues: Virtue Ethics for Liberatory Struggles* (New York: Oxford University Press, 2005), 159.

not the only pathway to economic opportunity, it is one that is closely aligned with existing LIS missions.

The final area of sustainability practice is *equity*, the overall degree to which a society is set up to operate in a manner that is fair for all members of that society. Fairness may manifest in economic terms, meaning that there could be some overlap with the economic applications of sustainability theory mentioned above. However, equity is about more than proving equal economic opportunity. Equity is only possible when those laws, policies, and social conventions that create asymmetrical burdens within a population are removed. Working for equity is another core form of social justice activism, in that social justice advocates often seek to disrupt instruments of hegemony. Antonio Gramsci is associated with the idea of cultural hegemony, which is the awareness that social institutions, when left unchallenged, can be used by elites in a society to limit and control an otherwise culturally diverse population. These acts of systematic oppression are usually perpetrated on portions of the population that have been historically marginalized, such as immigrant or migrant communities, racial or ethnic minorities, women, and persons working for the rights to define their own gender expression and sexual preferences. Seen in this light, advocating equity is essential in order to protect the legitimacy of representative democracy. Equity is a sustainability issue because systems of racial, gender, and other forms of bias wind up privileging ideas, strategies, and ways of thinking of one group or class for reasons other than merit. This chauvinism toward one way of being in the world can only serve to limit the adaptability of the species to ongoing and future challenges.

As with economic sustainability, there is also a more personal reason to promote equity due to the idea of flourishing. Asymmetrical enforcement of laws may lead to personal or communal suffering. Physical and mental abuse of people who wield less power in a society due to some facet of their identity may lead to suffering, impinging on the potential of entire segments of a population to flourish. Structurally, societies that are designed in such a way as to make use of hegemonic authority to set the norm for personal behavior not only limit the individual freedoms of members of their society, but negatively impact long term survivability by marginalizing cultures that contribute to the depth and complexity of the human species. Sustainability practices for equity in the LIS profession are well represented by existing LIS values such as democracy, the common good, social responsibility, intellectual freedom, and access to information. Continuing to act individually and collectively through interest groups and professional organizations in ways that are in line with those values will contribute to equitable sustainability practices.

The three core activities for sustainability practice reflect this anthropocentric, instrumentalist approach to our species' relationship with nature. At first it may seem like economic or socio-political systems have nothing to do with the "natural world," but if one does not apply the status of romanticized "other" to nature, but instead consider it to be the milieu in which all life on Earth operates, it makes intuitive sense to talk about economic or socio-political sustainability. For example, consider hunting to extinction a non-human species simply because their pelts are deemed valuable. This is an issue of ecology and economics. Consider policies that combine the mass incarceration of individuals on felony non-violent drug crimes, along with stripping their right to vote, the inability to get the same amount of access to student loans, and the difficulty of getting quality employment with a felony conviction. This is also a sustainability issue both on equity terms, because the burdens of this policy are asymmetrically born, and on ecological terms, because these policies may impair the flourishing of not only current the current generation but also their children and subsequent generations. With these examples, it is possible to see how seemingly disparate concepts like the health of the environment, the distribution of wealth, and sharing the burdens of living in a social order symmetrically are not isolated goals, but are instead complementary through an understanding of justice that takes into account both the present and future.

Sustainability as Justice Advocacy

Social justice is "educating ourselves and others, and taking action to change the status quo. Social justice is about giving voice to communities who have been forced into silence; social justice is about equity and equal access."[14] Construed in this way, justice is not an abstract set of principles, but it is instead a clear set of obligations between real persons. These persons are real and exist in a place and a time. Social justice movements have helped expand the understanding that humans have justice obligations to one another, even when remote in respect to place, be that in a different neighborhood or a different nation. However, justice obligations also exist between people who are remote in time as well. The results of an injustice committed today may affect people who have yet to be born. Given their contingent nature, those yet to be born are radically dependent upon the living to behave justly and ethically. While is it impossible to "give voice" in the present to those yet to be born, it is possible to protect the ability of future generations to have the same range of economic, political, and social choices we enjoy today. In effect, acting in the present to protect the range of choices available is protecting the viability of concepts like autonomy and freedom over the long-term future of our species.

Sustainability is a social justice orientation towards current generations as well. It provides a justification to oppose a particular injustice that exists today: that social, political, and economic institutions are increasingly normalizing the dominance of short-term thinking. Short-term thinking is the condition in which immediate, measurable consequences take precedence over more holistic, visionary ways of thinking. Typically short-term thinking manifests in a way where the immediate economic impacts of decisions are the primary concerns. In other words, how

---

14. L. A. Rodriguez and Tatiana Cummings, eds. "Cultural Times," (2007): 12, http://www.humboldt.edu /multicultural/Download/cultural_times/fall_2007.pdf, quoted in Nicole A. Cooke, Miriam E. Sweeney, and Safiya Umoja Noble. "Social Justice as Topic and Tool: An Attempt to Transform an LIS Curriculum and Culture." *Library Quarterly* 86, no. 1 (January 2016): 107–24.

does something affect the "bottom line" right now? Short-term thinking is dehumanizing and reductive, in that it reduces the wealth of ways to determine the worth and goodness of an action to only considering the immediate consequences. However, when short-term thinking is paired with neo-liberal thought it becomes particularly troubling. Neo-liberalism is a political theory whose adherents seek to replace government services and collective labor with markets. It likewise replaces local culture with market cultures, a combination of classical economic liberalism with ideals of individualism and personal responsibility that minimizes collective identity.[15] The ideology of neo-liberalism elevates the actions of the free market to be the prime factor in determining if policy is fair, meaning that if people can be shown to tolerate a policy, it is fair. The increasingly inexpensive availability of computation, networked communication, and micro-sensor technology means that it is possible to measure a wider range of human and natural environmental conditions than ever, in close to real time. This means that more facets of life could be subjected both to the neo-liberal project of letting the market determine fairness, combined with short-term thinking normalizing immediate consequences over long-term objectives, with the efect on environmental sustainability and human flourishing possibly being the kind of disaster Pierre Bourdieu critically labeled "a utopia of endless exploitation."[16]

Sustainability theory provides a context for justice that extends beyond the scope of any particular society, and yet insists that the only way to ensure future justice is to act in accord with one's ethical principles and rational beliefs in the present. Sustainability theory further provides us with a vision of humanity persisting into the remote future, or failing to do so, depending in part on our actions towards the biosphere in general, and one another in particular. Sustainability practice shows

15. Lisa Duggan, *The Twilight of Equality? Neoliberalism, Cultural Politics, and the Attack on Democracy* (Boston: Beacon Press, 2012), 12.

16. Pierre Bourdieu, "The Essence of Neoliberalism: Utopia of Endless Exploitation," *Le Monde Diplomatique* (1998), http://mondediplo.com/1998/12/08bourdieu.

us how acting responsibly in the realms of the economy, ecology, and social equity can promote flourishing as individuals and as a species. The greatest justice from the selected perspective of sustainability theory is to promote not just subsistence, but flourishing of the human species through prudential action. An injustice then would be anything that either lessens the human species' ability to flourish as a whole or creates an asymmetrical burden on one portion of the population relative to the other portions.

For a profession whose ethical obligations tend to focus on individual persons, communities, or the larger society, thinking not just in terms of seeking justice for the whole species today, but for all members of that species who are yet to be born, is a tremendous jump in responsibility. Is there any good that can come of assuming such a burden, one that it always just over the population horizon? As a profession that has established itself as the authority of preserving memory and facilitating discovery, there can be no clearer, no more important moral good than helping to sustain the species whose memories are being preserved, whose curiosity is driving the need for discovery. In particular, sustainability-as-justice is an approach that nurtures the awareness that all humans are a single species and that equity of origin implies that we have the same claim on the resources of the world. Sharing an origin and being the same species implies that we share a common destiny as a species as well. We are a united species across the artificial boundaries of nation-states. We are also united across the gulf of time – potentially into the deep future. If we hold to the idea of human rights, and we recognize the rights of human beings standing across from us, which they posses simply because they are human, then we must extend the same rights to a person living two hundred years from now on that same basis.

The advocacy imperative at the heart of sustainability-as-justice is this: it is right to question decisions that privilege short-term gains over long-term flourishing. It is expected and healthy to take care of your needs and the needs of your family, but to seek comforts in excess of the necessary requires awareness of the impacts of those comforts on non-renewable resources and on the health of the environment so that an informed decision can be made. A question to keep in mind that illustrates this imperative is: Can it be considered fair that humans who are alive today only by accident of birth are able to live in a consumer's paradise only if it means a far larger number from future generations must suffer austerity and privation? Consider the analogous situation where people of one nation live in opulence on plundered resources while people from all other nations toil on denuded lands with very little quality of life. Those people concerned with economic justice would likely call that scenario systematic exploitation at best and genocide at worst. Likewise, people with a well-developed sense of sustainability justice question the validity of allowing those born in certain nations in the present to thrive on far more than their fair share of resources at the expense of the population of the future.

Given the possibility that current consumptive lifestyles will lead not only to the depletion of resources, but to severe climate change, including a runaway greenhouse effect, ocean acidification, and mass extinctions of animal and plant life, this is not a matter of violating future generation's ability to flourish, but their ability to exist at all. Given what is at stake, for the benefit of the species as a whole, as many groups as possible should be engaged in sustainability justice work. The ultimate answer to the question of whether sustainability justice advocacy is a matter of LIS professional ethics is this: given the scope and complexity of the problem, the service orientation needed to identify with the needs of remote generations, the devotion to ethical principles needed to address asymmetries in the ecology, economy, and democracy, and the key role that knowledge and information are likely to play in addressing these challenges, there may actually be no profession that is more qualified to take the lead in sustainability practice as a form of justice advocacy.

Sustainability in the Curriculum

Many topics and skills commonly taught within the LIS curriculum could be easily adapted to incorporate sustainability concepts. Within user-services courses, what is key is an expanded idea of service that de-emphasizes the immediate, one-on-one encounter, and instead focuses on the collective self-sufficiency and autonomy needs of a community. This idea of service is expressed best in Durrani's position that to inform is to liberate, not only from ignorance but also from hegemonic control.[17] Human flourishing is impossible when people are unaware of the infrastructure that acts to limit their present and future choices by compelling one shortsighted vision of what is normal and acceptable. Simply by being aware of those infrastructural limits, LIS professionals can help communities push past them. Another important concept to include is awareness that information is not a neutral concept, and its use may instead be tied up with the neoliberal project of individuation. Osburn reflects on the degree to which "judgment, understanding, durability, and responsibility for others" have little functional place in a throwaway consumer culture.[18] By emphasizing knowledge services instead of information services, it is possible to insure that both the information and the context for making sense of that information are provided. In the realm of technical services, the key idea is to promote cognitive justice in information systems. Cognitive justice is the principle that recognizes that it is a moral duty to undo the damage colonial powers did when they used their dominance to propagate Western epistemologies.[19] This means that existing organizational structures, which only make Western European, hierarchical, scientific, and rigidly disciplined organizational standards available, should be replaced by organizational structures such as cataloging rules and classification schemes that recognize and accommodate multiple ontologies. From a technological and managerial standpoint, the greening of the library (which is a collection of policies and programs) with the intent of making decisions to lessen the ecological footprint of the library, provides an example for local communities.[20]

---

17. Shiraz Durrani, *Information and Liberation : Writings on the Politics of Information and Librarianship* (Duluth, MN: Library Juice Press, 2008), xxvii.

18. Charles B. Osburn, *The Western Devaluation of Knowledge* (Lanham, MD: Rowman & Littlefield Publishers, 2013), 117.

19. Boaventura de Sousa Santos, *Cognitive Justice in a Global World: Prudent Knowledges for a Decent Life* (Lanham, MD: Lexington Books, 2007), 12.

20. Antonelli and McCullough, *Greening Libraries*, 1.

Student Learning Outcomes

At least within the context of North American LIS programs, discussions of the curriculum exist within a context of master's degree program accreditation. In the LIS profession, individuals are not credentialed to work in LIS institutions on the basis of a competency exam; instead, professional jobs are available primarily to those who graduate from programs that achieve American Library Association (ALA) accredited status. The contributions of coursework to the accreditation process include both a program-level assessment of student learning outcomes and a review of the goals and objectives requirements of the curriculum.[21] Any class or module on sustainability theory or practice should therefore be shown to lead to these competencies, as well as to fulfill their own ethical and scholarly objectives.

Four essential student learning outcomes to consider when planning sustainability content are: 1.2.1 The essential character of the field of library and information studies; 1.2.2 The philosophy, principles, and ethics of the field; 1.2.5 The symbiotic relationship for library and information studies with other fields; and 1.2.6 The role of library and information services in a diverse global society, including the role of serving the needs of underserved groups.[22] The concept of essential character fits well with the prior discussion of the project of sustainability as being one that promotes flourishing for the entire species. Flourishing is a concept from character ethics which suggests that remaining true to one's character, whatever that character may turn out to be, is one pathway towards flourishing. When considering the ethics of the field, the moral imperatives of sustainability theory and the applications of sustainability practice discussed above may be presented alongside existing sources of ethical guidance, such as the "Core Values of Librarianship,"

21. Committee on Accreditation of the American Library Association, "Standards for Accreditation of Master's Programs in Library and Information Studies," 4–6, http://www.ala.org/accreditedprograms/standards.

22. These learning outcomes originate in the Standards cited above. Identification of the role of student learning outcomes and emphasis on these particular outcomes among others were presented by Clara Chu in her 2016 conference presentation, "Sustainable Development: Implications for LIS Education and Research."

the "Freedom to Read Statement," the "Library Bill of Rights," and the "Code of Ethics of the American Library Association."[23] Should the idea of incorporating sustainability theory into LIS practice gain traction, providing an overarching and unifying ethical goal, which is to promote the continued flourishing of the human species into the remote future, has the potential to unite the collected ethics of the profession into a more direct and ambitious narrative.

The learning objective concerning LIS service in a global setting is an explicit invitation to consider the implications of information services not only on individual communities around the world, but all those who rely on the Earth holistically. Considering underserved groups also opens an avenue for thinking about future generations who are radically dependent upon the decisions of the current population to determine what resources, including knowledge, are still available to them. Finally, when considering the symbiotic relationship between LIS and sustainability, new perspectives that clarify both emerge. As examples of this symbiosis, consider two works different in scope and approach, *Information Ecologies,* by Nardi and O'Day, and *Environmental Informatics,* edited by Avouris and Page.[24] What is encouraging about the symbiosis between LIS and sustainability is that both have the potential to be informed by either the theory or practice of the other, or by both the theory and practice of the other. Neither discipline need be subordinate, despite the practical reality that the guidelines of accreditation apply structural rules for how sustainability may be introduced within LIS.

---

23. American Library Association, "Core Values of Librarianship"; American Library Association, "The Freedom to Read Statement"; American Library Association, "Library Bill of Rights"; and American Library Association, "Code of Ethics of the American Library Association."

24. Bonnie A Nardi and Vicki O'Day, *Information Ecologies: Using Technology with Heart* (Cambridge, MA: MIT Press, 1999); Nicholas M. Avouris and Bernd Page, *Environmental Informatics: Methodology and Applications of Environmental Information Processing.*, Vol. 6. (Berlin: Springer Science & Business Media, 2013).

Developing Modules in Line with Course Goals and Objectives

While every LIS program determines the specifics of their curriculum, the ALA Standards for accreditation also provide guidance on the goals and objectives of those courses. This guidance includes the following points:

> II.2.1 Fosters development of library and information professionals who will assume a leadership role in providing services and collections appropriate for the communities that are served; II.2.2 Emphasizes an evolving body of knowledge that reflects the findings of basic and applied research from relevant fields; II.2.3 Integrates technology and the theories that underpin its design, application, and use; II.2.4 Responds to the needs of a diverse and global society, including the needs of underserved groups; II.2.5 Provides direction for future development of a rapidly changing field; II.2.6 Promotes commitment to continuous professional development and lifelong learning, including the skills and competencies that are needed for the practitioner of the future.[25]

These points may also provide guidance about what kinds of sustainability modules would be easily incorporated if developed, given that these objectives are guaranteed to be present within the curriculum regardless of program specifics. A module on sustainability leadership would meet criterion II.2.1 by promoting an expanded idea of services to include not just access to information services, but those economic opportunities and democratic rights that are fundamental for full participation in society. The module also has the potential to expand the notion of community to include the human species in its entirety. A module satisfying II.2.2 could emphasize the importance of providing access to knowledge as broadly as possible, since just as an awareness of the evolving body of LIS research promotes the vitality of the profession,

25. Committee on Accreditation of the American Library Association, "Standards for Accreditation of Master's Programs in Library and Information Studies," 5.

the human species also relies on ready access to new knowledge in order to make vital decisions. This is also an opportunity to discuss the limitations of the current models of scholarly publishing and electronic resource sharing, given the benefits of knowledge on equitable governance and economic opportunity. The theories that underpin design in II.2.3 present an opportunity to discuss the assumptions about the inevitability of progress and the myth of the intrinsic, almost salvific good of technology, and to expand the definition of what a technology is in relationship to the flourishing needs of individuals and the species. II.2.4 is traditionally the place in the curriculum to discuss the obligations of the LIS profession to better serve underserved populations. This is an important topic of discussion that should appear frequently in LIS courses. So in proposing to add a module including a different kind of diversity, in the ecological sense, it should only be done in a way that does not take away from the time devoted to diversity as a social justice issue. If possible, perhaps in addition to expressing the moral good of serving diverse populations, a module for II.2.4 could also provide a supplemental argument for the functional good of service to underserved populations as sustainability from economy and equity practices.

Point II.2.5 is the need to prepare LIS professionals for rapid change, and to provide the profession with a future towards which to develop. It is in this point that a module alone may not suffice. Instead, a case may be made that this objective provides the justification for offering an entire course on sustainability theory and practices in LIS. The main good that sustainability theory provides LIS is a sense of purpose in the present that yields results in the future. A sustainability course would provide a space to discuss the concept of rapid technological change and other technologically deterministic arguments, as well as the unintended consequences of leaving those narratives unchallenged. It would also provide an opportunity to discuss other forms of rapid change, such as the kind of changes brought about by the rapid degradation of biodiversity and the hospitable conditions our species relies on for flourishing and existence. Which skills for the storage and transmission of knowledge might be taught to promote sustainability in those kinds of conditions? Along those lines, the lifelong learning mentioned in II.2.6 does not have to mean lifelong consumption of education as a product, but learning to be self-sufficient, and to remove the economic and political barriers to the self-sufficiency of others as well. This would work equally well as a module in a foundations course, or potentially as its own elective course.

The Standalone Sustainability Course and The Long Game

While incorporating modules of sustainability theory and practice into the curriculum ensures that students cannot self-select away from being presented with key sustainability concepts, having a standalone sustainability course in an LIS program has distinct benefits. Most importantly, sustainability is a mindset, and it takes time to create a mindset. Adding modules to existing courses may facilitate a skills-based approach to teaching sustainability practices. Those skills are beneficial to possess if they do lead to better practices, but skills in context with a broader mindset have the potential to be transformative. One example of a mindset that may be transformed is that of hyperbolic discounting. Hyperbolic discounting is an economic principle wherein people tend to value a lesser reward that is available in the present more than a greater reward in the future. Another is the awareness of the ways that the concept of future transformation can be used by a hegemon to perpetuate inequity in the present. In a culture that has embraced the idea of inevitable progress, either towards utopia or dystopia, it takes time to learn a new mindset of personal responsibility for global events. What an awareness of sustainability provides is access to the idea of the long now, the awareness that humans never have experiential access to any time besides the now, the present moment. Thinking about the future as something that is fundamentally different from the present moment may lead to deferment of responsibility. Teaching sustainability in a standalone course, then, is more than teaching the moral obligations of sustainability theory or the ecological, economic, and equity activism associated with sustainability practice. It is teaching for the long game. The long game is the mindset that the fundamental unit of the human species is not the individual, not the family, not the nation or society of many nations, and not even the living human population. Instead, the fundamental unit of the human species is the human species—the entire run of the species from founder's mutation to whatever shared destiny awaits us all. This is a philosophy as well as an ethic, a mindset as well as a set of practices, that takes seriously this idea of the long game and uses it as an instrument to shape policy and practices in the here and now. Taking up a philosophy of this scope could easily lead to charges of delusions of grandeur for the LIS profession. However, few who self-identify as rationalists could look at the scope and depth of the changes human have made on the biosphere over the past 40,000 years, over the past 575 years, or over the past twenty years and still ignore thc transformative powers of the human species without wondering what we will do next. The real question, then, is who among us is willing to accept the moral burdens of having that much power, and then turn that power toward the project of human flourishing?

Bibliography

American Library Association. "Code of Ethics of the American Library Association." 2008. http://www.ala.org/advocacy/proethics/codeofethics/codeethics.

———. "Core Values of Librarianship." 2004. http://www.ala.org/advocacy/intfreedom/statementspols/corevalues.

———. "The Freedom to Read Statement." Accessed June 9, 2013. http://www.ala.org/advocacy/intfreedom/statementspols/freedomreadstatement.

———. "Library Bill of Rights." Accessed May 19, 2013. http://www.ala.org/advocacy/intfreedom/librarybill.

Antonelli, Monika, and Mark McCullough, eds. *Greening Libraries*. Los Angeles: Library Juice Press, 2012.

Avouris, Nicholas M., and Bernd Page. *Environmental Informatics: Methodology and Applications of Environmental Information Processing*. Vol. 6. Berlin: Springer Science & Business Media, 2013.

Bourdieu, Pierre. "The Essence of Neoliberalism: Utopia of Endless Exploitation." *Le Monde Diplomatique*, 1998. http://mondediplo.com/1998/12/08bourdieu.

Capeheart, Loretta, and Dragan Milovanovic. "Distributive Justice." In *Social Justice: Theories, Issues & Movements*, 29–44. New Brunswick, N.J.: Rutgers University Press, 2007.

Chu, Clara M. "Sustainable Development: Implications for LIS Education and Research." Paper presented at the ALISE 2016, Boston, MA, January 7, 2016.

Committee on Accreditation of the American Library Association. "Standards for Accreditation of Master's Programs in Library and Information Studies," February 2, 2015. http://www.ala.org/accreditedprograms/standards.

Cooke, Nicole A., Miriam E. Sweeney, and Safiya Umoja Noble. "Social Justice as Topic and Tool: An Attempt to Transform an LIS Curriculum and Culture." *Library Quarterly* 86, no. 1 (January 2016): 107–24.

de Sousa Santos, Boaventura. *Cognitive Justice in a Global World: Prudent Knowledges for a Decent Life*. Lanham, MD: Lexington Books, 2007.

Duggan, Lisa. *The Twilight of Equality? Neoliberalism, Cultural Politics, and the Attack on Democracy*. Boston: Beacon Press, 2012.

Durrani, Shiraz. *Information and Liberation: Writings on the Politics of Information and Librarianship*. Duluth, MN: Library Juice Press, 2008.

Floridi, Luciano. "LIS as Applied Philosophy of Information: A Reappraisal." *Library Trends* 52, no. 3 (2004): 658–65.

Henk, Mandy. *Ecology, Economy, Equity: The Path to a Carbon-Neutral Library*. Chicago: American Library Association Editions, 2014.

Nardi, Bonnie A., and Vicki O'Day. *Information Ecologies: Using Technology with Heart.* Cambridge, MA: MIT Press, 1999.

O'Neill, John. "The Varieties of Intrinsic Value." *Monist* 75, no. 2 (April 1992): 119–37.

Osburn, Charles B. *The Western Devaluation of Knowledge*. Lanham, MD: Rowman & Littlefield Publishers, 2013.

Preer, Jean L. *Library Ethics*. Westport, CT: Libraries Unlimited, 2008.

Rodriguez, L. A., and Tatiana Cummings, eds. "Cultural Times," 2007. http://www.humboldt.edu /multicultural/Download/cultural_times/fall_2007.pdf.

Tessman, Lisa. *Burdened Virtues: Virtue Ethics for Liberatory Struggles.* New York: Oxford University Press, 2005.

Warren, Karen. *Ecofeminist Philosophy: A Western Perspective on What It Is and Why It Matters*. Lanham, MD: Rowman & Littlefield, 2000.

Chapter 3

Transgressing LIS Education: A Continuing Journey Toward Social Justice

Robin Kurz

A Library Story

One evening, while shelving books in the children's nonfiction section, I overheard a conversation between a father and his daughter. The father, a white southern man in his mid-twenties, had told his daughter, who appeared to be around four or five years old, that she could select two DVDs to check out. She took her time, carefully examining the selection of movies, TV shows, and documentaries.

Her first selection was a *Little Bill* video. When she showed it to him for his approval, he said, "You're not watching any n----- movies." At this point, I stood speechless in an aisle less than five feet from the pair, both horrified at the exchange and thankful that no one else was in the children's room. The child replaced the DVD on the shelf and kept looking at the other choices. I knew that all of the possible interventions that immediately came to mind could cost me my job as head of children's services for the medium-sized public library system.

Soon, the girl had another choice, this time a *Dora the Explorer* DVD. When her father saw this one, he grabbed it from her hand and thrust it back onto the shelf. Saying "You won't be watching that little w--b--- [a racial slur primarily directed toward undocumented Latinx[1] immigrants] either," he grabbed her by the hand and told her they were leaving. She never protested as he pulled her from the room and toward the library's front exit.

I found another staff member to cover me on the desk, walked out behind the library, and called my future husband to tell him that I had decided to apply for a Ph.D. program after all.

Introduction and Background

Before the night described above, I had the naïve expectation that my generation would break the cycle, that we would be the ones who finally stopped passing on racist beliefs and language to our children. Seeing this interaction, with the parent younger than me, shattered that expectation. It was the final crack in the façade that white privilege had built around my life and my career in libraries.

Years earlier, after a brief stint in secondary education, I had embarked on a career in public libraries in my late twenties, starting as a circulation assistant then quickly moving to children's services. After four years as support staff, I left this position to earn my MLIS. Once I completed my degree, I was hired to head youth services for the medium-sized county library system where I witnessed the interaction. While this was the last blatantly racist moment I would witness as a public library employee, it was not the first.

In all of the places I had worked, there were countless examples of individual and institutional racism. These ranged from the codewords I had heard so often in circulation to the policies that gave African American and Latinx patrons extra barriers to access materials and services. There were microaggressions and macroaggressions without

1. "Latinx" is used throughout to be inclusive of all gender identities beyond the masculine/feminine binary represented by Latino/a or Latin@.

end. There were collections almost devoid of any mirrors[2] for the youth or the adults of color, who often formed the majority of these libraries' service areas. There were years and years of inaction and excuses, as I hit brick wall after brick wall. "Change doesn't happen overnight." "It's always been this way." "Just be patient." "Remember who pays the most taxes."

That evening, possibly even while witnessing this exchange, I had an epiphany. I could continue to work as a librarian and fight constantly to provide more equitable services to the people of a single county, or I could take a different route. With my Ph.D., I could teach hundreds, possibly thousands of future librarians. Those librarians would then go out into libraries around the country and effectively influence hundreds of thousands of lives. Together, we could provide more equitable services to so many more people than I could ever hope to reach alone.

This chapter details my journey in library and information science (LIS) education over the past seven years. After a look at my critical pedagogical foundations, I then explore the transformation of theory into praxis, the politics of course development, a snapshot of this praxis in practice, and the highs and lows of engaged pedagogy. Although I mention a few courses I have taught that have social justice[3] elements, most examples refer to a specific course on race in LIS. I have written this chapter as a first-person narrative in pursuit of reflexivity and in alignment with the critical and feminist epistemologies that underlie my teaching.

---

2. Rudine S. Bishop, "Mirrors, Windows and Sliding Glass Doors." *Perspectives* 6, no. 3 (1990): ix-xi.

3. For my teaching and research, I use Kathy Charmaz's concept of social justice, which she explains as "attentiveness to ideas and actions concerning fairness, equity, equality, democratic process, status, hierarchy, and individual and collective rights and obligations.... It means exploring tensions between complicity and consciousness, choice and constraint, indifference and compassion, inclusion and exclusion, poverty and privilege, and barriers and opportunities. It also means taking a critical stance toward actions, organizations, and social institutions." Kathy Charmaz, "Grounded Theory in the 21st Century: Applications for Advancing Social Justice Studies," in *The SAGE Handbook of Qualitative Research* (3rd ed.), ed. Norman K. Denzin and Yvonna S. Lincoln (Thousand Oaks, CA: Sage Publications Ltd), 510.

Pedagogical Foundations

As a teaching fellow in an LIS doctoral program, I would enter the graduate-level classroom years earlier than I had anticipated. Armed with a little secondary classroom experience, a doctoral course in pedagogy, and no shortage of conviction, I eagerly embraced course development in the fall of 2008. A faculty member's departure had left a vacancy in youth services, so I would spend the next four years teaching primarily two courses: young adult materials and materials and services for Latinx youth.

Even before I began the Ph.D. program, I had promised myself that I would always create my own syllabi for any courses I taught, regardless of how time-consuming this practice was. Besides having been the victim of faculty members who relied on inherited syllabi, assignments, and readings, I also wanted no one to question the integrity of my courses. Since I was ultimately responsible for the learning in my classroom, I had to take ownership of any course I taught, from syllabus development through final grade submission. Another promise was to update courses every time I taught them (even in consecutive semesters), not only to integrate newer readings, but also to implement changes based on feedback from students.

Events collided serendipitously in the 2008-09 academic year. While I was developing the syllabus for and then teaching the Latinx youth course for the first time, I had two transformational educational experiences, the only such experiences I have had as a student. Although I had some wonderful experiences in my LIS courses throughout both of my degrees in the field, none of them substantially transformed me as a person. However, two of the courses in my cognate of educational anthropology led to intrinsic changes in how I viewed our discipline, the academy, and society, as well as to my path as an educator, theorist, researcher, and activist.

Although there was not a department in educational anthropology at my institution, I was able to design my cognate through a combination of courses in the departments of anthropology and social foundations of education. In fall 2008, while I was developing my first graduate-level course, I was a student in Anthropological Theory. Adopting a seminar approach, the professor used Charles Lemert's *Social Theory: The Multicultural and Classic Readings* as a text and approached political economy and power through postcolonial and womanist perspectives. Thus began my first real contact with many of the theorists who would reshape my thinking: Antonio Gramsci, Trinh Minh-ha, Gayatvi Spivak, Patricia Hill Collins, Gloria Anzaldúa, and Paula Gunn Allen. Although she was not among those covered in that text, bell hooks was also among the readings.

These readings changed my course creation at a fundamental level. While I had taken the Latinx course at the master's level and had learned much from that professor's approach to the material, my readings in social theory allowed me to see that I could connect students with the material on a much deeper level. I was able to weave Spivak's thoughts on the subaltern voice and Anzaldúa's ideas on the borderlands identity and linguistic terrorism into the lectures and enable students to understand the larger social justice issues behind the need for library services and materials for Latinx.[4] Soon, I would realize that my direction for this course expanded it beyond its course description. This realization would lead to a new course once I had more latitude in course development as a junior faculty member at another institution.

In the spring of 2009, while I was teaching the Latinx course, I enrolled in another seminar course that would further change my path toward social justice in the LIS classroom. A special topics course in the social foundations of education department, Critical Race Theory (CRT) in Education, allowed me to expand my thinking and my teaching to address more directly the disciplinary and societal disparities that had led me to my doctoral program. The junior-level faculty member who taught this course was both inventive and courageous in her pedagogical

4. Gayatri C Spivak. *The Spivak Reader: Selected Works of Gayati Chakravorty Spivak.* ed. by Donna Landry and Gerald MacLean (New York: Routledge, 1995); Gloria Anzaldúa, *Borderlands/La Frontera: The New Mestiza* (San Francisco: Aunt Lute Books, 1987).

approach, setting an example for praxis that still informs my teaching. Besides tracing the evolution of CRT from legal studies to education, we also explored other forms of critical racial theories that transformed my research and teaching. These theories included critical race feminism and Latinx critical theory.

Similar to the readings in the prior semester's anthropology course, the readings in the CRT course led immediately to the evolution of my teaching approach. Two of the most transformational theories were intersectionality, as named by Kimberlé Crenshaw, and Tara Yosso's concept and model of community cultural wealth.[5] I wove both into that semester's Latinx course and into the young adult materials syllabus I was creating for the summer session.

Transforming Theory into Praxis

After these two instrumental courses and my first foray into implementing these theories into my pedagogy, my process began to evolve at a slower, more deliberate pace. I was embracing critical pedagogy, although I would not use that label for my teaching approach until a few years later.

Central among the many books that continue to inform my classroom practice are Paulo Freire's *Pedagogy of Freedom: Ethics, Democracy, and Civic Courage* and bell hooks' *Teaching to Transgress: Education as the Practice of Freedom*. Of all of Freire's works, *Pedagogy of Freedom* is the one that I most connect with in my continuing growth as an educator. Freire's emphasis on critical reflection on practice, risk-taking in the classroom, and teaching as a human act have directly influenced my course development, assignment construction, and interactions with students.

5. Kimberlé W Crenshaw, "Demarginalizing the Intersection of Race and Sex: A Black Feminist Critique of Antidiscrimination Doctrine, Feminist Theory, and Antiracist Politics" *University of Chicago Legal Forum* 1989, no.1 (1989): 139-167; Tara J. Yosso, *Critical Race Counterstories Along the Chicana/Chicano Educational Pipeline* (New York: Routledge, 2006).

In many ways, reading about hooks' engaged pedagogy validated some of the practices I had begun to apply in my courses already, such as removing myself as the sole purveyor of knowledge and recognizing the importance of experiential knowledge. I also connect with hooks on another level. While, as a white woman I will never fully understand her experiences as an African American woman, I do relate at an intrinsic level to her working-class, Southern background, feelings of familial alienation as a child, and the potential loss of my Southern vernacular speech. *Teaching to Transgress*, along with the rest of hooks' writings, empowered me to interrogate and subvert traditional LIS educational norms.

Critical race theory and Latinx critical theory (both of which I would use as the theoretical lens for future research) meshed well with hooks' works. Daniel Solórzano writes that "critical race theory has at least five themes that form its basic perspectives, research methods, and pedagogy:"[6]

1. The Centrality and Intersectionality of Race and Racism
2. The Challenge to Dominant Ideology
3. The Commitment to Social Justice
4. The Centrality of Experiential Knowledge
5. The Interdisciplinary Perspective[7]

In sections below, I will address how I incorporated each of these themes more specifically into various courses. On a more fundamental level, they run throughout my teaching in several ways. In almost all of my courses (which have now expanded far beyond the two mentioned above), race and racism are both centered and named. Even in courses where race would be less explicitly applicable to the stated learning outcomes, racism and other social injustices are named and addressed.

---

6. Daniel G Solórzano, "Images and Words that Wound: Critical Race Theory, Racial Stereotyping, and Teacher Education," *Teacher Education Quarterly* 24, no. 3 (1997): 5-19.

7. Ibid., 6-7.

The centering of race and racism in and of itself in the LIS classroom is a challenge to the dominant ideology,[8] where race (much less racism) is rarely mentioned. Often, when race is mentioned it is decontextualized and ahistoricized to the point of being useless for any meaningful discussion.

Based on my experiences, the experiences of my colleagues and students, and on a literature couched in terms of a neutrality that maintains the status quo, there is no tangible commitment to social justice in most LIS programs in the United States. With some notable exceptions, such as *Progressive Librarian* and much of the Litwin Books and Library Juice Press catalogs,[9] the current literature in our field is absent of any real action-oriented commitment to social justice. The literature remains relatively devoid of this work; however, those of us committed to social justice in LIS classrooms and practice are writing. Due to gatekeeping within the profession, these articles often find their way into journals in other disciplines or on other continents.

The centrality of experiential knowledge and the interdisciplinary perspective are closely aligned in the social justice-oriented LIS classroom. Due to the aforementioned lack of a discernible body of action-oriented social justice literature, LIS educators have to look beyond the boundaries of our discipline to bring experiential knowledge into the classroom. Thankfully, as an interdisciplinary field,[10] LIS aligns easily with many of the fields that hold this type of scholarship in higher regard.

---

8. Todd Honma, "Trippin' Over the Color Line: The Invisibility of Race in Library and Information Studies," *Interactions, UCLA Journal of Education and Information Studies* 1, no. 2 (2005): 1-22; Christine Pawley, "Unequal Legacies: Race and Multiculturalism in the LIS Curriculum," *Library Quarterly* 76, no. 2 (2006): 149-168.

9. Lorna Peterson, "Multiculturalism: Affirmative or Negative Action?" *Library Journal* 120, no. 12 (1995): 30-33. Other exceptions include the Honma and Pawley articles noted above.

10. The term "interdisciplinary" does not imply that LIS as a whole views all disciplines as equally important, as technical and scientific disciplines often are privileged above social and cultural disciplines in funding, publishing, etc. See, Safiya U. Noble et al., "Changing Course: Collaborative Reflections of Teaching/Taking 'Race, Gender, and Sexuality in the Information Professions,'" *Journal of Education for Library and Information Science* 55, no. 3 (2014): 212–22.

The Politics of Course Development

During my first semesters as a doctoral teaching fellow, the transgressive changes in the courses I taught were less comprehensive than I would have liked. Reflecting back upon my first tentative steps toward realizing social justice goals in the classroom, I am astounded that I had so few student complaints. I was operating in the "it's-better-to-ask-forgiveness-than-permission" mode, with hopes that positive student feedback would outweigh any complaints. The only major complaint I received was from one specific, tenured faculty member and my director supported me in that instance.

Once I had completed my Ph.D. and attained my first tenure-track faculty position, I felt empowered to make expansive changes throughout my assigned courses. Some courses lend themselves to a social justice lens more easily than others; however, the more I teach with the goal of helping students understand both the social justice issues facing society and the ways in which LIS professionals can address those issues, the more I realize that any course in an LIS curriculum can be taught through this lens. Like most critical pedagogy theorists, I believe that all education is political: education that claims neutrality maintains the status quo of inequity and perpetuates a culture of silence. I do not reject that I have an "agenda" in my courses. Instead, I assert that everyone does. My agenda just happens to be more explicit than most of my colleagues.[11]

Developing courses with social justice goals does not have to be contentious (although, based on my conversations with colleagues across the country, it is likely to be more contentious if you are a faculty member of color). I have had the support of all of my directors when creating courses around racial/ethnic issues. The only resistance I have had came from an LIS administrator who failed to acknowledge the need for a new LIS course on gender and sexuality.

11. "We found again and again that almost everyone, especially the old guard, were more disturbed by the overt recognition of the role our political perspectives play in shaping pedagogy than by their passive acceptance of ways of teaching and learning that reflect biases, particularly a white supremacist standpoint." bell hooks, *Teaching to Transgress: Education as the Practice of Freedom* (New York: Routledge, 1994), 37.

At my current institution, I have been successful in designing and gaining faculty approval for a new course on race in LIS. I also successfully implemented the same course under the special topics umbrella at a previous institution. One key to this success was the use of language that university faculty (mostly white) would find less objectionable than the word "race."[12] For the course title I purposefully used the word "multicultural" instead. Multicultural Resources and Services for Libraries is the title now in the catalog at my current institution, with the following course description: "The course introduces a wide range of multicultural resources in all formats. Students apply knowledge of educational theories to the design of readers' advisory services, library programs, and literacy activities in academic, public, and school library settings. Emphasis is given to meeting the recreational, cultural, informational, and educational needs of African American, Asian American, Latina/o, Native American, and bi/multiracial children, young adults, and adults."[13] Although the word "race" is absent from the course description, it is implicit there and in the approved learning outcomes.

While I likely could have obtained approval at the departmental level for a more strongly worded course title and course description, I also was aware of the layers of required approval at higher levels throughout the university and unsure of the reception at those various levels. As a tenure-track faculty member, I decided that using less potentially objectionable language seemed the best path to teaching the course in the near future. After all, my goal was not simply having a course on race in library and information science in the catalog, but in actually teaching such a course to students.

Before the course reached the departmental proposal stage, I began having one-on-one conversations with individual faculty members to

12. For a nuanced look at how the language around diversity has undermined racial equity and equality in LIS, see Lorna Peterson, "The Definition of Diversity: Two Views. A More Specific Definition," *Journal of Library Administration* 27, no. 1-2 (1999): 17-26.

13. "Course Descriptions," updated July 22, 2015, accessed August 16, 2015, http://www.emporia.edu/slim/studentresources/schedules/course-descriptions.html.

help them understand the relevance and importance of such a course to our students. I wanted to make sure I had individual conversations before bringing the proposed syllabus to a faculty meeting. While more time consuming, this approach allowed me to answer questions and concerns more conversationally than I would have been able to do in a group setting. As the course is also a part of a new certificate in youth services, it was contained within a larger curricular discussion at the faculty meeting, which alleviated some of the pressure that may have been present had it been the single course up for review and approval during that meeting.

A typical part of the course approval process is the sample syllabus. I was fortunate in that I had taught a version of the course at my prior institution and thus already had a syllabus. However, I did edit that syllabus somewhat from its original form, not only to account for newer readings but also to remove readings that could have been contentious. One of the most useful headings on any syllabus (sample or actual) is "Selected Readings." As society and the media have predisposed many administrators, faculty members, and students to view certain words and authors as controversial (e.g., Malcolm X, activist, whiteness), I removed many of the more controversial readings from the reading list on the sample syllabus. Most of them are on the final published syllabus for the course.

A Snapshot of Praxis in Practice

This fall marks the third year I have taught a course explicitly covering race and racism in libraries. The first year I taught the course was in a traditional classroom setting, in a three-hour night class of thirteen students. Since then, the course has been completely online and enrollment has grown considerably. This semester, there are two sections of the course due to the overwhelming amount of student interest. With every iteration of the course, I learn more and adapt the syllabus in response to my own learning and student feedback.

The final syllabus is a balanced mixture of seminal readings from LIS and diverse readings from writers of color and other marginalized voices across multiple disciplines. Whenever possible, as I explain to students, I have centered African American, Asian American, Latinx, Native American, and bi/multiracial voices in the classroom. This semester, I have also more purposefully included voices from modern diasporas. The course has had no required textbook, but I have decided that I will be adopting Charles Lemert's *Social Theory: The Multicultural, Global, and Classic Readings* in the future. As I already use many of the readings included in this collection, it only makes sense to use it as the course text. I will continue to supplement the readings from other disciplines with LIS-specific book chapters and articles that address specific collection and service areas.

The majority of my students have had little to no exposure to the writers I include in my syllabus, from W.E.B. Du Bois to Ronald Takaki, from Gloria Anzaldúa to Paula Gunn Allen. Many of them realize over the course of the semester just how pervasive the white voice has been throughout their educational experiences.[14] We discuss my attempts to compensate for my own white voice through the focus on these readings and interviews with practicing librarians and educators who represent other lived experiences. The course is divided into three reading tracks: children's, young adult, and adult. Students select a track at the beginning of the semester and must remain in that track throughout the term. I divide readings into two types: class-wide and track-specific. Each track also has a selection of African American, Asian American, Latinx, Native American, and bi/multiracial fiction titles, which students discuss in small groups as the semester progresses.

Honesty, reflexivity, and meaningful engagement are paramount in the classroom. I acknowledge from the first day of class that it will be a challenging but rewarding experience for everyone involved. I want to allow opportunity for those students unable or unwilling to invest

---

14. I begin class discussion on voice with: Chimamanda Ngozi Adichie, *The Danger of a Single Story*, TED video, 18:49, July 2009, http://www.ted.com/talks/chimamanda_adichie_the_danger_of_a_single_story.

in the learning process to leave the course during the first week. While forming a community in the classroom during the first few weeks, we work together to operationalize course terminology through readings and discussions and lay the groundwork for the remainder of the semester when the focus shifts to specific groups. As students become more comfortable with each other and me, discussions become more organic and require less initial input from me.

In the syllabus, I describe the course as a "highly participatory, seminar-style course" and divide the assignments into two categories: highly participatory and less participatory. The highly participatory assignments form a combined fifty-three percent of the graded activities for the course and include three assignments. Students record five-minute introductory videos describing their backgrounds, racial/ethnic heritages, and reasons for taking the course. They share these videos on an assignment-specific discussion board, which allows for peer-to-peer commenting. Additionally, the assignment allows me to better gauge what students expect from the course and (typically) start a conversation on the social construction of race, as at least a few students will describe themselves as solely white/caucasian.

Literature circles form the largest portion of each student's grade, at forty percent of the total course grade. Literature circles, which I have adapted from Jeff Whittingham,[15] are my attempt to remove some of the artificiality and repetitiveness of discussion board forums from online discussions. Literature circles also give students much deeper ownership of the learning and discussion process. Unlike more traditional literature circles often used in K-12 and undergraduate education, my literature circles do not allow for student selection of materials for discussion (each literature circle has a list of assigned fiction, nonfiction, and auto/biographical readings); however, students within each circle are able to decide on which of these readings to center their discussions and how those discussions evolve.

15. Jeff Whittingham, "Literature Circles: A Perfect Match for Online Instruction," *TechTrends* 57, no. 4 (May 2013): 53-58.

There are five literature circles over the course of the semester (one each for African American, Asian American, Latinx, Native American, and bi/multiracial readings), and each circle's members rotate between the roles of facilitator, passage selector, wordsmith, reporter, trendsetter, and encourager. I use the last two roles on an as-needed basis with groups of five or six students, since groups vary in size from four to six members. Each of the five circles cover the readings from two class weeks and occur over the course of a calendar week. Each group is able to select the platform that best fits the needs of its members. While I prefer that discussions take place synchronously, this is not required.

In addition to the literature circles, students and I engage in three class-wide discussions over the semester. Students have two options for these discussions: the traditional online discussion forum or a synchronous online video- and audio-enabled meeting. Two of these discussions take place early in the semester: one covering community, culture, and identity and the second on intersectionality and privilege. Toward the end of the semester, the final class-wide discussion covers creating meaningful, equitable collections, services, and programming and synthesizes all of the prior course readings, assignments, and discussions.

The less participatory assignments still often include participatory elements. The first of these is the identity narrative. In earlier versions of the class, this assignment had been solely a racial narrative. Although most students used the opportunity to reflect deeply upon the role of race in their lives, some white students used it to air their victimization by individual members of different races and ethnicities. I created the identity narrative not only to help students better focus their writing toward a more reflective narrative of the multiple layers of identity we each have, but to also better understand intersectionality in their own lives. The assignment instructions include ten types of identity: race, ethnicity, gender (biological), gender identity, class, sexual orientation, ability, language, and nationality. I ask students to address at least five of these identity types and give them the freedom to approach their narratives in a variety of ways, including thematically or chronologically. After the narratives are due, I create a discussion board where students share a paragraph from their papers that they feel particularly illuminates their individual identities.

Students continue to explore identity throughout the semester in their reflection journals, in which they write weekly entries reflecting upon each week's readings and media (my lectures, course interviews, online videos, etc.). These journals allow students to engage more deeply than the materials and class discussions. While the journals remain confidential between each student and me, students occasionally share a selection from their journals in pertinent class discussions. Students submit these journals twice during the semester so that I may address more completely any individual or class-wide concerns or misunderstood topics.

To expose students to more books than can be covered during the semester and to give them further practice in analytical reading, I created the long-form book review assignment. Students select from a list of sixty primarily non-fiction titles, ranging from Michelle Alexander's *The New Jim Crow: Mass Incarceration in the Age of Colorblindness* to Howard Zinn's *Voices of a People's History of the United States.* Students choose their titles on a first-come basis so that every student is reading a different book. Detailed instructions, including a PowerPoint slideshow, guide students through the process of writing a review in the style of *The New York Times Sunday Book Review.* Besides submitting the book reviews for grading, students also share their reviews with each other on the course blog.

Students begin to engage their classroom learning actively in two specific assignments: field visit reports and service-learning projects. Each student completes two field visit reports over the course of the semester. The purpose of this assignment is not to conduct actual research toward publication (although it could lead to ideas for independent studies) but to help students view libraries through different lenses. Students must visit two different library settings, neither of which can be their workplace. For each report, students conduct unobtrusive observations of library staff/patron interactions and evaluate physical and virtual library spaces through the lenses of African American, Asian American, Latinx, Native American, and/or bi/multiracial users. I have created a template for the field report so that students focus on and reflect upon specific topics most relevant to the class. Each field report concludes with a short reflection essay, and students share summaries of their reports on the course blog.

The final assignment for the class is the service-learning project. Robert G. Bringle and Julie A. Hatcher view service learning as "a credit-bearing educational experience in which students participate in an organized service activity that meets identified community needs and reflect on the service activity in such a way as to gain further understanding of course content, a broader appreciation of the discipline, and an enhanced sense of civic responsibility."[16]

I began using service learning as a required or optional part of many of my courses as a doctoral teaching fellow. This process became more formalized during my first tenure-track appointment, as that institution has a special designation for service-learning courses (which has both positive and negative implications), and I was able to gain that designation for the "multicultural" course when I taught it at that institution. Although my current institution has no formalized service-learning process, I was determined to keep these types of assignments as a part of my courses when possible, as I had witnessed their benefits for both students and community organizations.

Since the course is online and students live in various geographical locations across three time zones, I complete the preliminary groundwork for the projects with community partners to determine the best ways that students can help them on various projects. For the current semester, the community partner is a preexisting partnership of librarians, teachers, and community organizers working to address racism in the Kansas City metropolitan area. For background, the class is reading Tanner Colby's *Some of My Best Friends are Black: The Strange Story of Integration in America,* as Colby will be the center of the partnership's efforts in 2016. Based on the partnership's need, students will be creating

16. Robert G. Bringle and Julie A. Hatcher, "Implementing Service Learning in Higher Education," *Journal of Higher Education* 67, no. 2 (1996): 221-239.

public library program plans that either implicitly or explicitly connect to Colby's book. Students may work individually or in self-selected pairs for this assignment. Besides the program plan (for which a template is provided), students also reflect upon the assignment's connection to course content, the profession, and community collaboration. Students appreciate the experiential learning aspect of these service-learning assignments and previous community partners have been able to implement student work immediately into their organizations.

From the moment that the course begins, throughout all of the assignments, and until students submit their final assignments, I place importance on student ownership of the learning process. My courses are not easy, often requiring levels of readings for which students are unprepared, both quantitatively and qualitatively. In exchange for their commitment, I work with students to build a community[17] in which we can all grow through meaningful conversations, both peer/peer and student/faculty. I also allow room for exploration, evolution, and ownership in readings, discussions, and assignments, realizing that individual students will reach the course learning outcomes in different ways and not necessarily in concert with each other.

The Highs and Lows of Engaged Pedagogy

Pushing boundaries with readings, discussions, and assignments can lead to amazing growth as well as discouraging situations. Overall, I have had positive feedback from students, both during and long after these courses. When the feedback comes during or immediately following the course, I am able to talk with the students and learn exactly what they believe benefited them the most during the experience. Sometimes, I may not hear from a student until long after a course is complete. Students

17. For community building in the classroom, I look to hooks, *Teaching to Transgress*, 38-44, and Silvia Cristina Bettez, "Building Critical Communities Amid the Uncertainty of Social Justice Pedagogy in the Graduate Classroom," *Review of Education, Pedagogy, and Cultural Studies* 33, no. 1 (2011): 76-106.

reach out after graduation, often to tell me how they have been working (sometimes with success, sometimes without) to make changes in their libraries based on the inequities they learned about in one of my courses. Others give anonymous feedback through end-of-program and post-graduation surveys, speaking of how they wish my courses were required for all of that program's students. Through these personal and anonymous messages, I believe that my courses are making a difference in the lives of practitioners and the communities they serve.

As a doctoral teaching fellow, my expectation was that these social justice-centered courses would be transformative educational experiences for *all of my students*. I have learned since that this was a completely unrealistic expectation on my part as there must be willingness (or at least openness) on the part of the individual student toward transformation. I learned this in a very real way the first time I taught the multicultural course. Informed by my own experiences as a student, I believed that it would be a more successful learning experience in a traditional, face-to-face classroom setting. I was hesitant to consider teaching the course in the online, asynchronous model. My first, and only, time teaching the course in person quickly made me realize that most of my students had become disengaged in their own learning in traditional classroom spaces, instead seeing themselves as passive receptacles for information. It took additional time to engage them in meaningful classroom discussions, regardless of the topic, and establish a community of trust.[18]

One particular student, a white elementary school teacher who eventually dropped the course, hampered this community building further. Her remarks (sometimes microaggressive, other times blatantly racist) in every class meeting created such an unsafe space for the students that most discussions faltered before we exchanged any meaningful dialogue. I met privately with the student several times (about her language in class as well as the unacceptable quality of her written work), and she was never able to understand how her classmates could perceive any

18. Other students seemed to think that the course was going to be a series of professional development workshops taught from a colorblind perspective common in too many library settings using the term "multicultural."

of her comments, which she saw as benign, as hurtful. Her objectification of blackness (particularly black hair and black bodies) was the first time as an educator that I felt like one student was perpetrating actual harm in one of my classes.[19] I felt ill-equipped to address her comments effectively in such an intimate setting. While I was able to move the class discussions back to their previous threads, I still believe that I disappointed this entire group of students by not addressing those comments more immediately.

This semester was also the first (and last) time I allowed students to guide a service-learning project from start to finish. The students met with the library staff, learned about the communities the library served, brainstormed ideas for possible programs, and decided on an International Game Night. They planned, marketed, and carried out the entire event. The partnering library was amazed with the turnout for the event and the families enjoyed themselves, but the event itself failed to engage with library users in any meaningful, lasting way and did not have any social justice elements. Rather than stepping in and trying to guide the project to a more fulfilling end, I simply allowed it to run its course. After that class, I would always ensure that I collaborated more completely with community partners prior to the beginning of a project so that students would actually be working toward making lasting contributions in communities.

A final low (that has become a high) of engaged pedagogy has been finding the most effective way to address the emotional turmoil that students often experience in my courses, as they begin to see the world and people around them in new ways. Initially, I had no formal way of addressing the denial, anger, depression, despair, etc., that students may feel during the course of the semester. I would encourage students to contact me privately if they needed to talk or to talk to their peers. Now, I help prepare students for these emotions from the course's first

19. For further discussion of white objectification of blackness see, George Yancy, *Black Bodies, White Gazes: The Continuing Significance of Race* (Lanham, MD: Rowman & Littlefield, 2008).

week and incorporate related readings into the course.[20] Throughout the course, I share how my personal paradigms have shifted over the past seven years and encourage them to share how their lenses are changing how they view the world around them. As bell hooks writes, "This gives them both the opportunity to know that difficult experiences may be common and practice at integrating theory and practice: ways of knowing with habits of being. We practice interrogating habits of being as well as ideas. Through this process we build community."[21] This recognition and acceptance of emotional change has benefitted everyone in the course.

Conclusion

Even when things have not gone as planned or when I have had negative feedback from my fellow faculty members or from individual students, the rewards of teaching these courses have always been greater than the costs. I have grown just as much as my students have. On the last day of class, I give them advice that I have taken to heart myself. I ask them not to give up; even when something does not work the first time, try again and maintain hope that one day it will. I ask them to recognize that working toward social justice is a journey in which the destination often seems unreachable and traveling partners may be in short supply. I also let them know that, just as individual student growth empowers classroom growth (which empowers departmental growth, which in turn empowers institutional and societal growth), individual librarian growth empowers library growth (which empowers community and societal growth). When students leave my classroom, although they realize that they have finished just one short leg of a very long journey, they feel more empowered to face whatever obstacles they encounter along the way. As Paulo Freire writes, "I am a teacher full of the spirit of

20. These include selections from Ann T. Jealous and Caroline T. Haskell, eds. *Combined Destinies: Whites Sharing Grief about Racism* (Dulles, VA: Potomac Books, 2013).

21. bell hooks, *Teaching to Transgress*, 43.

hope, in spite of all signs to the contrary. I am a teacher who refuses the disillusionment that consumes and immobilizes. I am a teacher proud of the beauty of my teaching practice, a fragile beauty that may disappear if I do not care for the struggle and knowledge that I ought to teach."[22]

Bibliography

Adichie, Chimamanda Ngozi, *The Danger of a Single Story*, TED video, 18:49. July 2009, http://www.ted.com/talks/chimamanda_adichie_the_danger_of_a_single_story.

Anzaldúa, Gloria. *Borderlands/La Frontera: The New Mestiza.* San Francisco: Aunt Lute Books, 1987.

Bettez, Silvia Cristina. "Building Critical Communities Amid the Uncertainty of Social Justice Pedagogy in the Graduate Classroom." *Review of Education, Pedagogy, and Cultural Studies* 33, no. 1 (2011): 76-106.

Bishop, Rudine S. "Mirrors, Windows and Sliding Glass Doors." *Perspectives,* 6, no. 3 (1990): ix-xi.

Bringle, Robert G., and Julie A. Hatcher. "Implementing Service Learning in Higher Education." *Journal of Higher Education* 67, no. 2 (1996): 221-239.

Charmaz, Kathy. "Grounded Theory in the 21st Century: Applications for Advancing Social Justice Studies." In *The SAGE Handbook of Qualitative Research,* 3rd ed., edited by Norman K. Denzin and Yvonna S. Lincoln, 507-535. Thousand Oaks, CA: Sage Publications, 2005.

Colby, Tanner. *Some of My Best Friends are Black.* New York: Penguin, 2013.

22. Paulo Freire, *Pedagogy of Freedom: Ethics, Democracy, and Civic Courage,* trans. Patrick Clarke (Lanham, MD: Rowman & Littlefield, 1998), 94-95.

Crenshaw, Kimberlé W. "Demarginalizing the Intersection of Race and Sex: A Black Feminist Critique of Antidiscrimination Doctrine, Feminist Theory, and Antiracist Politics." *University of Chicago Legal Forum* 139 (1989): 139-167.

Freire, Paulo. *Pedagogy of Freedom: Ethics, Democracy, and Civic Courage.* Translated by Patrick Clarke. Lanham, MD: Rowman & Littlefield, 1998.

Honma, Todd. "Trippin' Over the Color Line: The Invisibility of Race in Library and Information Studies." *Interactions, UCLA Journal of Education and Information Studies* 1, no. 2 (2005): 1-22.

hooks, bell. *Teaching to Transgress: Education as the Practice of Freedom.* New York: Routledge, 1994.

Jealous, Ann T., and Caroline T. Haskell, eds. *Combined Destinies: Whites Sharing Grief about Racism.* Dulles, VA: Potomac Books, 2013.

Lemert, Charles, ed. *Social Theory: The Multicultural and Classic Readings.* 3rd ed. Boulder, CO: Westview, 2004.

Lemert, Charles, ed. *Social Theory: The Multicultural, Global, and Classic Readings.* 5th ed. Boulder, CO: Westview, 2013.

Noble, Safiya U., Jeanie Austin, Miriam E. Sweeney, Lucas McKeever, and Elizabeth Sullivan. "Changing Course: Collaborative Reflections of Teaching/Taking 'Race, Gender, and Sexuality in the Information Professions.'" *Journal of Education for Library and Information Science* 55, no. 3 (2014): 212–22.

Pawley, Christine. "Unequal Legacies: Race and Multiculturalism in the LIS Curriculum." *Library Quarterly* 76, no. 2 (2006): 149-168.

Peterson, Lorna. "The Definition of Diversity: Two Views. A More Specific Definition." *Journal of Library Administration* 27, no. 1-2 (1999): 17-26.

Peterson, Lorna. "Multiculturalism: Affirmative or Negative Action?" *Library Journal* 120, no. 12 (1995): 30-33.

Solórzano, Daniel G. "Images and Words that Wound: Critical Race Theory, Racial Stereotyping, and Teacher Education." *Teacher Education Quarterly* 24, no. 3 (1997): 5-19.

Spivak, Gayatri C. *The Spivak Reader: Selected Works of Gayati Chakravorty Spivak*. Edited by Donna Landry and Gerald MacLean. New York: Routledge, 1995.

Whittingham, Jeff. "Literature Circles: A Perfect Match for Online Instruction." *TechTrends: Linking Research and Practice To Improve Learning* 57, no. 4 (May 2013): 53-58.

Yancy, George. *Black Bodies, White Gazes: The Continuing Significance of Race*. Lanham, MD: Rowman & Littlefield, 2008.

Yosso, Tara J. *Critical Race Counterstories Along the Chicana/Chicano Educational Pipeline*. New York: Routledge, 2006.

SECTION TWO:
TEACHING SOCIAL JUSTICE IN THE CLASSROOM

Chapter 4

Examining Race, Power, Privilege, and Equity in the Youth Services LIS Classroom

Sandra Hughes-Hassell and Katy J. Vance

"...the problem of the Twentieth Century is the problem of the color-line."
-W.E.B. DuBois[1]

W.E. DuBois' oft-quoted words remind us that the United States is not, and never has been, a colorblind society. Racism, defined as "a system of privileges that works to the advantage of whites and to the detriment of people of color,"[2] has played and continues to play a dominant role in determining inequity in the United States. Students of color[3] and Native youth are more likely to attend segregated schools than whites;[4] to receive a disproportionate amount of poor teaching,

1. W.E. DuBois, *The Souls of Black Folk* (New York: Bantam, 1989. Originally published in 1903).

2. Jonda C. McNair, "Innocent Though They May Seem...A Critical Race Theory Analysis of Firefly and Seesaw Scholastic Book Club Order Forms," *Multicultural Review* 17, no. 1 (2008): 24.

3. The authors prefer the terms *students of color*, *youth of color*, or *people of color* to refer to people of African descent, people of Asian descent, and people of Latin American or Mexican descent, as opposed to the terms non-white or minority. The term non-white normalizes whiteness and reinforces the privileged position of whites in the U.S. As demographic data shows, the term minority is inaccurate.

4. Gary Orfield, *Schools More Separate: Consequences of a Decade of Resegregation* (Cambridge, MA: Harvard Civil Rights Project, 2001).

including teachers with less experience, fewer advanced degrees, and higher rates of absenteeism;[5] or to be tracked even if they attend more racially and ethnically diverse schools.[6] According to the Annie E. Casey Foundation, compared to the treatment received by white youth, policies, practices, and stereotypes within the juvenile justice system work against youth of color and expose them to greater vulnerability for juvenile detention and compromised outcomes.[7] The list of inequities goes on. Ladson-Billings and Tate argue that these inequalities are "a logical and predictable result of a racialized society in which discussions of race and racism continue to be muted and marginalized."[8]

Adding to the challenges facing youth of color and Native youth is the fact that much of the public discourse concerning these young people is based on a cultural deficit model—a stance that minimizes, or even ignores, the structural forces that have led to the unequal distribution of resources, lack of opportunity, and other forms of oppression and discrimination that negatively affect the lived experiences of these youth and their communities.[9] Cabrera argues that educators and policy-makers who do not recognize the racial disparities that exist in society, who buy into this cultural deficit viewpoint, contribute to the continuation of inequitable practices and the further marginalization of these youth.[10]

---

5. United States Department of Education, Office for Civil Rights, *Revealing New Truths about Our Nation's School* (Washington, D.C.: U.S. Department of Education, 2012).

6. Patricia A. Edwards, Gwendolyn T. McMillon and Jennifer D. Turner, *Change is Gonna Come: Transforming Literacy Education for African American Students* (New York: Teachers College Press, 2010).

7. Annie E. Casey Foundation, *Race Matters: Unequal Opportunities for Juvenile Justice* (Baltimore: Annie E. Casey Foundation, 2006).

8. Gloria Ladson-Billings and William F. Tate, IV, "Toward A Critical Race Theory of Education," *Teachers College Record* 97, no. 1 (1995): 47-68.

9. See Natasha J. Cabrera, "Minority Children and Their Families" in *Being Black is Not a Risk Factor: A Strengths-Based Look at the State of the Black Child* (Washington, D.C.: National Black Child Development Institute, 2013); Kafi D. Kumasi, "Roses in the Concrete: A Critical Race Perspective on Urban Youth and School Libraries," *Knowledge Quest* 40, no. 4 (2012): 32-37.

10. Ibid.

Furner contends that, since race is inarguably embedded in most major social systems, it is reasonable to assume that libraries as institutions are also "infected with racism."[11] He points to several possible manifestations of race and racism in the library, including inadequate staffing and provision of library services to communities of color, as well as low levels of user satisfaction among communities of color. Kumasi found that many youth of color "feel like outsiders in library spaces and deem the school library as sole 'property' of the school librarian."[12] She asserts that these feelings of disconnect and exclusion must be attended to if librarians want to make all of their students feel welcome. Pawley agrees, arguing that if we want to create libraries that meet the needs of people of color and Native groups, libraries must become "'race-neutral'…spaces, where whiteness is no longer central and people of color are no longer marginalized."[13]

While it can be difficult to create spaces for productive conversations about topics such as equity, race, power, and privilege, as Nieto argues, if a low level of discourse remains the norm, "neither unfair individual behaviors nor institutional policies will change. The dilemma is how to challenge the silence about race, racism, and power so that teachers [and librarians] can enter into meaningful and constructive dialogues with their students [patrons, and their colleagues]."[14] While attempting to explore these issues in the professional world can be intimidating and fraught with missteps, the graduate classroom provides "a particularly meaningful forum in which [students] can take the time to reflect and explore the problems and tensions they have experienced...while also exploring their hopes and aspirations."[15] For students who have been

11. Jonathon Furner, "Dewey Deracialized: A Critical Race-Theoretic Perspective," *Knowledge Organization* 34, no. 3 (2007): 144.

12. Kumasi, "Roses in the Concrete," 36.

13. Christine Pawley, "Unequal Legacies: Race and Multiculturalism in the LIS Curriculum," *Library Quarterly* 76, no. 2 (2006): 153.

14. Sonia Nieto, *Language, Culture and Teaching: Critical Perspectives*, 2nd ed. (New York: Routledge, 2010).

15. Jenny Foight-Cressman, *Introducing a Critical Perspective into a Graduate*

targeted by bias and inequity, the graduate classroom provides an opportunity for them to challenge the dominant narrative and counter their peers' misperceptions. At the same time, students who have enjoyed more privileged identities begin to examine their own implicit biases and analyze stereotypes that may be influencing their views of marginalized people in their communities.[16]

This chapter will describe *INLS 735: Youth Services in a Diverse Society*, a graduate level course that is currently being taught in the School of Information and Library Science at the University of North Carolina at Chapel Hill. The purpose of the course, developed in 2011, is to prepare students to work as youth services librarians in today's increasingly diverse society. Through the course, students develop a theoretical base in critical race theory (CRT) and other cross-disciplinary theories and conceptual frameworks, while they explore issues relevant to working as Library and Information Science (LIS) professionals with diverse and often marginalized communities. This chapter will:

- provide an argument for including this course in the LIS youth services curriculum,
- define Critical Race Theory, the conceptual framework which serves as the framework for the course,
- explain three key elements of the course: the learning outcomes, the classroom environment, and the course assignments, and
- address challenges presented by the course.

Why This Course, Now?

> "*...one of the fundamental tasks of educators is to make sure that the future points the way to a more socially just world, a world in which critique and possibility—in conjunction with the values of reason, freedom, and equality—function to alter the grounds upon which life is lived.*" —Henry Giroux[17]

Course in Children's Literature (Ph.D. diss., University of Pennsylvania, United States, 2005).

16. Paul C. Gorski and Kathy Swalwell, "Equity Literacy for All" *Educational Leadership* 72, no. 6 (2015): 34-40.

17. Henry A. Giroux, "Lessons From Paulo Freire," *Chronicle of Higher*

For the first time in U.S. history, youth of color made up the majority of students attending American public schools in the 2014-2015 school year.[18] According to an analysis of the 2010 census data completed by the Annie E. Casey Foundation, there are currently 74.2 million children under the age of eighteen in the United States; forty-six percent of them are children of color.[19] All of the growth in the child population since 2000 has been among groups other than Non-Hispanic whites. Three major groups experienced significant increases between 2000 and 2010:

1. Children of mixed race grew at a faster rate than any other group over the past decade, increasing by forty-six percent.
2. The number of Hispanic children grew by thirty-nine percent.
3. The number of non-Hispanic Asian and Pacific Islander children grew by thirty-one percent.[20]

Today, more than one-fifth of America's children are immigrants or children of immigrants.[21] If these trends continue, demographers conclude, "soon there will be no majority racial or ethnic group in the United States—no one group that makes up more than fifty percent of the total population."[22]

As the number of people of color in the United States continues to increase, the diversity of LIS graduates around the United States remains stagnant. The current demographics for librarians are relatively homogenous: as a profession, we are overwhelmingly white, middle-aged,

---

Education (Oct 17, 2010).

18. Jens M. Krogstad and Richard Fry. "Dept. of Ed. Projects Public Schools Will Be 'Majority-Minority' This Fall," *Fact Tank— Our Lives in Numbers,* 2014.

19. William O'Hare, *The Changing Child Population of the United States: Analysis of Data From the 2010 Census* (Baltimore, MD: The Annie E. Casey Foundation, 2011).

20. Ibid.

21. Ibid.

22. Ron Crouch and Sally Banks Zakariya, *The United States of Education: The Changing Demographics of the United States and Their Schools* (Alexandria, VA: Center for Public Education, 2012).

able-bodied, employed full time, and female.[23] *The ALA Diversity Counts* report shows that eighty-eight percent of librarians are white, eighty-three percent identify as female, and only four percent identify as having a work disability.[24] Consequently, the profession of librarianship is becoming increasingly dissimilar from library users.

There are currently a variety of approaches for dealing with this disconnect, most focusing on recruitment and retention, such as the ALA Spectrum Scholars program, the ARL Initiative to Create a Diverse Workforce, and the LITA/OCLC Minority Librarian Scholarship in Library and Information Technology. Additionally, ALA funds diversity research grants and the ARL funds the Leadership and Career Development program. These essential initiatives are helping to develop a more diverse future workforce.

Efforts in recruitment and retention however, do not address two pressing issues facing the profession. One, the need for immediate preparation of librarians, both those currently employed as well as pre-service librarians enrolled in LIS programs, to not only meet the information needs of diverse populations, but to also recognize, respond to, and redress the inequities that deny these youth access to the opportunities and privilege enjoyed by youth who belong to the dominant group. As Mestre notes, "Many librarians are now struggling to connect with a completely new set of learners, with cultural backgrounds distinctly different from each other and from their teachers. It may be a challenge for the [librarian] who has only used teaching strategies and examples based on his or her life experiences."[25]

Marcoux agrees, stressing that the "tension between groups with an idea of 'us and them'" has the potential to negatively affect the ability of librarians to work effectively with youth with different culture,

23. American Library Association, *Diversity Counts Report 2009-2010 Update* (Chicago, IL: ALA, 2012).

24. Ibid.

25. Lori S. Mestre, "Culturally Responsive Instruction for Teacher-Librarians," *Teacher Librarian* 36, no. 3 (2010): 8.

language, learning styles, and backgrounds.[26] Two, no matter how varied the personal background and experience of any individual librarian, there will always be patrons who hail from a different background and/or life experience. Additionally, even if the LIS workforce becomes more diverse, since racism is embedded in American institutions, issues of power, privilege, and inequity will still exist and pre-service librarians need to know how to address them.

Although the 2008 American Library Association's "Standards for Accreditation of Master's Programs in Library and Information Studies" requires that program objectives reflect "the role of the library and information services in a diverse, global society, including the role of serving the needs of underserved groups," research shows that students graduating from LIS programs have taken few, if any, classes related to diversity.[27] The availability of diversity-related courses varies from one LIS program to another, with iSchools offering the fewest.[28] Across all types of LIS programs, the vast majority of diversity-related courses are electives that are offered infrequently, if at all.[29] Mestre found that nearly eighty percent of the students graduating from LIS programs indicated that they had not taken even one class related to diversity.[30]

In order to serve patrons' information needs, librarians, particularly school and public librarians who work with youth, need to have positive

26. Elizabeth Marcoux, "Diversity and the Teacher-Librarian, *Teacher Librarian* 36, no. 3 (2010): 6.

27. American Library Association, *Standards for Accreditation of Master's Programs in Library and Information Studies* (Chicago: ALA, 2008).

28. Mega Subramaniam and Paul Jaeger, "Modeling Inclusive Practice? Attracting Diverse Faculty and Future Faculty to the Information Workforce," *Library Trends* 59, no. 1 (2010): 109-127.

29. Mega Subramaniam and Paul Jaeger, "Weaving Diversity into LIS: An Examination of Diversity Course Offerings in iSchool Programs." *Education for Information* 28, no. 1 (2011): 1-19.

30. Lori S. Mestre, "Librarians Working with Diverse Populations: What Impact Does Cultural Competency Training Have on Their Efforts," *The Journal of Academic Librarianship* 36, no. 6 (2010): 479-488.

attitudes towards, strong beliefs about, and a solid commitment to diversity, equity, and social justice. We believe it is incumbent on LIS education programs to support the development of this skill set.

Pre-Service Librarians

As Dietrich and Ralph point out, "developing a personal philosophy of multicultural education does not happen in isolation."[31] LIS education must ensure that issues of diversity and equity are implicit in the curriculum in order to prepare librarians to serve our diverse society.[32] Davis and Hall argue, "The very existence of libraries rests on our ability to create institutions and resource centers where would-be users see their information needs and themselves reflected."[33] This means that in order to develop collections, programs, and services that reflect and support their patrons' increasingly diverse backgrounds, life experiences, and information needs, pre-service librarians must be culturally competent and equity literate.

Cultural competence is the ability to recognize the significance of culture in one's own life and in the lives of others; to come to know and respect diverse cultural backgrounds and characteristics through interaction with individuals from diverse linguistic, cultural, and socioeconomic groups; and to fully integrate the culture of diverse groups into services, work, and institutions in order to enhance the lives of both those being served by the library profession and those engaged in service.[34] More simply, "cultural competency goes beyond cultural

---

31. Deborah Dietrich and Kathleen S. Ralph, "Crossing Borders: Multicultural Literature in the Classroom," *Journal of Educational Issue of Language Minority Student* 15, (1995). Accessed May 13, 2015 from https://castl.duq.edu/Conferences/Urbanlearnr/Crossing_Borders.pdf.

32 Claudia Gollop, "Library and Information Science Education," *College & Research Libraries* 60, no. 4 (1999): 385-395.

33. Denise Davis and Tracie Hall, *Diversity Counts Report 2007* (Chicago: American Library Association, 2007).

34. Patricia M. Overall, "Cultural Competence: A Conceptual Framework for Library Information Science Professionals," *Library Quarterly* 79, no. 2 (2009): 175-204.

awareness. It denotes an individual's ability to effectively interact with and among others whose values, behaviors and environments are different from your own."[35]

Gorski argues that cultural competence is not enough—that adults who work with youth must be equity literate, which he defines as being "proficient, not just with culture, but with the skills necessary for creating an equitable learning environment for all students and their families."[36] That is, they must be able to recognize biases and inequities in materials, interactions, and policies; respond to biases, discrimination, and inequities in a thoughtful and equitable manner; redress biases and inequities in the long term by studying how bigger social change can happen; and create and sustain a bias-free equitable learning environment.[37] The development of cultural competence and equity literacy within LIS education will lead to more equitable access to information for minority and underserved populations, improve the effectiveness and relevance of library services to library users, and increase library use by diverse populations.[38] It will also position librarians as active participants in creating the more socially just world that Henry Giroux describes.

The first step for pre-service librarians in becoming culturally competent and equity literate, particularly those who belong to the dominant culture, is to develop fully formed personal racial and cultural identities. Pre-service librarians, just like pre-service educators, need to have a strong sense of their cultural identity in order to support and serve diverse populations. Successful incorporation of diversity into LIS coursework supports students in identifying and deconstructing their personal biases, assumptions, and stances. Without this self-reflection,

---

35. Michigan Education Association, *What is Cultural Competence?* Accessed May 13, 2015 from http://www.mea.org/diversity/index.html

36. Paul C. Gorski, *Reaching and Teaching Students in Poverty: Strategies for Erasing the Opportunity Gap* (New York: Teachers College Press, 2013).

37 Paul C. Gorski and Kathy Swalwell, "Equity Literacy for All" *Educational Leadership* 72, no. 6 (2015): 34-40.

38. Overall, "Cultural Competence: A Conceptual Framework for Library Information Science Professionals."

these future librarians cannot effectively and accurately understand, represent, and portray their patrons' multicultural identities.[39]

Reflective self-knowledge is only the first step in the path towards becoming culturally competent. Pre-service librarians must also build knowledge of diverse communities. Overall suggests a number of ways that cultural knowledge can be built, including planned instruction that incorporates historical, demographic, linguistic, and social information about diverse communities, encounters with people from diverse communities, and interactions with confidants who are able to provide insights into cultural differences between community members and LIS professionals.[40] Gaining cultural knowledge about communities moves librarians beyond a stereotyped, deficit-oriented understanding of their patrons, gives them insight into the cultural capital that shapes the lives of their patrons, and is critical if librarians are going to be able to develop trusting relationships upon which responsive services and programs can be built.

Understanding their own cultural identity and the culture of diverse communities is not enough, however. Pre-service librarians must "identify, analyze, and transform those structural and cultural aspects of society that maintain the subordination and marginalization of People of Color."[41] Specifically, pre-service librarians need to examine these issues as they relate to their future spheres of work, identifying ways in which libraries are contributing to—and can alleviate—problems related to racism and inequity.

Service learning is key to cultivating LIS students' understanding of issues such as race, power, and privilege and how they relate to access for diverse communities. Service learning is defined as "a teaching and

---

39. Froight-Cressman, *Introducing a Critical Perspective into a Graduate Course in Children's Literature*.

40. Overall, "Cultural Competence: A Conceptual Framework for Library Information Science Professionals."

41. Daniel G. Solórzano, "Images and Words that Wound: Critical Race Theory, Racial Stereotyping, and Teacher Education," *Teacher Education Quarterly* 24, no. 3 (1997): 6.

learning strategy that integrates meaningful community service with instruction and reflection to enrich the learning experience, teach civic responsibility, and strengthen communities."[42] Its goals are "strikingly congruent with librarianship's long-standing commitment to improving the lives of citizens within communities."[43] The real life experiences students gain through their service learning experience push students to move beyond an academic understanding to a deeper understanding of the lived experiences of diverse communities and to recognize how these communities are often shaped by bias, prejudice, discrimination, oppression, and inequity. That said, service-learning experiences could also have the effect of validating stereotypes that students hold about diverse communities, rather than disrupting them.[44] For this reason, it is important that these experiences be carefully planned and require LIS students to engage in ongoing, critical reflection, mediated by the instructor teaching the course.

The journey to cultural competence and equity literacy is certainly not the work of one semester; rather, it is "a developmental process that evolves over an extended period."[45] A semester of intense work examining the issues of race, power, privilege, and equity during graduate school, however, can form the basis of life-long learning in this area for students. We believe the long-term nature of this process, and the potential impact that a course like INLS 735 can have on pre-service librarians' future work with youth, is even more reason why it needs a place in the education of pre-service librarians.

---

42. National Service Learning Clearinghouse, *What is Service Learning?* 2001. Accessed April 5, 2011 from http://www.servicelearning.org/what_is_service-learning/service-learning_is/index.php.

43. Elaine Yontz and Kathleen de la Peña McCook, "Service-Learning and LIS Education," *Journal of Education for Library and Information Science* 44, no. 1 (2003): 58-68.

44. Cameron McCarthy, "Multicultural Discourses and Curriculum Reform: A Critical Perspective," *Educational Theory* 44, no. 1 (1994): 81-98.

45. Mestre, "Culturally Responsive Instruction for Teacher-Librarians."

Conceptual Framework: Critical Race Theory

In planning the course, we recognized the need to adopt a critical perspective—one that would challenge students to examine and understand issues related to equity, race, power, and privilege—and critical race theory (CRT) provided the framework we were seeking. CRT is a multidisciplinary epistemology developed by legal scholars in the 1970s to address the effects of race and racism in the U.S. legal system.[46] As Mendoza and Reese explain, "CRT challenges the dominant view that White European American experience is or should be the normative standard; it is presented as a form of oppositional scholarship that is grounded in the ways people of color in the United States have experienced racial oppression."[47]

CRT researchers argue that the effects of race are real and can be devastating to populations who belong to the subordinate group.[48] CRT also contains an activist dimension. It not only tries to understand our social situation, but to change it; it sets out not only to ascertain how society organizes itself along racial lines and hierarchies, but also to transform it for the better.[49] This activist sentiment is at the core of the course. Just as "lawyers use critical race theory ideas to advocate on behalf of clients and to expose bias within the system,"[50] the goal of the course is to prepare pre-service librarians to employ CRT throughout their careers to effect real change within their libraries, communities,

---

46. Derrick Bell, *Faces at the Bottom of the Well: The Permanence of Racism* (New York: Basic Books, 1992); Richard Delgado and Jean Stefanic, *Critical Race Theory: An Introduction* (New York: New York University Press, 2001).

47. Jean Mendoza and Debbie Reese, "Examining Multicultural Picture Books for the Early Childhood Classroom: Possibilities and Pitfalls," *Early Childhood Research & Practice* 32, no. 2 (2001): 20.

48. Beverly Tatum uses the term "dominant" to refer to white people and the term "subordinate" to refer to people of color and others who have been oppressed in her book, *Why Are All the Black Kids Sitting Together in the Cafeteria?* (New York: Basic Books, 2003).

49. Delgado and Stefanic, *Critical Race Theory: An Introduction.*

50. Ibid, 101.

and the LIS profession, thus making a lasting difference in the lives of underrepresented and marginalized populations.[51]

Solórzano identifies five key themes that form the basis of CRT.[52] We briefly define each below, and then show how they are embodied in the course.

The centrality of race and racism. CRT scholars assert that race and racism are defining characteristics of American society— that both are embedded in the structures, policies, and practices of most American institutions and that they work to the detriment of people of color. Solórzano identifies four dimensions of racism that must be understood and examined: (1) micro and macro components, (2) institutional and individual forms, (3) conscious and unconscious elements, and (4) the cumulative impact on both the individual and the group.[53] While CRT scholars focus on the centrality of race and racism, they also recognize that racism intersects with other forms of subordination and discrimination such as gender, class, ability, and sexual orientation.[54]

Interdisciplinary perspective. CRT scholars argue that to be truly understood, race and racism must be analyzed in both an historical and contemporary context.[55] They argue that understanding the historical development of race as a construct in this country, as well as how the current biracial system continues to be reproduced, are critical to dismantling institutional and structural racism and creating equitable opportunities for people of color and Native peoples.

The challenge to the dominant ideology. CRT challenges the traditional claims that social institutions and systems are objective, colorblind,

51. See Sandra Hughes-Hassell, Heather A. Barkley, and Elizabeth Koehler, "Promoting Equity in Children's Literacy Instruction: Using A Critical Race Theory Framework to Examine Transitional Books," *School Library Research* 12 (2009). Accessed May 13, 2015 from http://www.ala.org/aasl/sites/ala.org.aasl/files/content/aaslpubsandjournals/slr/vol12/SLMR_PromotingEquity_V12.pdf.

52. Solórzano, "Images and Words that Wound."

53. Ibid.

54. Ibid.

55. Ibid.

and race neutral, and that as a result, equal opportunity is available to all Americans. If people of color are not successful, according to the traditional perspective, it is because of a deficiency in them; that is, their race is intellectually inferior, their cultural values are dysfunctional, or they are just not working hard enough.[56] CRT disrupts this deficit model ideology by recognizing that the sources of inequality are not located within people of color, but instead are imposed on them by racial oppression and inequitable social and political policies and practices.[57]

The centrality of experiential knowledge. CRT views the experiential and cultural knowledge of diverse communities as a strength and embraces it through concepts such as counter-storytelling and culturally relevant pedagogy. Counter-storytelling is "a method of telling the stories of those people whose experiences are not often told," including people of color, women, gays, and the poor.[58] CRT scholars believe that by giving voice to marginalized communities, counter-stories validate their life circumstances and serve as powerful ways to challenge and subvert the versions of reality held by the privileged. Delgado, who introduced the concept, outlines a number of ways that counter-storytelling benefits groups that have traditionally been marginalized and oppressed in the United States. By telling (and hearing) counter-stories, members of marginalized groups:

- gain healing from becoming familiar with their own historic oppression and victimization,
- realize that they are not alone; that others have the same thoughts and experiences,

56. Ibid.

57. See: Paul Gorski, "Imagining Equity Literacy," *Teaching Tolerance* website, April 10, 2014, http://www.tolerance.org/blog/imagining-equity-literacy?elq=c186689bf1984d34a8e3f8fa951e870b&elqCampaignId=248; Lawrence Parker and David O. Stovall, "Actions Following Words: Critical Race Theory Connects to Critical Pedagogy," *Educational Philosophy* 36, no. 2(2014): 167-182.

58. Daniel G. Solórzano and Tara J. Yosso, "Critical Race Methodology: Counter-Story Telling As An Analytical Framework For Education," *Qualitative Inquiry* 8, no. 1 (2002): 26.

- stop blaming themselves for their marginal position, and
- construct additional counter-stories to challenge the dominant story.[59]

Members of the dominant culture also benefit from hearing counter-stories. Delgado argues that counter-stories can help them overcome their "ethnocentrism and the unthinking conviction that [their] way of seeing the world is the only one—that the way things are is inevitable, natural, just, and best."[60]

Youth's experiential and cultural knowledge is also embraced through the practice of culturally relevant teaching. Ladson-Billings defines this practice as a pedagogy that "empowers students intellectually, socially, emotionally, and politically by using cultural referents to impart knowledge, skills, and attitudes."[61] It recognizes the linguistic, literacy, and cultural practices of communities of color as resources to honor, explore, extend, and build on in formal educational settings. In practice, culturally relevant pedagogy uses the "cultural knowledge, prior experiences, frames of reference, and performance styles" of students of color to make learning more relevant, meaningful, and validating.[62] Key principles of culturally relevant pedagogy include:

- an authentic belief that students from culturally diverse backgrounds are capable learners and can become intellectual leaders,
- legitimization of students' real-life experiences as part of the curriculum,
- a commitment to enabling students to explore and make connections between their multiple identities,

---

59. Richard Delgado, "Storytelling for Oppositionists and Others: A Plea for Narrative," *The Michigan Law Review Association* 87, no. 8 (1989): 2437.

60. Ibid, 2439.

61. Gloria Ladson-Billings, *The Dreamkeepers: Successful Teaching of African American Children,* 2nd ed. (San Francisco: Jossey Bass, 2009): 20.

62. Geneva Gay, *Culturally Responsive Teaching* (New York: Teachers College Press, 2000), 29.

- the creation of a community of learners,
- engagement of students and teachers in a collective struggle against the status quo, and
- the recognition of the political nature of teaching.[63]

The commitment to social justice. A key goal of critical race theory is to bring about change that will lead to social justice.[64] CRT challenges us to envision social justice as the struggle to eliminate racism, poverty, classism and other forms of oppression while empowering groups that have been oppressed.[65] Social justice is a goal shared by the LIS community. As Furner explains, a "just library is one whose resources are put to active, deliberate use in support of social change and in the recognition of the special rights of oppressed groups."[66] He goes on to argue that it is only in this way "that the library can demonstrate a serious commitment to principles of social justice."[67] His challenge to librarians is to be agents of change, working for equity in their communities.

Integrating CRT into the Course

Table 1 provides concrete examples of how the five principles of CRT are embedded into the course readings, assignments, and discussions. CRT is explicitly taught in the early stages of the course. Students read and discuss writings by key leaders in CRT including Derrick Bell, Richard Delgado, Gloria Ladson-Billings, William F. Tate IV, and Daniel Solórzano. As the course progresses, they are introduced to LatCrit,

63. Ladson-Billings, *The Dreamkeepers,* 126-128.

64. Jessica T. DeCuir and Adrienne D. Dixson, "'So When It Comes Out, They Aren't That Surprised That It is There': Using Critical Race Theory as a Tool of Analysis of Race and Racism in Education," *Educational Researcher* 33, no. 5 (2004): 26-31.

65 Daniel G. Solórzano and Deloris Delgado Bernal, "Critical Race Theory and Transformational Resistance: Chicana/o Students in an Urban Context," *Urban Education*, 36, no. 3 (2001): 308-342.

66. Furner, "Dewey Deracialized," 11.

67. Ibid.

TribalCrit, and QueerCrit, derivatives of CRT developed to highlight the oppression and discrimination faced by the Latino, Native, and LGBT communities. Students also examine the concept of white privilege as articulated by Peggy McIntosh.

Elements of the Course

Key Learning Outcomes

Often diversity courses focus on simply embracing multiculturalism or celebrating diversity. These efforts, while well-intentioned, often reinforce a false sense of colorblindness and do little to disrupt the serious equity issues that exist in our society or to prepare pre-service LIS students to work toward justice and equity through libraries.[68] Placing CRT at the center of the course prepares pre-service youth services librarians to recognize the racist legacies of LIS structures and how racism and privilege still impact youth and libraries today, and, then, to devise ways to transform libraries into equitable institutions.[69] The key learning goals for the course include:

- Becoming well versed in the theory and implementation of Critical Race Theory, and its offshoots, such as TribalCrit, LatCrit, and QueerCrit, as they relate to librarianship, education, and community building.
- Utilizing cross-disciplinary theories and conceptual frameworks to understand the lived experiences of marginalized young adult and children's populations as related to information access and literacy development, and to develop and deliver services that respond to their experiences and needs.
- Developing racial and cultural identity on a personal level and understanding it on a societal level.

68. Christine Pawley, "Unequal Legacies," 162.
69. Ibid, 165.

Element of CRT	Students...
Centrality of race and racism	▪ Define and examine terms such as race, racism, white privilege, microaggression, implicit bias and power ▪ Examine their implicit biases (e.g., complete Harvard's Implicit Bias Tests - https://implicit.harvard.edu/implicit/takeatest.html) ▪ Explore their racial, ethnic, and cultural identity and its intersection with our other identities (e.g. Cultural Autobiography Assignment) ▪ Examine library policies and procedures for evidence of implicit biases and inequitable outcomes ▪ Examine youth literature for stereotypes, implicit bias, and prejudice
Interdisciplinary perspective	▪ Read historical and contemporary accounts of discriminatory, inequitable practices and their impact on diverse communities ▪ Discuss current events and their connection to issues of power, race, privilege, and equity (e.g., the debate currently taking place about law enforcement's relationship with the African American community and how this impacts libraries)
Challenge to the dominant ideology	▪ Unpack concepts such as funds of knowledge, cultural capital, and the Afro-cultural ethos ▪ Discuss articles and papers that uncover the structural forces that have led to the unequal distribution of resources, lack of opportunity, and other forms of oppression and discrimination that negatively affect the lived experiences of these youth and their communities (e.g., "A Critical Race Analysis of Latina/o and African

	American Advanced Placement Enrollment in Public High Schools"[1]) ▪ Analyze the concept of colorblindness and the negative impact it has on both youth of color and white youth
Centrality of experiential knowledge	▪ Examine the power of story to disrupt the dominant narrative ▪ Read and discuss articles, books, and papers written by researchers of color and Native scholars (e.g. *Why are All the Black Kids Sitting in the Cafeteria? And Other Conversations About Race*[2]) ▪ Interact with guest speakers from diverse communities (e.g., African American and Latino teens from the Blue Ribbon Mentor Advocate program) ▪ Watch documentaries, TEDTalks, news programs presenting the viewpoints of diverse communities (e.g., "When Your Hands are Tied"[3]) ▪ Follow blogs and other social media maintained by individuals from diverse communities (e.g., American Indians in Children's Literature[4]) ▪ Learn about and implement culturally relevant teaching strategies during their service-learning experience
Commitment to social justice	▪ Examine the ALA Diversity Statement[5] and the ALISE Diversity Statement[6] ▪ Participate in service-learning project ▪ Foster conversations with their colleagues outside the class about equity concerns in their communities

Table 1. Elements of CRT and their representation in INLS 735

Table Notes: 1.Daniel G. Solórzano and Armida Ornelas, "A Critical Race Analysis of Latina/o and African American Advanced Placement Enrollment in Public High Schools," *High School Journal* 87, no. 3 (2004): 15-26.
2. Beverly Tatum, *Why are All the Black Kids Sitting Together in the Cafeteria? And Other Conversations About Race* (New York: Basic Books, 2003).
3. "When Your Hands are Tied" is a film that explores how American Indian youth are expressing themselves in the contemporary world while maintaining strong traditions. Boccella Productions, "When Your Hands are Tied," accessed May 14, 2015, https://vimeo.com/10752418.
4. On her website, Debbie Reese "provides critical perspectives and analysis of Native peoples in children's and young adult books, the curriculum, popular culture, and society." Debbie Reese, *American Indians in Children's Literature* (blog), accessed May 14, 2015, http://americanindiansinchildrensliterature.blogspot.com/
5. American Library Association, "ALA Policy Manual – Diversity," accessed May 14, 2015 http://www.ala.org/aboutala/governance/policymanual/updatedpolicymanual/section2/diversity.
6. Association of Library & Information Science Educators, "ALISE Diversity Statement," accessed May 14, 2015 http://www.alise.org/alise---alise-diversity-statement.

- Examining libraries through a CRT lens, and understanding how to recognize and dismantle racism within libraries as organizations.
- Working for social justice in youth and children's services by participating in outreach to underserved youth and children's populations in the state of North Carolina.

Classroom Environment

Michelle Alexander argues that "a new social consensus must be forged about race and the role of race in defining the basic structure of our society"[70] if we hope to create a socially just world. She goes on to say that "this new consensus must begin with dialogue, a conversation that fosters a critical consciousness, a key prerequisite to effective social action."[71] INLS 735 is a seminar course, with the bulk of each class devoted to exploring essential questions like these:

- What local, regional, and global inequities exist and how have they been sustained over time?
- How is racism manifested in social institutions in the U.S.?
- What role does race and ethnicity play in the development of identity for youth of color?
- How are our assumptions about educational level and ability influenced by the language, culture, or socioeconomic status of an individual?
- What is white privilege and how can those with privilege use their power and resources to make positive change?
- What individual and collective responsibilities do we have towards creating a just society?

Recognizing that these conversations will undoubtedly involve strongly held beliefs and may include current political and social controversies, we have adopted four strategies aimed at creating a classroom environment conducive to critical examination of issues related to race, racism, equity, power, and privilege:

- We sit in a circle as a way to reduce the barriers that have the potential to separate us.
- Drawing on the Quaker tradition, we begin and end each class with a brief period of silence. At the beginning of the class, the silence serves to center us in the moment/in the topic. At the

70. Michelle Alexander, *The New Jim Crow: Mass Incarceration in the Age of Colorblindness* (New York: New Press, 2011), 15.

71. Ibid.

end of the class it allows us to reflect on what we have seen, heard, read, and discussed and prepares us to reenter the world outside the classroom.

- We use a set of class norms to guide our work together as a group (see **Table 2**). These norms are designed to keep our discourse focused, respectful, and brave, and to help us resist the feeling or temptation to back away from or to compartmentalize the uncomfortable dialogue that is a precursor to deeper understanding and growth.
- We build in time for reflection before and after class. Students journal about the readings prior to class. Specifically, they are asked to discuss what stood out to them in the readings, think about connections they are making (i.e., with other readings, their own experiences, current events, etc.), pose one or two questions they would like to discuss in class, and suggest possible applications the concepts in the readings will have to their future role as librarians. They are also asked to sketch or draw the ideas discussed in the reading. At the end of each class period, students are given ten minutes to complete a post-class discussion reflection.

1. View this circle as a liberated zone.
2. Listen to one another.
3. Respect one another.
4. Maintain confidentiality.
5. Use "I" statements; speak about your own thoughts and experiences, not those of others.
6. Focus on a broad definition of diversity.
7. Bring questions/comments/concerns to the circle.
8. Pay attention to how YOU feel.
9. Recognize that we are all teachers and learners.
10. Recognize that this class is the beginning of a journey.

Table 2. INLS 735 class norms

Major Assignments

There are two major assignments for the class—creation of a personal cultural autobiography and participation in a service learning experience. The personal narrative asks students to explore their own personal history, including the formation of their identity, beliefs, perspectives, and values. Who we are as individuals dramatically affects how we interact with others and affects our work with youth. The purpose of the narrative is to heighten students' awareness of their racial and cultural identity as a step in better understanding children and teens who come from different backgrounds. One of the assumptions underlying the assignment is that things do not simply happen to us, we are active in interpreting and assigning meaning to experiences in our lives. These experiences in turn influence the way we see the world and what we value. The goal of the autobiography is to reveal to students their experiences with issues related to race, ethnicity, socioeconomic class, religious differences, sexual orientation, gender identification, ability or disability, etc., in their past and to help them gain insight into their journey towards cultural competence and equity literacy. For the cultural autobiography, students may write a traditional essay or use any other format. Students are encouraged to use their arts, technology, and personal skills creatively to tell their story. The instructor for the course is the only one who reads the autobiographies, but we do discuss aspects of them in class.

Discussing diversity issues in academic isolation becomes an echo chamber if students do not have a place to apply their learning. For this course, students spend thirty hours of service learning in a local public or school library. As Montague, Wolske, and Larke explain, "connecting service learning with LIS curriculum allows students to gain hands-on skills, interact with diverse populations, and gain a deeper understanding for the conceptual basis of the course."[72] Perhaps more importantly,

---

72. Rae A. Montague, Martin Wolske, and Beth Larkee, "Three Views on Service Learning," *American Libraries, Digital Supplement* Winter (2009). Accessed May 13, 2015 from http://www.eslarp.uiuc.edu/news/American-Libraries2009.pdf

to be equitable librarians, students not only need to be knowledgeable about CRT and proficient with culture, but as Gorski points out, they must also have the skills necessary for creating an equitable learning environment for all students and families.[73]

Students work with the librarian at their site to select a group of youth to work with, identify a need, and then design and lead a program that addresses that need. Development of the program is informed by a community analysis that the student performs, spending time with the youth and listening to them, as well as the course readings and discussions. **Table 3** includes a few of the projects students have undertaken.

Students reflect on their service learning experience throughout the term. After each visit, they write a blog entry reflecting on the experience: their observations, the challenges and successes they experienced, and questions or concerns they have. Each post includes not only a summary of the tasks accomplished, but also a critical reflection on the experience in which they draw connections between the theory we discuss in class and the real life application of their service learning opportunity. For example:

> Both of these conversations [with the students I'm working with] reinforced to me several aspects from the reading. First, that leaving issues of race and inequity without being discussed is only making racism and inequity worse. Teenagers are noticing these problems, and from the reactions from my students, they absolutely want to talk about them. Even though I know the reading we did for class was more directed towards younger children, I think it's important to remember that no matter what the age of the child/young person, they do notice these issues, and that they want to talk about them, and may be more willing to talk about them than adults. And, basing off the developmental characteristics we talked about in the YA Lit class, the teen years are a great time to have these discussions. As teens develop they are forming their identities and thinking about how their race and ethnicity shapes how they see themselves and how others view them.

73. Gorski, *Reaching and Teaching Students in Poverty.*

Project	Type of Library	Youth Involved
Mad scientists afterschool club	Public	Children & teens; African American; lower socioeconomic status
Technology afterschool club	School	Children; African American; lower socioeconomic status
Student run radio show	School	Teens; African American, Latino, & White; socioeconomically diverse
Mini-course on rights & responsibilities of teens	School	Teens; African American, Latino, & White; socioeconomically diverse
Digital storytelling	School	Children; Burmese; lower socioeconomic status
Literacy program	Public – Juvenile Detention Center	Teens; African American, Latino, & White; socioeconomically diverse
Library Youth Partnership program	Public	Teens; African American, Latino, & White; lower socioeconomic status
Poetry unit	School	Teens; African American, Latino, & White; socioeconomically diverse; cognitive disabilities
Literacy program	School	Teens; English Language Learners (Latino, Arabic); socioeconomically diverse

Table 3. Sample service learning projects INLS 735 (2012-2015)

> Throughout the whole planning period for my program, I've been constantly reminded of the importance of setting high expectations for individuals, no matter what. [The students I am working with] are similar to the students described in our different readings - the ones that don't have high expectations given to them by those in authority over them (like teachers, etc.). It's been absolutely amazing to see the change that has taken place in the students, since I raised expectations. Expectations really are key - they have the power to encourage and empower teens, and to show them that you are invested in them, and believe in their potential.
> —Excerpt from student blog post[74]

Everyone in the class (students and the instructor) reads the weekly posts and comments on them. One purpose of these posts is to allow the instructor and other students in the class to challenge the post author to maintain an asset-based approach to their work; that is, to not fall back on stereotypes of communities of color or let their implicit biases guide their work.

For the final class session, students give a presentation on the service learning experience. Like the cultural autobiography, this presentation may take any format. In this presentation, students summarize their service project, critically evaluate their work in terms of the needs of the community, and connect their service learning to the theory and research we have studied over the course of the semester. The following is a summary of one student's reflections and demonstrates her integration of the concepts discussed in class with her work with youth:

> The LYP program has changed because I now...
> ▪ Give teens a voice, use their strengths and cultural backpacks
> ▪ Have the LYP teens be the storytellers
> ▪ Realize that every teen has different strengths; I have learned ways to play off and emphasize those strengths (Funds of Knowledge, asset based approach; capital in communities)
> ▪ Know fair is not always equal! - Some LYPs needed different approaches; i.e., work schedules, meeting times, roles in the group
> ▪ SET HIGH EXPECTATIONS! And communicate them early, often, and clearly
> ▪ Value proximity to the students

---

74. All excerpts from student work presented in this chapter are anonymized and used with student permission.

- Show that I am willing to have difficult conversations and tackle current issues such as racism, bullying, etc.
- Give teens time to think and act (relates to cultural backpacks and high expectations; I only jump in when its visibly uncomfortable for teens)
- Practice transparency in my communication and tell the teens why I feel certain things are important
- Incorporate teaching strategies that show LYP teens I value feedback and their active participation (write around, surveys)
- Recognize my implicit biases, and when I am making decisions or judgments that do not empower the teens
- Step out of my comfort zone, and meet people where they need to be met (speaking Spanish, talking about difficult topics, asking difficult questions)
- Increase my awareness of issues

For her service-learning project, the student incorporated the service learning experience with her position as the Library Youth Partnership (LYP) Coordinator at a local public library. The Library Youth Partnership is a grant-funded program that allows the library to hire underserved teens as Library Youth Partners. Their job is to create and perform story times in the public school after-school care programs. The teens she hired this year are all low income teens; eight are African American and one is white. The students in the after-school care programs are predominantly African American and Latino. Understanding the importance and value of giving teens voice, the student asked the Library Youth Partners to reflect on their work at the end of the semester. The following are comments from two of the teens:

> "Something I've liked about [the LYP program] so far this semester is the meaning/lessons behind the programs. We've started to have a meaning, a point we're getting at." –Library Youth Partner, 2015 (*identifies as an African American female*)

> "I like how the program has changed in the ways that the kids are more interactive now in the stuff we do, and the stuff we do is more cultural, as opposed to more generic story books…I think we are in a diverse area, so it's really important for kids to understand the cultures of other people around them as they are growing up, and not just be boxed in their own culture. I think that's really cool." –Library Youth Partner, 2015 (*identifies as a white male*).

Challenges to Teaching Social Justice in the LIS Classroom

Teaching a course in which race, racism, power, privilege, and equity are in the foreground is not without challenges. Modeling how to navigate these challenges, however, is important and benefits students by allowing them to experience these potential difficulties. This prepares them for opportunities to successfully embed the following issues— in spite of inherent challenges— in their own library practice:

- Not imposing instructor viewpoints/opinions on students but instead facilitating their journey.
- Being okay with silence.
- Supporting students in their discomfort and nudging them to continue to move forward.
- Making sure students know they will make mistakes, but also holding them accountable for being aware of their embedded and unconscious biases and/or privilege.
- Ensuring that students who are members of a subordinate group are not made to feel like they are being asked to speak for that group.
- Managing the intensity of the discussion.
- Translating the theory into actionable practices.

Another potential challenge (which is not one we have faced at UNC) is pushback against the political nature of teaching for equity literacy and introducing social justice into the LIS curriculum. In responding to this rebuke it is important to point to the diversity statements from ALA and ALISE, both of which challenge members of the LIS profession to actively combat racism, prejudice, discrimination, and oppression, and emphasize the critical role libraries can play in empowering diverse communities. It is also important to ask ourselves, as Gorski and Swalwell[75]

75. Gorski and Swalwell, "Equity Literacy for All."

suggest: is teaching about racism, power, and privilege more political than pretending they do not exist and omitting them from the curriculum? How might we explain the politics of *not* teaching about these issues when the statistics shared at the beginning of this chapter, as well as the current events in Ferguson, Baltimore, and New York, suggest that the lives of many of the youth our students will work with are framed by these inequities? How can we prepare our students to create programs and services that respond to the needs of these youth and their families if they do not understand the complex, systemic, and historical nature of racism in American institutions, including libraries?

Conclusions

The Wall of Tolerance found at the Civil Rights Memorial Center in Montgomery, Alabama, digitally displays the names of more than half a million people who have pledged to take a stand against hate and work for justice and tolerance in their daily lives. According to the Southern Poverty Law Center's website, "the Wall demonstrates that individuals, not government or organizations, are responsible for continuing the march for social justice. It stands as a dynamic representation of the strength of the movement in America."[76] Visitors to the Civil Rights Memorial Center have the opportunity to take the pledge and add their names to the Wall during their visit:

> By placing my name on the Wall of Tolerance, I pledge to take a stand against hate, injustice and intolerance. I will work in my daily life for justice, equality and human rights—the ideals for which the Civil Rights martyrs died.[77]

---

76. Southern Poverty Law Center, *Civil Rights Memorial, Wall of Tolerance.* Accessed May 23, 2015 from http://www.splcenter.org/civil-rights-memorial/wall-tolerance

77. Ibid.

INLS 735: Youth Services in a Diverse Society is our Wall of Tolerance, where we and our students make public our pledge as LIS professionals to work for social justice—to ensure that youth of color and Native youth have access to the liberties, rights, opportunities, and successes that have been denied them through institutional inequities built on racism, power, and privilege; to create library programs and services that build on the strengths found in these communities; and to empower youth whose voices have been historically silenced to trust their voice and the truth they seek.

Bibliography

Alexander, Michelle. *The New Jim Crow: Mass Incarceration in the Age of Colorblindness.* New York: New Press, 2011.

American Library Association. *ALA Policy Manual—Diversity* (Chicago: American Library Association). Accessed May 14, 2015. http://www.ala.org/aboutala/governance/policymanual/updatedpolicymanual/section2/diversity.

American Library Association. *Standards for Accreditation of Master's Programs in Library and Information Studies.* Chicago: American Library Association, 2008.

American Library Association. *Diversity Counts Report 2009-2010 Update.* Chicago: American Library Association, 2012. Accessed May 12, 2015. http://www.ala.org/offices/diversity/diversitycounts/2009-2010update.

Annie E. Casey Foundation, *Race Matters: Unequal Opportunities for Juvenile Justice.* Baltimore: Annie E. Casey Foundation, 2006. Accessed May 12, 2015. http://www.aecf.org/upload/publicationfiles/fact_sheet12.pdf.

Association of Library and Information Science Educators. *ALISE Diversity Statement.* Seattle: ALISE, 2013. Accessed May 14, 2015. http://www.alise.org/alise---alise-diversity-statement.

Bell, Derrick. *Faces at the Bottom of the Well: The Permanence of Racism.* New York: Basic Books, 1992.

Boccella Productions. "When Your Hands are Tied." Accessed May 14, 2015. https://vimeo.com/10752418.

Cabrera, Natasha J. "Minority Children and Their Families." In *Being Black is Not a Risk Factor: A Strengths-Based Look at the State of the Black Child.* Washington, D.C.: National Black Child Development Institute, 2013.

Crouch, Ron, and Sally Banks Zakariya, *The United States of Education: The Changing Demographics of the United States and Their Schools.* Alexandria, VA: Center for Public Education, 2012. Accessed May 12, 2015. http://www.centerforpubliceducation.org/You-May-Also-Be-Interested-In-landing-page-level/Organizing-a-School-YMABI/The-United-States-of-education-The-changing-demographics-of-the-United-States-and-their-schools.html.

Foight-Cressman, Jenny. "Introducing a Critical Perspective into a Graduate Course in Children's Literature." PhD diss., University of Pennsylvania, 2005.

Davis, Denise, and Thomas Hall. *Diversity Counts Report 2007.* Chicago: American Library Association, 2007.

DeCuir, Jessica T., and Adrienne D. Dixson. "'So When it Comes Out, They Aren't That Surprised That it is There': Using Critical Race Theory as a Tool of Analysis of Race and Racism in Education." *Educational Researcher* 33, no. 5 (2004): 26-31.

Delgado, Richard. "Storytelling for Oppositionists and Others: A Plea for Narrative." *The Michigan Law Review Association* 87, no. 8 (1989): 2411-2441.

Delgado, Richard, and Jean Stefanic. *Critical Race Theory: An Introduction.* New York: New York University Press, 2001.

Dietrich, Deborah and Kathleen S. Ralph. "Crossing Borders: Multicultural Literature in the Classroom," *Journal of Educational Issue of Language Minority Student* 15, (1995). Accessed May 13, 2015. https://castl.duq.edu/Conferences/Urbanlearnr/Crossing_Borders.pdf.

DuBois, W.E.B. *The Souls of Black Folk.* New York: Bantam, 1989. Originally published in 1903.

Edwards, Patricia A., Gwendolyn T. McMillon and Jennifer D. Turner. Ch*ange is Gonna Come: Transforming Literacy Education for African American Students.* New York: Teachers College Press, 2010.

Furner, Jonathon. "Dewey Deracialized: A Critical Race-Theoretic Perspective," *Knowledge Organization* 34, no. 3 (2007): 144-168.

Gay, Geneva. *Culturally Responsive Teaching.* New York: Teachers College Press, 2000.

Giroux, Henry A. "Lessons from Paulo Freire." *Chronicle of Higher Education* (Oct 17, 2010).

Gollop, Claudia. "Library and Information Science Education." *College & Research Libraries* 60, no. 4 (1999): 385-395.

Gorski, Paul C. *Reaching and Teaching Students in Poverty: Strategies for Erasing the Opportunity Gap.* New York: Teachers College Press, 2013.

Gorski, Paul C. "Imagining Equity Literacy." *Teaching Tolerance* website. April 10, 2014. http://www.tolerance.org/blog/imagining-equity-literacy?elq=c186689bf1984d34a8e3f8fa951e870b&elqCampaignId=248.

Gorski, Paul C., and Kathy Swalwell. "Equity Literacy for All." *Educational Leadership* 72, no. 6 (2015): 34-40.

Hughes-Hassell, Sandra, Heather A. Barkley, and Elizabeth Koehler. "Promoting Equity in Children's Literacy Instruction: Using a Critical Race Theory Framework to Examine Transitional

Books." *School Library Research* 12 (2009). Accessed May 13, 2015. http://www.ala.org/aasl/sites/ala.org.aasl/files/content/aaslpubsandjournals/slr/vol12/SLMR_PromotingEquity_V12.pdf.

Krogstad, Jens M., and Richard Fry. "Dept. of Ed. Projects Public Schools Will Be 'Majority-Minority' This Fall," *Fact Tank—Our Lives in Numbers,* 2014. Accessed May 12, 2015. http://www.pewresearch.org/fact-tank/2014/08/18/u-s-public-schools-expected-to-be-majority-minority-starting-this-fall/.

Kumasi, Kafi D. "Roses in the Concrete: A Critical Race Perspective on Urban Youth and School Libraries." *Knowledge Quest* 40, no. 4 (2012): 32-37.

Ladson-Billings, Gloria. *The Dreamkeepers: Successful Teaching of African American Children,* 2nd ed. San Francisco: Jossey Bass, 2009.

Ladson-Billings, Gloria, and William F. Tate, IV. "Toward A Critical Race Theory of Education," *Teachers College Record* 97, no. 1 (1995): 47-68.

Marcoux, Elizabeth. "Diversity and the Teacher-Librarian. *Teacher Librarian* 36, no. 3 (2010): 6-7

Mestre, Lori S. "Culturally Responsive Instruction for Teacher-Librarians." *Teacher Librarian* 36, no. 3 (2010): 8-12.

Mestre, Lori S. "Librarians Working with Diverse Populations: What Impact Does Cultural Competency Training Have on Their Efforts." *Journal of Academic Librarianship* 36, no. 6 (2010): 479-488.

McCarthy, C. "Multicultural Discourses and Curriculum Reform: A Critical Perspective." *Educational Theory* 44, no. 1 (1994): 81–98.

McNair, Jonda C. "Innocent Though They May Seem…A Critical Race Theory Analysis of Firefly and Seesaw Scholastic Book Club Order Forms." *Multicultural Review* 17, no. 1 (2008): 24-29.

Mendoza, Jean, and Debbie Reese. "Examining Multicultural Picture Books for the Early Childhood Classroom: Possibilities and Pitfalls." *Early Childhood Research & Practice* 32, no. 2 (2001): 1-38.

Michigan Education Association. *What is Cultural Competence?* Accessed May 13, 2015. http://www.mea.org/diversity/index.html.

Montague, Rae E., Martin Wolske, and Beth Larkee, "Three Views on Service Learning," *American Libraries; Digital Supplement* Winter (2009). Accessed May 13, 2015. http://www.eslarp.uiuc.edu/news/AmericanLibraries2009.pdf.

National Service Learning Clearinghouse, *What is Service Learning?* 2001. Accessed April 5, 2011. http://www.servicelearning.org/what_is_service-learning/service-learning_is/index.php.

Nieto, Sonia. *Language, Culture and Teaching: Critical Perspectives*, 2nd ed. New York: Routledge, 2010.

O'Hare, William. *The Changing Child Population of the United States: Analysis of Data from the 2010 Census.* Baltimore: The Annie E. Casey Foundation, 2011.

Orfield, Gary. *Schools More Separate: Consequences Of A Decade Of Resegregation.* Cambridge: Harvard Civil Rights Project, 2001. Accessed May 12, 2015. http://www.civilrightsproject.ucla.edu/research/deseg/separate_schools01.php.

Overall, Patricia M. "Cultural Competence: A Conceptual Framework for Library Information Science Professionals." *Library Quarterly* 79, no. 2 (2009): 175-204

Parker, Lawrence, and David O. Stovall. "Actions Following Words: Critical Race Theory Connects To Critical Pedagogy." *Educational Philosophy* 36, no. 2(2014): 167-182.

Pawley, Christine. "Unequal Legacies: Race and Multiculturalism in the LIS Curriculum." *Library Quarterly* 76, no. 2 (2006): 149-168.

Solórzano, Daniel G. "Images and Words that Wound: Critical Race Theory, Racial Stereotyping, and Teacher Education." *Teacher Education Quarterly* 24, no. 3 (1997): 5-19.

Solórzano, Daniel G., and Deloris Delgado Bernal. "Critical Race Theory and Transformational Resistance: Chicana/O Students in an Urban Context." *Urban Education*, 36, no. 3 (2001): 308-342.

Solórzano, Daniel G., and Armida Ornelas. "A Critical Race Analysis of Latina/o and African American Advanced Placement Enrollment in Public High Schools." *High School Journal* 87, no. 3 (2004): 15-26.

Solórzano, Daniel G., and Tara J. Yosso. "Critical Race Methodology: Counter-Story Telling as an Analytical Framework for Education." *Qualitative Inquiry* 8, no. 1 (2002): 23-44.

Southern Poverty Law Center. *Civil Rights Memorial, Wall of Tolerance.* Accessed May 23, 2015. http://www.splcenter.org/civil-rights-memorial/wall-tolerance.

Subramaniam Mega, and Paul Jaeger. "Modeling Inclusive Practice? Attracting Diverse Faculty and Future Faculty to the Information Workforce." *Library Trends 59, no. 1 (2010):* 109-127.

Subramaniam. Mega, and Paul Jaeger. "Weaving Diversity into LIS: An Examination of Diversity Course Offerings in iSchool Programs." *Education for Information 28, no. 1 (2011)*: 1-19.

Tatum, Beverly. *Why are All the Black Kids Sitting in the Cafeteria? And Other Conversations about Race.* New York: Basic Books, 2003.

United States Department of Education, Office for Civil Rights, *Revealing New Truths about Our Nation's School.* Washington, D.C.: U.S. Department of Education, 2012. Accessed May 12, 2015 from http://www2.ed.gov/about/offices/list/ocr/docs/crdc-2012-data-summary.pdf.

Yontz, Elaine and Kathleen de la Peña McCook. "Service-Learning and LIS Education." *Journal of Education for Library and Information Science* 44, no. 1 (2003): 58-68.

Chapter 5

Social Justice in Action: Cultural Humility, Scripts, and the LIS Classroom

Julie Ann Winkelstein

Introduction

In my fifties, I went back to school for my master's degree, then my Ph.D. in library science. I had been a public librarian for twenty years, working in jails and prisons, as a family literacy coordinator, on a bookmobile, and in a small city branch as a children's and young adult librarian. As I started writing this chapter, I looked back over these twenty years and asked myself: In my work as a librarian, what would I have wanted to know about social justice? What information or training would have made a difference in the way I practiced my librarianship? In summarizing my research and my experience as a public librarian and LIS teacher to answer these questions, I have focused this chapter on cultural humility as a basis for social justice librarianship and the ways in which the study of children's literature can create an opening for transformative learning in the LIS curriculum.

Libraries are intended to be regarded as safe and information rich spaces, yet the people who have the fewest alternatives for meeting their safety and information needs often do not experience public libraries as secure, and may not even find access to the information they are seeking. It is the responsibility of librarians to correct these systemic inequalities, and that starts with knowing who is not being served (even when the library appears to be busy and functioning more or less smoothly) and why the library is not functioning for them. To help build this knowledge and social justice analysis, we as educators need to provide curricula that question and destabilize cultural scripts about the roles of librarians and patrons. This is a way public librarians can make a real difference through their work, so that public libraries can meet their commitment to being these safe and useful spaces.

In retrospect I see that I, like many of my colleagues, engaged in what could be called "social justice librarianship," though it never occurred to me to apply that term. I was simply doing my job, fueled by anger at the outcome of our criminal justice system (when working as a jail and prison librarian), concern about the lack of relevant resources (when working in family literacy), and the need to meet the expressed and apparent needs of the community (when working in a branch). It is only now, that I am away from public librarianship and engaged in work that is highly related to social justice, that I can see this theme running throughout my career. This kind of awareness existed on the periphery of my library work, but without specific acknowledgement of the ramifications of the challenges my community faced in the larger world. I would have liked to have been more aware of this concept and to have had more tools to address social justice in my daily work life. I hope this chapter—and this book—will contribute to an increased knowledge of the importance of social justice in all the work we do as librarians.

The Social Justice Potential of Public Libraries and Library Schools

To begin talking about the largely untapped social justice potential of libraries and LIS curricula, I first want to address the gap that often exists between library services and public awareness of them, by way of an example. Sir Michael Marmot, Director of the International Institute for Society and Health and a researcher on the health impacts of social inequalities, gave a talk in 2015 at the David Brower Center in

Berkeley, California. He began his remarks by saying: "Inequality strains the binds that bring us together as a society."[1] He went on to explain that health and the distribution of health are indicators of how well a nation or community is doing. These effects can be ameliorated, he continued, by interventions that include early education for children, higher education for adults, meaningful and adequate employment, and exposure to ideas that help us discuss and further our understanding of how our societies work.[2]

Public libraries have resources to help build access to all of these protective health factors, yet the public is largely unaware of this. This can mean resources that are available at public libraries for finding employment, applying to schools and colleges, processing immigration, legal, and tax documents, completing homework assignments, preparing young children for school, attending discussion groups or other programs, may not be accessed. We need our librarians to be cognizant of the impact of social inequalities on the lives of their community members and to understand that redressing these inequalities is an institutional and a personal responsibility. In addition, we need to prepare our future librarians to be aware of the gaps between what they offer and what the community expects and uses, and to offer tools for closing these gaps.

Feedback from students and other communities about how libraries are perceived can inform future librarians of what their public does not know about them. It is important to emphasize that the lack of awareness of the potential public libraries have to forward social justice work acts not only as a constraint on our abilities, as librarians, to perform our social justice work, but it can also act as a filter for those entering our profession. Those with a social justice agenda may be less inclined to choose librarianship and more apt to choose fields more commonly associated with social justice, such as public health and social work.

---

1. Sir Michael Marmot, "The Health Gap: The Challenge of an Unequal World" (lecture, David Brower Center, Berkeley, CA, November 6, 2015).

2. Ibid.

By centering on social justice, library schools can provide the basis for both an introduction to and a deepening of this type of knowledge and perception, and can attract social justice-oriented students who may not otherwise have considered LIS. For example, on the whole, the students who signed up for my undergraduate Information Studies and Technology (IS&T) minor class at the University of Tennessee, Knoxville (UTK), "Race, Gender and Technology," already had an interest in addressing social justice, especially as related to gender and race. This class has an obvious social justice theme, since the title includes both "race" and "gender." Similarly, the UTK graduate-level multicultural children's and young adult literature class, "Valuing Diversity: International and Intercultural Resources for Youth," attracted students with explicit social justice interests, including anti-racist work; the word "diversity" is often used in the library world for talking about differences, and is frequently equated to race. While many students were interested in social justice, most of the IS&T minor students were not planning to enter the library profession, although by the end of each semester there were usually two to three students considering the field.

One of the most repeated comments in the final exercise of that class, which was to describe one insight they gained through the class, was the newly perceived power of the public library to address social justice issues, such as race, unemployment, access to technology, and literacy. The students all lived in communities with public libraries, yet their awareness of what these libraries could offer was limited. They were surprised to find out what was there and became eager to promote libraries.

Social Justice as Librarianship: Learning from Other Fields

My current work is primarily related to lesbian, gay, bisexual, transgender, and queer or questioning (LGBTQ+) youth experiencing homelessness. My research in this area has been about linking social justice, libraries, and librarianship, and bringing together community organizations and libraries to create a stronger support network for these young people. Through this process, I have realized that much of the theory written in other fields of social justice readily translates to LIS, since the information conveyed through social justice writing relates to stigma, social exclusion, and the concept of marginalization.

One way to bring these ideas into a library is to begin with culture: the cultures of those who have been socially excluded, stigmatized, or misrepresented, and the cultures of libraries and those who work for these libraries. Here is an exercise I use in classes and presentations that offers the opportunity to look at some of our cultural connections. It is called "Circles of My Multicultural Self" and it is from a useful website called "EdChange."[3]

Circles of My Multicultural Self

This activity highlights the multiple dimensions of our identities. It addresses the importance of individuals self-defining their identities and challenging stereotypes.

- Place your name in the center circle of the structure below. (See **Figure 1**).Write an important aspect of your identity in each of the satellite circles – an identifier or descriptor that you feel is important in defining you. This can include anything: Asian American, female, mother, athlete, educator, Taoist, scientist, or any descriptor with which you identify.
- Write one or two sentences about a time you were especially proud to identify yourself with one of the descriptors you used above.
- Write one or two sentences about a time it was especially painful to be identified with one of your identifiers or descriptors.

3. Paul C. Gorski, "Critical Multicultural Pavilion Awareness Activities: Circles of My Multicultural Self," *EdChange,* accessed November 8, 2015, http://www.edchange.org/multicultural/activities/circlesofself.html.

- Name a stereotype associated with one of the groups with which you identify that is not consistent with who you are. Fill in the following sentence:

I am (a/an) ________________________ but I am NOT (a/an)____________________.

My Example: So if one of my identifiers was "middle-aged," and I thought a stereotype was that all middle-aged people are slow to adopt new ideas, my sentence would be: *I am middle-aged, but I am not slow to adopt new ideas.*

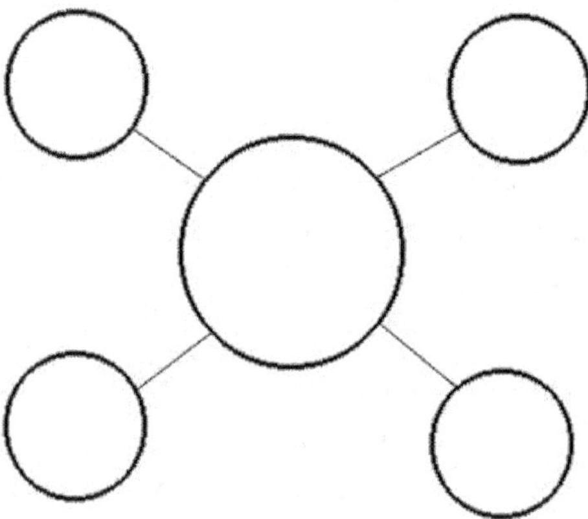

Figure 1.

This exercise is designed to take about twenty to thirty minutes and can be done as a homework assignment, an in-class small group exercise, or in any way you can incorporate it into your curriculum. It can be a good way to start out the semester, so students can begin to learn more about themselves as well as their classmates. I have done this exercise in librarian trainings and some of the responses were: "I'm a librarian but I'm not an introvert" and "I'm second generation but I'm not torn between two cultures." I like this exercise because it is an excellent first step toward understanding culture and cultural humility.

It involves articulating parts of our own culture and at the same time hearing about others.

The term "culture" has a range of definitions. Anthropologists Alfred L. Kroeber and Clyde Kluckhorn offer an oft-cited definition:

> Culture consists of patterns, explicit and implicit, of and for behavior acquired and transmitted by symbols, constituting the distinctive achievement of human groups, including their embodiments in artifacts; the essential core of culture consists of traditional (i.e., historically derived and selected) ideas and especially their attached values; culture systems may, on the one hand be considered as products of action; on the other hand, as conditioning elements of further action.[4]

The *attached values* at the "essential core of culture" have key significance in examining library culture. Taking a functional and psychological view of culture, interculturalist Stella Ting-Toomey evokes this value element as she describes two of its functions that contribute to an understanding of the role of culture in social justice librarianship. First, "culture serves the *group inclusion function*, satisfying our need for membership and belonging. Culture creates a comfort zone in which we experience in-group inclusion and in-group/out-group differences."[5] Second, "*culture's intergroup boundary regulation function* shapes our in-group and out-group attitudes in dealing with people who are culturally dissimilar."[6] When we combine these two descriptions, we can see that an awareness of our own cultures, as individuals, as community members, and as librarians or future librarians, is a crucial part of the social justice work of libraries. It is not always easy to become aware of our own cultures, and possibly our concomitant privilege and/or power, and their profound impact on our personal and institutional behavior.

---

4. Alfred K. Kroeber and Clyde Kluckhorn, *Culture: A Critical Review of Concepts and Definitions*, Papers of the Peabody Museum of Archaeology and Ethnology 47, no. 1 (Cambridge, MA: Harvard University, 1952): 181.

5. Stella Ting-Toomey, *Communicating Across Cultures* (New York: Guilford Press, 1999): 13.

6. Ibid.

Partly for that reason, this awareness is not yet adequately integrated into the discipline of LIS.

If you do an Internet search for the term "social justice," librarianship does not appear anywhere near the top of the results, unlike health, education, and social work. Yet social justice is just as central to accessibility and effectiveness in library science as it is in these other fields. These other fields have moved forward more quickly in incorporating the social justice concepts of equal opportunities, defining and examining privilege, and addressing barriers to what is frequently called "meaningful access"—access that is not based on tokenism or an inaccurate or incomplete perception of what is needed for a particular person. For example, if you offer circulating laptops to public library users without confirming they have regular access to the Internet, basic and technological literacy skills needed to take advantage of this technology, a supportive and safe space in which to explore and use the laptop, and adequate housing, healthcare and food, then despite your good intentions, your library patrons may still not have meaningful access.

The checklist below is adapted from Fisher-Borne et al., who, as social work educators, created this list to offer guidance to social workers in incorporating cultural humility into their work. (In the adapted list below, all references to social workers and clients have been changed to terms relating to libraries.) This list may serve as a useful guide to creating meaningful access in libraries by adapting existing social justice theory.

Asking Ourselves: Addressing Power Imbalances

Individual level

- What social and economic barriers impact a library patron's ability to receive needed library services?
- What specific experiences are my library patrons having that are related to oppression and/or larger systemic issues?
- How does my library work to actively challenge power imbalances and involve communities considered on the margins of the dominant culture?

- How do I extend my responsibility beyond individual library patrons and advocate for changes in local, state, and national policies and practices?

Institutional level

- How do we actively address inequalities both internally (i.e., policies and procedures) and externally (i.e., legislative advocacy)?
- How do we define and live out the core library values of intellectual freedom, diversity, and the public good?
- What are the organizational structures we have that encourage action to address inequalities?
- What training and professional development opportunities do we offer that address inequalities and encourage self-reflection about power and privilege?
- How do we engage with the larger community to ensure community voice in our work? What organizations are already doing this well? [7]

An important example of how commuting social justice knowledge to LIS can help librarianship move forward comes from practical advice given by researcher, author, and Associate Professor of English at Florida International University, Linda Spears-Bunton, whose work focuses on the relationships among literacy, literature, and culture. Writing about the teaching of multicultural literature in grades 6 through 12, she offers this suggestion:

> It is important to make a self-assessment about what you know about African American, Asian/Pacific American, Latino, and Native American people. Concurrently, it is necessary to critically examine the source(s) of your prior knowledge. A simple way to begin is to survey the books, magazines, newspapers, works of art, and music in your home. Consider

---

7. Marcie Fisher-Borne, Jessie Montana Cain, and Suzanne L. Martin, "From Mastery to Accountability: Cultural Humility as an Alternative to Cultural Competence," *Social Work Education: The International Journal* 34, no.2 (2015): Table 2, 176.

> the films and television shows you watch and examine them for the kinds of images they present about people of color. Look at your network of friends and acquaintances and the social and cultural activities in which you regularly participate; examine this network in light of the ways in which it influences how you read the 'word and the world.'[8]

Self-examination like this needs to have a central place in library school, which tends to be dominated by white people, as does librarianship in the U.S.[9] This kind of inquiry can yield insights into students' lives, assumptions, and preconceptions as they strive to understand what it is they do not know and how to move forward with their own self-education. Racism is an enormously impactful structural issue that must be addressed in schools, as it affects students and faculty, and in libraries, as it affects librarians and library users. The "Black Lives Matter" movement[10] and the campus protests in late 2015 related to race,[11] as well as books like the National Book Award winner *Between the World and Me* by Ta-Nehisi Coates, and the cumulative works of many, many other social justice activists, such as Michelle Alexander,[12] bell hooks,[13] and Iris Young,[14] have created a highly visible wave of political awareness of ongoing structural oppressions that disproportionately affect

8. Linda Spears-Bunton, "All the Colors of the Land: A Literacy Montage" in *Teaching Multicultural Literature in Grades 9-12: Moving Beyond the Canon*, ed. Arlette E. Willis (Norwood, MA: Christopher-Gordon Publishers, 1998): 25.

9. Denise M. Davis and Tracie D. Hall "Diversity Counts," (Chicago: ALA Office for Research and Statistics, ALA Office for Diversity, 2007), accessed December 28, 2015, http://www.ala.org/offices/diversity/diversitycounts/divcounts.

10. *Black Lives Matter*, accessed December 28, 2015, http://blacklivesmatter.com/about/.

11. Keeanga-Yamahtta Taylor, "Black Lives Matter on Campus, Too," *Aljazeera America*, November 29, 2015, http://america.aljazeera.com/opinions/2015/11/black-lives-matter-on-campus-too.html.

12. Michelle Alexander, *The New Jim Crow: Mass Incarceration in the Age of Colorblindness* (New York: The New Press, 2012).

13. bell hooks, *Race, Gender and Cultural Politics* (Boston: South End Press, 1990).

14. Iris M. Young, *Justice and the Politics of Difference* (Princeton, NJ: Princeton University Press, 1990).

people of color. Libraries are a part of this system, and they need to participate fully in the movement for equality. For example, librarians can bring in speakers, partner with local agencies and faith groups, host discussions on race, and provide a range of resources such as books, websites, movies, and contact information for local and national organizations. They can ask themselves: "What other organizational structures can we put in place to encourage action to address inequalities? What is the role of a public library in the community's awareness? What is our role, as librarians, in this awareness?"

Another example of applying social justice knowledge in LIS relates to gender. It is critical for those who identify as transgender or gender nonconforming or who reject the gender binary to feel safe in their bodies and in their identities. Yet this safety is too often lacking; trans patients have reported being shoved, hit, and shouted at in doctor's offices when they try to talk about themselves. "Injustice at Every Turn," a report from the National Center for Transgender Equality and the National Gay and Lesbian Task Force, offers many examples of this kind of discrimination.[15] Interacting with a health practitioner who is uncomfortable, uneducated, or even hostile is a barrier to sharing personal details about their bodies and their lives, with potentially life-threatening results: they may not have a Pap smear or prostate exam because they do not feel safe enough to reveal that the sex they were assigned at birth has never matched their gender identity. The Callen-Lorde Community Health Center in New York City[16] offers a model for providing services that promote safety and wellbeing by affirming identity. The medical staff there, as well as the posters on the wall and the kinds of programs and information offered, reflect these services. Patient treatment is personal and individual, but it is also driven by institutional and societal attitudes

---

15. Jaime M. Grant, Lisa A. Mottet, Justin Tanis, Jack Harrison, Jody L. Herman, and Mary Keisling, "Injustice at Every Turn: A Report of the National Transgender Discrimination Survey" (Washington, D.C.: National Center for Transgender Equality and National Gay and Lesbian Task Force, 2011).

16. *Callen-Lorde Community Health Center*, accessed December 29, 2015, http://callen-lorde.org/.

that affect expectations, assumptions, training, rules, regulations, policies, and procedures. To be able to create this environment, the staff at Callen-Lorde receive training that provides insights into the culture of the people they are serving. They are also expected to be aware of their own cultural expectations and experiences, by asking themselves: "What is the information we want to impart? How do we expect to be able to offer that information? Which cultural norms are we drawing from?" The Callen-Lorde medical staff members have to look at the barriers created by the power differentials between themselves and the patients they want to serve. Libraries can learn from this type of example as they work toward creating a culture that promotes meaningful access by addressing power imbalances at individual and institutional levels, and library schools can also teach from such a model.

Cultural Humility in the Library

Many people have attended trainings or workshops on cultural sensitivity, which are trainings focused on understanding that there are human differences and how to interact in a respectful and inclusive way with those who are different. This is certainly a good starting point, but beyond working to establish communication across cultures, we also need to look critically at our own culture and how it fits into larger patterns of inequity.

The concept of "cultural humility" moves us beyond navigating our immediate and ingrained intercultural interactions to taking this crucial step back. "Cultural humility" emphasizes the recognition and dismantling of power relationships inside and outside institutions that can affect a person's ability to provide services and resources. This term was originally developed in the healthcare field by Dr. Melanie Tervalon and Dr. Jann Murray-Garcia. In 1998, they wrote the groundbreaking article, "Cultural Humility Versus Cultural Competence: A Critical Distinction in Defining Physician Training Outcomes in Multicultural Education." As the authors state: "Cultural humility incorporates a lifelong commitment to self-evaluation and self-critique, to redressing the power imbalances in the patient-physician dynamic, and to developing mutually beneficial and non-paternalistic clinical and advocacy partnerships with communities on behalf of individuals and defined populations."[17]

When I read this excerpt from their abstract, I substitute "patient" with "patron," "physician" with "librarian," and "clinical" with "library-based." The result is a good description of cultural humility as it applies to librarianship. This description contrasts with the cultural competence model with its particular focus on knowledge, as presented by authors such as Overall[18] and others.

Borrowing from social work, we can add to this definition the three core elements of cultural humility introduced by interculturalists Fisher-Borne, Cain, and Martin in their social work article, "From Mastery to Accountability: Cultural Humility as an Alternative to Cultural Competence." These are: institutional and individual accountability, lifelong learning and critical reflection, and mitigating power imbalances.[19] The authors' emphasis on individual and institutional accountability may be where we, as librarians, have the biggest challenges, and where universal LIS education about cultural humility and cultural scripts could make a profound difference.

In her pre-health lecture on cultural humility as an assistant adjunct professor at the Betty Irene Moore school of nursing at the University of California, Davis, Dr. Murray-Garcia describes the pre-existing "scripts" that influence our expectations related to individuals, groups, and even

17. Jann Murray-Garcia and Melanie Tervalon, "Cultural Humility Versus Cultural Competence: A Critical Distinction in Defining Training Outcomes in Multicultural Education," *Journal of Health Care for the Poor and Underserved* 9, no.2 (1998): 117.

18. Patricia Montiel Overall, "Cultural Competence: A Conceptual Framework for Library and Information Science Professionals," *Library Quarterly* 79, no. 2 (2009): 175-204.

19. Marcie Fisher-Borne, Jessie Montana Cain and Suzanne L. Martin, "From Mastery to Accountability: Cultural Humility as an Alternative to Cultural Competence," *Social Work Education: The International Journal* 34, no. 2 (2015): 165-181, accessed July 5, 2015, http://dx.doi.org/10.1080/02615479.2014.977244.

institutions who we may perceive as "the other." As she explains in the video of her presentation:

> Some of the scripts we learn pretty early in our lives are pretty faithfully reproduced...All of us have internalized the scripts that get played out, that generation after generation produce unequal results, whether it's in health care, the criminal justice system, school system...This is a lifelong process. You will never have mastery in someone else's culture or their life experience. So the issue is not competence; for me, it's a stance of humility where you are aware of your own scripts for that person, you are aware of the scripts they might bring to you, maybe they are from a group that has been historically mistreated by institutions ...You've got to develop a relationship for that person to tell you. For me, that's more about humility than it is about competence.[20]

Murray-Garcia points out these scripts exist independent of any particular group. They produce stereotypes, but the stereotypes can be attached to various groups at different times, depending on the institutional, personal, or historical context. In one example, Irish immigrants in the mid- to late-nineteenth century were described in the U.S. media as drunken, pugnacious semi-savages and represented in cartoons as small, ugly, and simian-like. Dr. Murray-Garcia asks the audience: "How do we use that script today, and for which group of people?" She also asks: "When terms like 'disadvantaged,' 'underserved,' or 'underprivileged' are used, are these people who need to be fixed, or is it a system in which we are all implicated?" Another example she uses is that of Koreans in Japan, who were brought forcibly as slaves and who have experienced second-class citizenship, whose children go to less resourced schools, whose test scores as a group are lower, who have higher dropout rates and poorer economic and health outcomes, who have higher incarceration rates, and whose communities experience more violence and victimization. "Does that sound like a familiar script we use in the U.S.?" she asks. The students begin to understand the pattern: the script stays the same, but the groups change. In libraries, the script for a contaminated, inferior

20. Jann Murray-Garcia, *Cultural Humility and the Pre-Health Professions Student: Preparing NOW to Eliminate Disparities during Your Career*, video, 55:52, December 23, 2013, https://www.youtube.com/watch?v=NZUP6CrHAXA.

"other" from which "normal" people need protection is all too often played out faithfully; in my field of study, this tenacious script shows up in the treatment of people who are experiencing homelessness and people who have mental health diagnoses.

While librarians may acknowledge that some people are living in unstable housing, sometimes to the extent that they are sleeping under a freeway overpass at night, we frequently want to adhere to our rules about requiring a permanent address for a library card or not allowing people to doze off while they are at the library. We may know that there are a range of mental health diagnoses and we may in fact be privately living with mental health challenges ourselves, but when someone comes to our reference desk and waves their arms around or when they talk quietly to themselves at the computer, many librarians become uncomfortable and want to call the police or bring in the security guard, even though the person is not behaving violently.

When we as librarians enforce rules, policies, procedures; when we design our collections; when we decide whose needs we will strive to meet and whose are not legitimate or not our problem; when we create programs; and when we simply interact with our library users, we can ask ourselves: "What script am I using for this situation or for this person? Are there certain people who have the rules bent for them and others who do not? Are there expectations I have the minute someone enters the library and am I willing to question an expectation, whether it is a positive or negative belief or a belief that someone is exceptional because they do not fit with my script?" For example, if a person looks like they are experiencing homelessness but they are reading Faulkner, a common script regarding people who live on the streets would say that this person presents a contradiction. What other scripts may play out in libraries? What do they have to say about the role libraries play in the life of a community? If these scripts are limited by the vision we have of libraries, how might they affect what kinds of programming libraries offer? When we teach our future librarians, what script are we expecting them to follow?

Scripts that dictate a role for "us" and "the other" are related to the concept of marginalization, wherein one group perceives themselves to reside safely within some margins— for instance, racial, behavioral, economic, cultural, or geographical—while another group, the "outsiders," are considered outside of those designated margins. But what if you looked at it the other way around? What if the people who have been marked as "outsiders" perceive themselves within their own margins? Then who is marginalized?

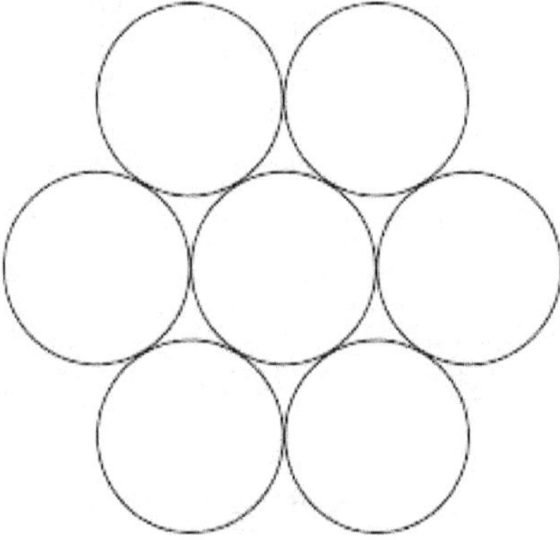

Figure 2.

Who is marginalized in this illustration? Which circle is the "standard" one?

We are all always on the margins of some groups and in the center of others. UC Berkeley professor of rhetoric and gender and women's studies, Minh-Ha Trinh asks: "Marginality: *Who* names? *Whose* fringes?"[21] We can ask the same: "Whose margins are we talking about?" In fact, margins describe not the person or group indicated, but power relationships, attitudes, perceptions, and assumptions about that person or group relative to another. For this reason, we need to look closely at library cultures and their margins, and at what scripts we use for dealing with those who do not fall within them. For example, when

21. Minh-Ha Trinh, *When the Moon Waxes Red* (New York: Routledge, 1991): 14.

we say "public libraries are reaching out to marginalized youth," whose margins are we using?

We probably know the answer to this question—that statement uses the margins of the dominant culture, the ones in power, and for librarians, that may be us. It may not feel that way on a daily basis, and it may be that there are ways we do not feel we have power in our professional lives. But as part of the institution of a library, we do have power, because it is a part of the U.S. culture. In this society, books and knowledge and libraries are associated with power and privilege. Library employees use a prescribed vocabulary and clearly worded expectations of our library users. We have rules, policies, and procedures, and we enforce them. We are in charge. Thus, without cultural humility, without an ongoing critical self-reflection of ourselves and our institutions, without an awareness of the scripts we are following— personal, institutional, and societal— we will fall short of serving our entire community well.

We must be able to identify our own preferences and comfort zones and then be willing to step outside of them. We must check our scripts and interrupt them, even if it feels awkward or uncomfortable at first, because through the scripts we unknowingly follow we carry out not only our own expectations and power dynamics but also those of our institutions. We must commit to lowering institutional and societal barriers by holding ourselves and our institutions accountable, so the experiences our library users have are consistent throughout—*all* library users feel welcome by *all* library staff.

Children's and Young Adult Literature

In children's literature courses, we have opportunities to talk about power and privilege as they relate to gender, race, age, bodies, health, sexual orientation, space and how it is occupied, and all the other ways we categorize ourselves and other people. In the children's literature classes I teach, one of the concepts I present is that when we decenter the dominant culture in acquisition choices, we allow an antidote to images that may be presented, subtly and not so subtly, about people's lives.

Noted scholar, lecturer, and author Na'im Akbar, known for his research in African American psychology, comments on this: "A great deal of what constitutes self-concept grows out of the social images that are projected about people... One of the consequences of oppression is the loss of control over those projection of images..."[22] A fuller understanding of the role of race and ethnicity in our society and the impact these concepts have on children's self-images, as well as their understanding of others, can help us examine our current collections with fresh perceptions and our potential acquisitions with new strategies. Without this understanding, our selections may be less representative of the cultures in our society. This knowledge can both act as a way to diminish potential barriers and provide the impetus to critically examine the books we choose for our collections, so that they act as windows and mirrors for our public.

Three Children's Literature Classes

I provide here some examples of the ways in which I incorporate social justice thought into three children's literature classes: the previously mentioned synchronous online graduate class, "Valuing Diversity: Multicultural and International Resources for Youth"; an asynchronous online undergraduate class, "Books and Related Materials for Children"; and a four-week asynchronous online continuing education class called "Multicultural Children's Literature."

"Valuing Diversity" is taught every other summer for current MLS graduate students. There are about twenty students in this class, and it has been taught by both full-time and adjunct faculty. "Books and Related Materials for Children" is offered for students in the IS&T undergraduate minor through the School of Information Sciences and is taught by both doctoral students and adjunct faculty. Class enrollment averages between forty and fifty students, many of whom are planning to become teachers.

---

22. Na'im Akbar, interview quote, in Michael D. Harris, *Colored Pictures: Race & Visual Representations* (Chapel Hill, NC: University of North Carolina Press, 2003): 14.

"Multicultural Children's Literature" was part of a grant-funded continuing education project called "The Infopeople Project," and most of the fifteen students were practicing librarians. This class was offered once, after which the class recordings and materials were archived online and made freely accessible to the public. By comparing these three classes, I offer an overview and some specific examples of ways in which LIS education can foster social justice awareness.

One of the questions for library schools is whether to offer a specific social justice-related class or to incorporate social justice into all classes. One example of this conversation was the 2014 iConference session titled "Social Justice in Library and Information Science," where panelists engaged the audience in discussions about how to approach this topic.[23] There are advantages to both approaches and the ideal would be to do both. The following are examples of the two approaches.

"Valuing Diversity: Multicultural and International Resources for Youth"

In this synchronous online class we look at statistics and background information related to select cultures, such as Latinx, African American and Afro Caribbean, LGBTQ+, Asian and Asian American, and Native American. We also look at ageism, physical abilities, and body awareness. These are the groupings I use, but it is important to stress that they were convenient for teaching this course; of course no one falls perfectly into any one particular category. We address all of these through assigned readings, fiction, class discussions, student writings, and a final paper. The students' insights and comments were perceptive and thoughtful, and it was an extremely rewarding class to teach.

Here are two samples of student comments which were both reactions to assigned articles. The first article, "Why I'm Not Thankful for

23. Miriam E. Sweeney, Nicole A. Cooke, Melissa Villa-Nicholas, K.R. Roberto, and Safiya U. Noble, "Social Justice in the Library and Information Science," in iConference 2014 Proceedings (2014): 1202-1203, doi:10.9776/14213.

Thanksgiving,"[24] was about the use of Native American stereotypes. On the class discussion board, one student commented that she had been underestimating the impact of stereotypes by considering some to be unimportant or "less bad," until she confronted the historical context of the Atlanta Braves symbol of the tomahawk. As she put it:

> The symbol for the Braves is the tomahawk, and every Braves game has the tomahawk chop, where every Braves fan in the stadium chops with their arm while chanting. Nonsensical chanting is a major Native American stereotype and a mockery of the traditional practices of some Native American tribes. The tomahawk and the tomahawk chop became repulsive when viewed from a historical standpoint. Native Americans were abused in many ways by the European settlers, including but not limited to being defeated in battles. A stadium full of predominantly white baseball fans pretending to be the Native American warriors that were almost entirely wiped out by their ancestors seems glaringly offensive, but like me for so long, most of those fans have no clue.

Other students replied, citing their own experiences with Thanksgiving celebrations in school, and with sports teams such as the Cleveland Indians. Another student responded to an article about the representation of Muslims in children's literature, noting that growing up with a best friend who was Muslim, with whom she connected as a Christian because both friends were religious, probably served a protective function in helping her resist the negative stereotyping of Muslims in the U.S. post-9/11. "Perhaps," she noted, "children's literature could have a similar effect by giving children the opportunity to find common ground and cultivate personal relationships with people from cultures other than their own." One of her classmates responded to her posting, interested in her point of view and pointing out the importance of accuracy in the representation:

24. Michael A. Dorris, "Why I'm Not Thankful for Thanksgiving" in *Through Indian Eyes: The Native Experience in Books for Children*, eds. Beverly Slapin and Doris Seale (Philadelphia: New Society Publishers, 1992), 19-22.

> If Muslims are included in children's literature, the author just needs to make sure the depiction is accurate and written from an authoritative point of view. Otherwise, it will be misconstrued as being racist. Just like the very first article we read about Taco Night, we would have to get rid of the stereotypes of Muslims and concentrate on the authentic side of Muslim life. Every elementary, middle and high school should have some type of race relations or tolerance class. This would be a perfect opportunity to be reminded that everyone is different and should be treated with respect regardless of your views and opinions.

Both of these comments showed a willingness to discuss, question, and learn from the examples offered and from each other.

The final assignment for this class is to choose a topic relevant to the course and write about it, drawing on course materials as well as outside resources. One example of a paper subject was: "Who has the right to write about a particular culture?" This was a topic we discussed throughout the semester, with students offering their views on both sides; the majority of students felt someone who takes the time to be well informed might write about a culture other than their own. This student offered a thoughtful and balanced paper in which she grappled with the complexities of this question, supporting her answers with quotes from a range of authors, including Amy Tan and Walter Dean Myers. Whatever her conclusions, it was apparent to me that this discussion will be carried into her future work as a librarian. This class seemed to help her better understand the importance of culture and how its representation can affect readers. This is the kind of background that librarians need to be able to incorporate social justice into their library work.

Another student chose to write about cross-cultural friendships in children's literature, comparing three children's books. Her examples highlighted children's books in which apparent racial differences are only evident in the illustrations. Yet another student examined the controversy around Julius Lester's novel about slavery, *Day of Tears: A Novel in Dialogue.*

As a teacher, my goal is to bring forward topics and allow the space for students to reach their own conclusions. Although I am sure my social justice bent is obvious, I want my students to feel free to express their opinions, as long as they can support what they say. This kind of dialogue is necessary if we are going to have librarians who are able to carry this knowledge forward and apply it in their future jobs.

A course like this gives not only direct knowledge of available multicultural literature but it also— and more importantly— gives students the opportunity to read and discuss in-depth articles about terms such as cultures, nations, ethnicity, race, and religion, as well as how these concepts are interpreted by individuals and societies. These tools will serve educators, librarians, children, and ultimately society, because they provide the critical framework necessary for making decisions about a collection. There is a tendency for those who are selecting materials to rely on book lists and reviews garnered from various usually highly reputable sources. This is a start, but in the long run what is most essential is a commitment to the ongoing assessment and acquisition of materials that are current, authentic, and excellent. In fact, in class discussions, several students acknowledged the challenge of selecting multicultural children's literature, expressing a lack of confidence in their ability to do so. They are committed to creating a diverse collection, yet they are afraid of choosing inappropriate materials. This class helped them feel better prepared to make these choices.

This is what it means to be a professional librarian—someone who serves the community wisely and with in-depth knowledge and understanding. As Professor Emerita of Education at Ohio State University, Rudine Sims Bishop, tells us: "That is the underlying purpose of multicultural education, to change the world by making it a more equitable one. Multicultural literature can be a powerful vehicle for accomplishing that task."[25] This is social justice in action.

In this class, the students who were enrolled were either interested in social justice issues and considering whether or not librarianship would be the venue for their social action, or they were already working

---

25. Rudine Sims Bishop, "Multicultural Literature for Children: Making Informed Choices," in *Teaching Multicultural Literature in Grades K-8*, ed. Violet J. Harris (Norwood, MA: Christopher Gordon Publishers, 1992), 52.

in libraries but looking for ways to incorporate social justice into their daily work lives. This class offered tools for doing just that.

"Books and Other Materials for Children"

As previously noted, the other possibility is to include social justice issues in classes where that is *not* expected, such as research methods or undergraduate children's literature classes. Through these classes, educators have the opportunity to teach core LIS material with social justice as the default lens, rather than dominant narratives that perpetuate inequality. This causes real change in the way students feel and think about the material and also about themselves. The changes may be incremental, or even infinitesimal, but exposure to other ways of looking at the world begins to uncover assumptions and increase awareness of societal inequities. For example, students in a children's literature class may never have considered the implications of a "norm" for children's book characters, characters who are assumed, without any discussion, to be able-bodied, slim, white, cisgender, straight, and housed. There are, of course, exceptions to this, but frequently these exceptions are spelled out for us and are, in many cases, the focus of the book.

The undergraduate "Books and Other Materials for Children" is an example of this type of course. The brief course catalog description states: "Materials for children in leisure time or classroom activities. Criteria for selecting books, magazines, recordings, films, and related materials. Storytelling and other devices for encouraging reading." The only indication that there may be a social justice component to this class is the seventh of eight course objectives listed on my syllabus: "Recognize stereotypes and cultural biases in children's literature." It is interesting to note that, since it is not required, not all instructors of this course include this as one of the course objectives. Like graduate level classes in children's literature, this class is reading and writing intensive, and when I teach it, offers a wide range of book titles and articles. One of the sixteen weeks is focused primarily on diversity and children's literature, including the range of meanings we can associate with the word "culture," such as race, nationality, ability, socioeconomic status, and bodies. It is an extremely abbreviated version of the graduate class, yet it works well in laying the groundwork for learning to think about the characters in our books and what their lives are like.

One way I approach this is through children's and young adult book awards. I include the traditional awards, such as the Caldecott and the Newbery, but also less mainstream ones, such as the Middle Eastern Book Award, sponsored by the Middle East Outreach Council; the Jane Addams Book Award, sponsored by the Jane Addams Peace Association; the Schneider Family Book Award, which focuses on the representation of the disability experience in children's and adolescent literature and is administered by the American Library Association (ALA); and the American Indian Youth Literature Award, sponsored by the American Indian Library Association (AILA). I introduce the students to these awards and then their final project for the semester is called the "Picture Book Project" in which they write briefly about ten picture books chosen from twenty-seven lesser-known awards.

Another way that students are encouraged to think about representation in children's book collections in libraries is with an assignment which requires that they visit the children's section of their local public library and answer specific questions. These questions include:

- Describe this section.
- Does it feel welcoming to you?
- To whom might it feel welcoming or not welcoming?
- If there are displays, which books are included?
- If children's book awards are highlighted, which ones have been selected?

Again, this exercise encourages students to be aware of assumptions that are being made about books, library users, children, parents, and library staff. This assignment is completed about three quarters of the way through the semester, and the impact of conversations about diversity up to this point can be seen in the student responses. In 2015, several of the students commented in particular on the lack of displayed books that represent a range of physical abilities, in addition to a lack of racial diversity. None of the libraries they visited displayed any of the lesser known awards. These observations were indicative of how these students are using social justice concepts to observe and think about the world around them.

Infopeople: "Multicultural Children's Literature"

The Infopeople Project is a grant-funded project that provides continuing education trainings through the California State Library. This third class had a format that was quite different from the previous two. The lectures and attendant materials were prepared in advance and posted to the Infopeople website. The four lectures were presented as text, to be read by the students. Links were embedded in the lectures, and each class ended with a list of possible assignments. Unlike the university classes, there was no grading but there were assignments that had to be done to receive the completion certificate at the end of the class. Students worked at their own pace and all discussions were via discussion boards.

I used the same basic groupings as in the graduate class, providing a background on each group. Exercises were more practical and applicable to the daily lives of librarians, since most participants were working librarians. Examples of assignments included:

- Search a public library catalog for children's fiction about various religions and then report on which religions were easiest to find and which ones were more challenging.
- Evaluate a popular children's book for gender bias.
- Assess a popular children's picture book for ageism.
- Based on the class resources and lectures, select five children's books you would like to add to your collection and explain why you chose those.

- Identify three goals you have for making your children's collection more diverse, list one barrier you might encounter for each goal, and offer one way to address each of these barriers.

Comments from the Infopeople students can provide insights into the impact of the material and the exercises. Evaluations from various students included observations on: the lack of multicultural children's books in her library's collection; why some children's "classics" could be considered offensive because of the stereotypes; imagining her own religious group being incorrectly portrayed and how that would feel to her; an appreciation for the opportunity to closely examine her own perspective on the world and how that affects the way she evaluates books; the importance of extensive reading of excellent multicultural children's books; and the impact of thinking about ageism in children's literature. As these students continue their library work, they will apply these insights and more into their daily lives. Whether or not they call it social justice, these insights will strengthen the ability of their libraries to help create a more equitable society.

Social Justice and LIS Curricula: Moving Forward

The incorporation of social justice into LIS curricula is critical to serving and supporting our communities. We must understand how our libraries and their lives intersect and what barriers to responsive service may exist on either side. In this chapter I use children's literature as a vehicle for demonstrating how we can create this kind of awareness and how we can offer our future and current librarians the tools they need. I look at this through the lens of cultural humility practice in public librarianship.

If we look at our libraries, our library organizations— like ALA, the Public Library Association (PLA), state organizations, the Association for Library and Information Science Education (ALISE)— and even our library schools, we can see that there are particular ways of doing things, and specific assumptions that are made. I frequently encounter this in my work with people experiencing homelessness. ALA has the Library Services to the Poor policy,[26] as well as the Office for Diversity and Outreach Services, and the Social Responsibilities Round Table's Hunger, Homelessness and Poverty task force. In addition, there is the Library Bill of Rights[27] with its many interpretations.[28] However, the reality is that there is no enforcement, and little institutional and organizational leadership, regarding the social justice aspect of working with our communities in ways that are culturally appropriate, respectful, and helpful. As noted in the fields of social work and health care, it is more than learning to communicate; it is more than a passing self-examination; it is more than making statements and posting them on a website. We have to be willing to take on our institutions and question the very assumptions being made about who we are as an institution and whom we are serving. This is a challenge, and it is one we need to begin to face in library schools and continue to face throughout our careers.

Each LIS student, each LIS professor, and each librarian has the potential to be an active participant in ensuring meaningful access to library-based resources. Libraries reside in communities and as librarians it is our job to work with our communities to make sure each person has the opportunity to thrive. Without the lens of social justice, our efforts will fall short. With a social justice perspective built into the process of becoming librarians, our work is powerful, sustainable, and life-changing.

---

26. American Library Association, "ALA Policy Statement: Library Services to the Poor," *Extending Our Reach: Reducing Homelessness Through Library Engagement*, accessed December 30, 2015, http://www.ala.org/offices/extending-our-reach-reducing-homelessness-through-library-engagement-7.

27. American Library Association, "Library Bill of Rights," accessed December 30, 2015, http://www.ala.org/advocacy/intfreedom/librarybill.

28. American Library Association, "Interpretations of the Library Bill of Rights," accessed December 30, 2015, http://www.ala.org/advocacy/intfreedom/librarybill/interpretations.

Acknowledgements

I'd like to express my huge gratitude to my daughter, Rae Winkelstein, for her editing and support as this chapter came to fruition.

Bibliography

Alexander, Michelle. *The New Jim Crow: Mass Incarceration in the Age of Colorblindness.* New York: The New Press, 2012.

American Library Association. "ALA Policy Statement: Library Services to the Poor," Extending Our Reach: Reducing Homelessness through Library Engagement. Accessed December 30, 2015. http://www.ala.org/offices/extending-our-reach-reducing-homelessness-through-library-engagement-7.

American Library Association. "Interpretations of the Library Bill of Rights." Accessed December 30, 2015. http://www.ala.org/advocacy/intfreedom/librarybill/interpretations.

American Library Association. "Library Bill of Rights." Accessed December 30, 2015. http://www.ala.org/advocacy/intfreedom/librarybill.

Bishop, Rudine Sums. "Multicultural Literature for Children: Making Informed Choices." In *Teaching Multicultural Literature in Grades K-8*, edited by Violet J. Harris, 37-53. Norwood, MA: Christopher Gordon Publishers, Inc., 1992.

Callen-Lorde Community Health Center. Accessed December 29, 2015. http://callen-lorde.org/.

Davis, Denise M., and Tracie D. Hall. "Diversity Counts." Chicago: ALA Office for Research and Statistics, ALA Office for Diversity, 2007. Accessed December 28, 2015. http://www.ala.org/offices/diversity/diversitycounts/divcounts

Dorris, Michael A. "Why I'm Not Thankful for Thanksgiving." In *Through Indian Eyes: The Native Experience in Books for Children*, eds. Beverly Slapin and Doris Seale, 19-22. Philadelphia: New Society Publishers, 1992.

Fisher-Borne, Marcie, Jessie Montana Cain, and Suzanne L. Martin. "From Mastery to Accountability: Cultural Humility as an Alternative to Cultural Competence." *Social Work Education: The International Journal* 34, no. 2 (2015): 165-181. Accessed July 5, 2015. http://dx.doi.org/10.1080/02615479.2014.977244.

Gorski, Paul C. "Critical Multicultural Pavilion Awareness Activities: Circles of My Multicultural Self." Accessed November 8, 2015. http://www.edchange.org/multicultural/activities/circlesofself.html.

Grant, Jaime M., Lisa A. Mottet, Justin Tanis, Jack Harrison, Jody L. Herman, and Mary Keisling. "Injustice at Every Turn: A Report of the National Transgender Discrimination Survey." Washington, D.C.: National Center for Transgender Equality and National Gay and Lesbian Task Force, 2011.

Harris, Michael D. Harris. *Colored Pictures: Race & Visual Representations*. Chapel Hill, NC: University of North Carolina Press, 2003.

hooks, bell. *Race, Gender and Cultural Politics*. Boston: South End Press, 1990.

Kroeber, Alfred L., and Clyde Kluckhorn. *Culture: A Critical Review of Concepts and Definitions*. Papers of the Peabody Museum of Archaeology and Ethnology 47, no.1. Cambridge, MA: Harvard University, 1952.

Marmot, Michael. "The Health Gap: The Challenge of an Unequal World." Lecture presentated at the David Brower Center, Berkeley, CA, November 6, 2015.

Murray-Garcia, Jann. "Cultural Humility and the Pre-Health Professions Student." YouTube video, 55:52 minutes. December 23, 2013. https://www.youtube.com/watch?v=NZUP6CrHAXA.

Murray-Garcia, Jann, and Melanie Tervalon. "Cultural Humility Versus Cultural Competence: A Critical Distinction in Defining Physician Training Outcomes in Multicultural Education." *Journal of Health Care for the Poor and Underserved* 9, no. 2 (1998): 117-125.

Overall, Patricia Montiel. "Cultural Competence: A Conceptual Framework for Library and Information Science Professionals." *Library Quarterly* 79, no. 2 (2009): 175-204.

Spears-Bunton, Linda. "All the Colors of the Land: A Literacy Montage." In *Teaching Multicultural Literature in Grades 9-12: Moving Beyond the Canon*, edited by Arlette E. Willis, 17-36. Norwood, MA: Christopher-Gordon Publishers, 1998.

Sweeney, Miriam E., Nicole A. Cooke, Melissa Villa-Nicholas, K.R. Roberto, and Safiya U. Noble, "Social Justice in the Library and Information Science." In iConference 2014 Proceedings (2014): 1202-1203. doi:10.9776/14213.

Taylor, Keeanga-Yamahtta Taylor. "Black Lives Matter on Campus, Too," *Aljazeera America*, November 29, 2015. http://america.aljazeera.com/opinions/2015/11/black-lives-matter-on-campus-too.html.

Ting-Toomey, Stella. *Communicating Across Cultures*. New York: Guilford Press, 1999.

Trinh, Minh-Ha. *When the Moon Waxes Red*. New York: Routledge, 1991.

Young, Iris M. *Justice and the Politics of Difference*. Princeton, NJ: Princeton University Press, 1990.

Chapter 6

Dismantling Racism: Teaching LIS Social Justice Courses to Non-LIS Undergraduate Students

Sarah Park Dahlen

Introduction

I have always considered my scholarship, teaching, and service to be a form of activism; as such, it is necessary to reflect on and evaluate whether or not they actually result in social change. I have also long believed that social justice topics need to be introduced as early as is developmentally appropriate so that young people will grow up informed, and with more empathy and compassion. Therefore, although I have exclusively taught graduate students in the Master of Library and Information Science (MLIS) program at St. Catherine University (St. Kate's), in 2013 I sought an opportunity to teach a social justice and children's literature course to undergraduate students. Because the course was based on my graduate level social justice and children's literature course, it is useful to evaluate the execution of the course according to the characteristics and components of the Association for Library and Information Science Education (ALISE) Diversity Statement (discussed later in the chapter). I experienced significant challenges, such as some student resistance to course content, but overall the class caused students to think differently about race and children's literature, and therefore I believe it will eventually lead to social change.

The Global Search for Justice

The mission of St. Catherine University, which is one of the largest women's undergraduate colleges in the country, is to "[educate] students to lead and influence... Committed to excellence and opportunity, St. Catherine University develops ethical, reflective and socially responsible leaders, informed by the philosophy of the women's college and the spirit of the founders."[1] St. Catherine University (aka St. Kate's) believes that justice education is an essential part of the curriculum, and faculty are expected to integrate justice into all courses. In particular, St. Kate's offers a Liberal Arts Core Curriculum in the College for Women, which is committed to preparing students to be "leaders for social justice" with "skills in critical thinking, communication and understanding diversity."[2] The curriculum is bookended with two courses marking the beginning and end of a student's education at St. Kate's: "The Reflective Woman" (TRW) and "The Global Search for Justice" (GSJ). TRW is a "discussion-based course intended to develop knowledge, values and skills in critical and creative inquiry, effective communication and an understanding of diversity." Additionally, the course explores "ways to work toward community and justice."[3] It is usually the first course a student takes upon matriculation and, as stated, it is supposed to lay the foundation for later courses.

At the other end, GSJ is focused on "an in-depth examination of the conditions of justice experienced by a people or peoples outside of European/North American majority culture."[4] Specifically, the Dismantling Racism section assumes that racism is at the core of our society, that white privilege exists in the U.S., and that it is impossible to separate class and gender from racism. Students work toward dismantling racism

1. "St. Catherine University Mission and Vision." *St. Catherine University*. Accessed August 31, 2015. https://www.stkate.edu/about/mission-and-vision

2. "Liberal Arts Core Curriculum of the St. Catherine University College for Women." *St. Catherine University*. No date, 1.

3. Ibid, 4.

4. Ibid, 8.

by understanding its historical roots, developing a personal commitment to social justice, and finding strength in community organizing.[5] It is expected that by the time students take a GSJ course, they have accepted these assumptions and are committed to working toward dismantling racism.

As an assistant professor in a graduate program, I have encountered graduate students who have not taken courses in or had any formal training on anti-racism work, diversity, or cultural competence. Because of this, I was thinking that justice education needed to begin earlier than graduate school. This core requirement at my university seemed like a good way for me to expand the reach of my teaching to younger students— specifically, teaching my course at the undergraduate level was one way to introduce the intersections of children's literature, social justice, and library and information science (LIS) to a broader audience. Therefore, I revised my graduate-level "Social Justice and Children's/YA Literature" course and named it "Dismantling Racism: Social Justice and Children's Literature." It was a perfect fit, but as with any first-time effort, I faced considerable challenges and learned much upon reflection.

TRW and GSJ courses are typically taught by St. Kate's faculty and staff, and anyone volunteering to teach a core course must take a two-day training in the month of May, preceding the academic year in which the core class will be taught. I participated in the May, 2013 training in preparation to teach a GSJ course the following fall. With the university's emphasis on "[developing] ethical, reflective and socially responsible leaders," this training would benefit all faculty and staff. It would also help permeate the university with an understanding of the need to discuss justice issues in all classes, and provide instructors with the tools to do so.

Since students enrolling in GSJ classes are in their third and fourth year, and since core classes are expected to be rigorous, the adjustments I made to my existing graduate level course were mostly to bring it in line with the core requirements. I eliminated library practice-related

5. "GSJ Topics and Faculty," *St. Catherine University*, n.d., 1.

assignments such as book talks and flyers, and instead added intensive writing assignments, readings out of *The Global Search for Justice Reader*,[6] and a final project to be showcased at the Justice Symposium at the end of the semester. The syllabi for my graduate level courses are already comprehensive; based on experience, I err on the side of being thorough and fill my syllabus with details that will help students fully understand assignment expectations.[7]

Integrating *The Global Search for Justice Reader* into my GSJ syllabus was a major adjustment from my graduate level course, especially because the course is already reading-heavy. *The Reader* contains chapters written by St. Kate's core faculty on topics such as the prison industrial complex, oppression, justice frameworks, etc., and these provided a larger framework for the justice issues we discussed in and through children's literature. I also assigned chapters from the book *Diversity in Youth Literature: Opening Doors through Reading*, [8] which I co-edited with Dr. Jamie Campbell Naidoo. The first few chapters from this text set a foundation specifically for diversity and children's literature, and subsequent chapters address the children's books I assigned.

I included the quote addressing racism assumptions on the first page of the syllabus[9] and adjusted my course description to be less library-focused and more general:

> In this course, students will learn how to select, evaluate and analyze depictions and aspects of social justice and injustice, particularly but not exclusively, as they relate to race, in and through children's and young

---

6. Marla Martin Hanley, Nancy A. Heitzig, Sharon Doherty, Robert Grunst, and Russell B. Connors, Jr., eds. *The Global Search for Justice Reader*, 4th ed. (St. Paul, MN: St. Catherine University, 2009).

7. Despite this, and despite giving students samples of assignments, I'm fairly certain that some students did not pay attention, did not read the syllabus, did not care, or a combination of all three. I measure how clear my assignment descriptions are based on the fact that almost all students complete the work according to my expectations.

8. Jamie Campbell Naidoo and Sarah Park Dahlen, eds., *Diversity in Youth Literature: Opening Doors through Reading* (Chicago: ALA Editions, 2012).

9. "GSJ Topics and Faculty," 1.

> adult literature, and then communicate their learning to others in an effort to promote social change. We will consider topics such as power, racism, diversity, violence, perspective, publishing trends, authorship, illustrations, and ideology.

While the course was interdisciplinary and drew upon resources in sociology, literature, history, cultural studies, and more, the students who enrolled in my class came mostly from science backgrounds (such as nutrition and nursing); none expressed an interest in a career as a future librarian, though one was an education major.

The ALISE Diversity Statement's ABCs

In 2011, recognizing the long-standing need for more action related to diversity issues, the Association for Library and Information Science Education (ALISE) established a Diversity Statement Task Force, which drafted a diversity statement that was approved by the ALISE Board in 2012[10] and by the membership in 2013. The Diversity Statement states that ALISE is committed to the active recruitment and equitable and full participation of members of all backgrounds, the promotion of diversity and its benefits in library and information science education, research and service by its personal and institutional members, and their full participation in the profession.[11] Similarly, the GSJ courses are intended to prepare students to understand the need for and to work toward the "equitable and full participation of members of all backgrounds." According to the ALISE Diversity Statement:

---

10. Renate Chancellor, Clara M. Chu, Nicole A. Cooke, Delicia T. Greene, and Shari Lee, "ALISE Diversity Statement Proposal," *Association for Library and Information Science Education*, accessed August 31, 2015, http://www.alise.org/assets/documents/alise-diversitystatement-proposal4members.pdf.

11. Clara Chu, "ALISE Diversity Statement," *Association for Library and Information Science Education,* accessed August 31, 2015, http://www.alise.org/assets/documents/alise-diversitystatement-board_approved4member_vote.pdf.

> ALISE has an ethical compass that points to equity, inclusion and social responsibility. By definition, diversity "is the difference among us" (Lee, Shari and Chancellor, Renate. January 18, 2011). Diversity refers to the representation of the wide variety of backgrounds (including racial, cultural, linguistic, gender, religious, international, socioeconomic, sexual orientation, differently-abled, age among others) that people possess and is often used to address quantitative requirements/agendas/goals...[12]

Discussing diverse ideas and perspectives in the classroom and among LIS faculty, students, and staff will resonate throughout the wider profession. Rather than staying silent on potentially difficult and uncomfortable issues, the open discussion and circulation of different perspectives, ideas, and stories will increase our repertoire of knowledge and expand our capacity for critical, creative thinking and problem solving. Listening to and believing one another's stories will help us be more compassionate, open hearted, and open-minded. This, then, will help us be better, more effective LIS professionals in an increasingly diverse and global community.[13] Again, these benefits are not unlike the anticipated benefits of a GSJ course focused on Dismantling Racism. Discussing diverse ideas and promoting mutual respect are core values in a GSJ class, especially one focused on dismantling racism.

A major component of ALISE's Diversity Statement is the ABCs—the Affective, Behavioral, and Cognitive dimensions that impact what we know, how we think, and how we behave in terms of diversity. In the following section, I analyze my course and the students' reactions according to these characteristics, to share the challenges and successes of my class, and to advocate for the ongoing need for diversity education at all levels of learning.

KNOW (Cognitive)

Many students admitted that one of the reasons they enrolled in my class was because the title sounded interesting—they had never

12. Ibid.

13. Ibid.

considered issues of racism in children's literature. So by knowing the class existed, and then taking it, students had their eyes opened to the reality that first, racism exists, and second, that it's a huge part of children's literature. They had thought of children's literature as innocent and politically neutral, but during the class many shared that they were learning more than they had expected.

As long as students did the readings and came to class, they were probably most transformed at the basic level of knowing: in their cognitive characteristics. For example, most students did not know that the Roma were an oppressed people group until they read Brian W. Sturm and Meghan Gaherty's article "The Door has Never Opened for Us: The Roma in Recent Children's Fiction for Grades 4-6"[14] and applied some of its concepts to analyze the picture book *Madeline and the Gypsies*;[15] or that 120,000 Japanese Americans were interned during World War II until they read *Dear Miss Breed: True Stories of the Japanese American Incarceration During World War II and a Librarian Who Made a Difference* by Joanne Oppenheim[16] and *A Different Mirror for Young People: A History of Multicultural America*[17] by Ronald Takaki; or that Rosa Parks was not in fact the first person to stay seated on a bus until they read *Claudette Colvin: Twice Toward Justice*[18] by Phillip M. Hoose. Unless they were absent from class, they now know and have new information regarding these histories and people, as well as different theories, ideologies, and frameworks. In other words, they didn't know what they didn't know until they took this

14. Brian W. Sturm and Meghan Gaherty, "The Door has Never Opened for Us: The Roma in Recent Children's Fiction for Grades 4-6," in *Diversity in Youth Literature: Opening Doors Through Reading*, eds. Jamie Campbell Naidoo and Sarah Park Dahlen (Chicago: ALA Editions, 2012).

15. Ludwig Bemelmans, *Madeline and the Gypsies* (New York: Puffin Books, 2000).

16. Joanne Oppenhein, *Dear Miss Breed: True Stories of the Japanese American Incarceration During World War II and a Librarian Who Made a Difference* (New York: Scholastic, 2006).

17. Ronald Takaki, *A Different Mirror for Young People: A History of Multicultural America.* (New York: Triangle Square, 2012).

18. Phillip M. Hoose, *Claudette Colvin: Twice Toward Justice* (New York: Farrar, Straus, Giroux, 2009).

class. During our mid-semester check-in, they shared how surprised they were in learning about some of these untold histories. Once they knew, there were responsible for what they learned—or were they?

THINK *(Affective)*

It was encouraging to be able to use children's literature for the important purpose of introducing silenced voices, marginalized histories, and new ideas to students who had not been previously exposed. And though I saw evidence that they were beginning to think differently—to think critically—about the information regarding oppression and the injustices as relayed in the children's literature we read together and about what they had been taught and not taught during their K-12 education, I am not entirely confident about the extent to which their thinking was radically transformed. Therefore, I believe there were limited gains in affective and behavioral characteristics.

In being unable to move past "think," some struggled to accept diversity or difference, and to let their new knowledge impact their lives. For example, one student was reluctant to discuss the racism in the Skippyjon Jones picture books, a popular series that Martínez-Roldán criticizes for its use of mock Spanish that actually "devalues and ridicules Latinos and their culture."[19] In "Skippyjon Jones: Transforming a Racist Stereotype into an Industry," Beverly Slapin traces the development of the faux-Mexican stereotype from Speedy Gonzalez, the Frito Bandito, and the Taco Bell Chihuahua to *Skippyjon Jones*. She agrees with Martínez-Roldán, claiming that the picture books are actually "condescending and mocking to Mexican and Mexican-American people and the Spanish language."[20]

---

19. Carmen M. Martínez-Roldán, "The Representation of Latinos and the Use of Spanish: A Critical Content Analysis of *Skippyjon Jones*," *Journal of Children's Literature* 39, no. 1, (2013): 5-14.

20. Beverly Slapin, "Skippyjon Jones: Transforming a Racist Stereotype into an Industry," *De Colores: The Raza Experience in Books for Children* (blog), April 6, 2013, http://decoloresreviews.blogspot.com/2013/04/skippyjon-jones-and-big-bones.html.

Despite discussing these issues during class, we did not come to a productive conclusion regarding the one student who had so loved the books that she had named her own Chihuahua "Skippyjon Jones." Admittedly, it was an awkward (and unanticipated) moment, but we could have benefited from this as a teaching moment. For example, Slapin writes, "If Judy Schachner is capable of any shame, now would be a good time to post a public apology, shut down her business and turn over all of her profits to the courageous young Mexican American students in Arizona who are fighting to liberate themselves from the racist 'education' they are receiving at the hands of the Tucson Unified School District."[21]

Admitting mistakes in one's writing or illustrating is not unheard of; in 2014, award-winning graphic novelist Gene Luen Yang created and shared a comic in which he shared an error in his critically acclaimed *The Shadow Hero*: "So. I screwed up… In the essay that accompanies the first printing of *The Shadow Hero*, I repeatedly refer to Chu F. Hing, the creator of the Green Turtle, as if Hing were his familial name. This is incorrect. Hing is his individual name. His familial name is Chu."[22]

He goes on to explain how he came to learn the truth, and that his publisher, First Second Books, corrected the mistake in subsequent printings. Similarly, in my class, we could have walked through the steps of what the student could do now that she had learned new information —she could have re-named her dog, shared with people about the racism in the books and why she felt compelled to change the name of her dog, or taken other positive steps. Instead, the student dropped the class, and we lost an opportunity to continue discussing and learning how children's literature—and the study of children's literature—can have a real impact on our lives.

---

21. Ibid.

22.. Gene Luen Yang, "A Mistake in The Shadow Hero," Diversity in YA (tumblr), http://diversityinya.tumblr.com/post/104604090974/a-mistake-in-the-shadow-hero.

ACT (Behavioral)

If it is difficult to think differently based on new things we know, it is even less likely that we will act differently. While I know that many people are unreceptive— indeed, resistant—to discussions of diversity or to accusations that they committed a racist act, such as naming their dog after a problematic character, I was still hopeful that my course would be transformative. That said, I have no illusions that all of my students are going to go out into the world as change agents in the world of children's literature, though they may be the ethical and reflective leaders St. Catherine expects them to be in the world in general. It was fantastic that some students were already invested in anti-racism work; they contributed much to the course and, hopefully, also gained additional tools and concrete ideas for how children's books could dismantle racism. But for others, perhaps they remained stuck at the knowing and couldn't move fully toward thinking and acting differently, in part because they did not see the relevance of the course in their lives. The GSJ class was a requirement, a course outside their majors, an additional class that they may have considered a burden. Perhaps they just wanted to finish classes, graduate, and be reflective and ethical leaders in nursing and fashion, and while they may have found justice issues important (they did, after all, choose St. Catherine University), they did not like politicizing children's literature. Still, because most students had non-education-related career plans, I often asked them to consider how this course was relevant beyond our classroom and in their majors. It was during these discussions that we brainstormed what to them would be the most applicable and realistic solutions, and the typical response was that they would think twice when buying books for the young people in their lives. For example, after reading and discussing Sherman Alexie's *The Absolutely True Diary of a Part-Time Indian*, and discussing the critical need for more contemporary and insider-authored Native stories, students shared that they would avoid romanticized and inaccurate texts, and instead look for Native-authored texts. In order to more easily facilitate their access to books, and because publishers need to see demand for diverse books, I often recommended resources such as the book lists on Debbie Reese's American Indians and Children's Literature blog.[23] So I hope my students' dollars will push the publishing industry to diversify the books they publish, and cause a ripple effect to push information providers—authors, editors, teachers, librarians, the media, and others— to write, publish, and promote more diverse perspectives and stories.

Students now *know* of a lot of racist events that they were not taught in their K-12 education, in their other undergraduate courses, or from the media, and they know it because they read and discussed children's literature and critical articles on children's literature. Their lack of knowing is a failure on the part of our education system and the larger information industry for privileging certain voices and stories and silencing others, and we LIS educators play a role in this. My students now know that we all have, perhaps unintentionally, been perpetuating whiteness in children's literature, and that we must advocate for more diverse voices. With this new information, I hope my students will act toward changing the kinds of stories they accept about our world. I hope that, at a minimum, students will take what they now *know*, *think* differently, and *act* radically after the class, at least by being more critical readers and consumers of the media around them, whether directed at children or adults. Perhaps after they completed my course, they began to see more instances of misrepresentation in various media, such as the controversy that erupted when Emma Stone was cast as a mixed race Native Hawaiian and Chinese American character in the movie *Aloha*.[24] Perhaps, although I did not see much fruit initially, my course planted seeds that will blossom later.

23. Debbie Reese, *American Indians in Children's Literature* (blog), accessed December 5, 2015, http://americanindiansinchildrensliterature.blogspot.com/.

24. Keith Chow, "These Actresses are Not Asian or Pacific Islanders," *The Nerds of Color*, June 3, 2015, accessed December 5, 2015, http://thenerdsofcolor.org/2015/06/03/these-actresses-are-not-asian-or-pacific-islanders/.

One semester was quite short and I had to respect the parameters of the core curriculum, so I was limited in the kinds of assignments I could design; GSJ courses must have specific points of commonality in order to maintain integrity across the different classes. Also, the fact that it was my first time teaching in the core means, almost by definition, that I made mistakes, and will learn from them and do better next time. In an ideal world, courses that challenge worldviews and interrogate racism should be taught over multiple semesters, so that proper scaffolding can prepare students for the very intense discussions that are sure to emerge. For any topic, there is a long, complex history to be learned, ideologies to unlearn, and multiple perspectives to consider. For example, I could teach an entire course on the politics of children's literature publishing, and then teach a course addressing various perspectives on dismantling racism and children's literature. After teaching those courses, I could teach a class on dismantling racism in Asian American children's literature or Native American children's literature, for example, or a service learning course where students work with bookstores, libraries, and schools to diversify collections, promote diverse books, and plan culturally appropriate programming and curriculum.

Challenges

My course was not without some very big challenges. Courses with words such as "racism" or "justice" in the title tend to attract students who are already invested in racial justice work. However, as mentioned previously, all St. Kate's undergraduate students must take a GSJ class, and they have diverse but limited options. In this case, I believe that some students saw the words "children's literature" in the course title, "Global Search for Justice, Dismantling Racism: Social Justice and Children's Literature," and thought the course would be easy because it was about "children's literature." Before classes had even begun, one irate student emailed me demanding to know how I expected her to purchase and read all the assigned books and readings. I recommended she check the books out from the library and, actually, she turned out to be one of my most hard-working and thoughtful students.

Two main challenges emerged during the semester. The first is a specific student challenge—the worst during the entire semester— and the second is a more general observation of the students that I began to believe as the semester progressed. Teaching challenges can, and should, be what Davis and Steyn conceptualize as potentially productive, as "meaning-making," because teaching challenges can become "teaching moments."[25] These challenges were definitely learning moments for me, and I hope for the students as well.

The course is under the pod "Dismantling Racism," so we used this language in class. We spoke explicitly about topics such as racism, white privilege, and microaggressions, using the language from the *GSJ Reader*, the scholarly articles I assigned, and the core curriculum. For example, the core's description of the "Dismantling Racism" pod, which should be included in all GSJ syllabi, include phrases such as "racism" and "white privilege." Therefore, because these concepts shaped the very nature of the course, I was unafraid to use the language openly during class and expected students to do so as well.

One major assignment in the course required each student to present on two of our texts, either alone or in pairs, depending on how many students were in the class and how many texts we would read and discuss. The assignment required them to address the following: historical/social/political/cultural context of the texts; authors'/illustrators' biographies; reception of the text (reviews, awards, criticisms); censorship and access issues; and how this text serves to dismantle racism in our world. At the beginning of the semester, students chose the two books on which they would present.

I assigned the information book *Dear Miss Breed: True Stories of the Japanese American Incarceration During World War II and a Librarian Who*

25. Danya Davis and Melissa Steyn, "Teaching for Social Justice: Reframing Some Pedagogical Assumptions," *Perspectives in Education* 30, no 4 (2012): 31.

Made a Difference,[26] which is about the work of the San Diego librarian Clara Breed. Miss Breed was the public librarian to a large community of Japanese Americans who, during the hysteria of World War II, were interned in Poston, Arizona. The author writes about Miss Breed's relationship with her patrons and how she kept in touch with them during their internment, sent them books and other materials, and advocated for their political rights. In short, she was the type of white, ally librarian we hope will work in our libraries. The student who selected this book concluded her otherwise excellent presentation by saying, "While Miss Breed's work dismantles racism, this book doesn't." The student could see how an event was racist, and that a librarian featured in a book worked toward dismantling racism, but she couldn't see how the book itself— the existence of the book, the reading of the book, and discussions of the book—was dismantling racism. She did not acknowledge the transformative potential a book holds, and therefore missed one major goal of the class.

My response to this situation was, in my mind, clear. It would be unethical for me to allow a student to present to the class that, for example, the earth is not round, so it was clear to me that it was also unethical to leave a statement such as "This book does not dismantle racism" without comment. So I questioned the student on her concluding statement, but she repeated that only the work of Miss Breed and not the book dismantled racism. I continued to push her, asking her again and again why she didn't think the book itself dismantled racism. I walked through the steps, asking scaffolding questions such as: "Do you think the Japanese internment was racist? Do you think Clara Breed did anti-racist work? Do you think learning about the internment is a step toward dismantling racism? Does this book do the work of teaching about the internment?" As the questioning progressed, we both became more adamant, and it was clear that neither of us wanted to relent. She finally conceded, however: "Fine, you're right, it dismantles

26. Joanne Oppenheim, *Dear Miss Breed: True Stories of the Japanese American Incarceration During World War II and a Librarian Who Made a Difference* (New York: Scholastic, 2006).

racism," and then turned and walked out of the classroom. I followed her and we sat down in my office, but she started shouting at me that I was always "picking on" her and ran out again, saying she was going to speak to the core directors. Immediately after class ended, I contacted the directors to let them know what had happened. I was honest about my own role in allowing the situation to escalate, and admitted that I could have handled it better. As promised, the student also contacted them, and they were prepared to talk with her about the situation—they supported my assertion that *Dear Miss Breed* dismantles racism and that I was the authority of the topic and the class. Her view of me as less-than was evident in her question to them, "Why does Sarah think she's so smart? Just because she has a Ph.D.?" One core director quickly responded, "Well, yes." The connection here is too easy; in her overview of the existing research, Lazos demonstrates "that both minorities and women are presumed to be incompetent as soon as they walk in the door."[27] And, as in my case, "Showing irritation or anger backfires."[28]

That brings me to my second challenge. There is a lot more going on here than just the fact that we had a major disagreement about a book. I was already fighting an uphill battle because I am 1) non-white, 2) relatively young, 3) not very tall, and 4) female. Student perceptions of non-white, female faculty as being less authoritative have been well documented, as have the consequences of such thinking—non-white female faculty are more often challenged and receive lower course and teaching evaluations.[29] As Angela P. Harris and Carmen G. González write in the introduction to *Presumed Incompetent: The Intersections of Race and Class for Women in Academia*, "Those who differ from this norm [white, heterosexual, and middle- and upper-class] find themselves, to

27. Sylvia R. Lazos, "Are Student Teaching Evaluations Holding Back Women and Minorities? The Perils of 'Doing' Gender and Race in the Classroom," in *Presumed Incompetent: The Intersections of Race and Class for Women in Academia*, eds. Gabriella Gutiérrez y Muhs, Yolanda Flores Niemann, Carmen G. González, and Angela P. Harris (Boulder, CO: The University Press of Colorado, 2012), 177.

28. Ibid., 176.

29. Ibid.

a greater or lesser degree, 'presumed incompetent' by students, colleagues, and administrators."[30] In other words, "Whites and men start from a presumption of competence; minorities and women do not and have to deal with a multitude of unconscious biases that put them at a disadvantage."[31]

The larger context of all this, of course, is that starting to talk about justice work, dismantling racism, and related topics in college is actually quite late, and talking about it in-depth during a third or fourth year is very late. I echo Grace Chang when she writes, "I have learned a great deal from my students' responses about what American students are prepared to learn in college, what they expect—often simply to be entertained—and what they resist or refuse to study or even consider."[32] St. Catherine University boasts a student body that is 29.5 percent "multicultural,"[33] but these numbers are conflated with international students, so one can assume that the domestic student body is less diverse than 29 percent. Minnesota itself is the sixteenth whitest state in the country,[34] and while we have a progressive voting streak, with the nation's highest voter turnout and a very active, politically engaged citizenry, St. Kate's surveys are finding that in recent years our incoming students are identifying as more politically conservative. Students' lack of previous justice education (some students admitted that my class was

---

30. Angela P. Harris and Carmen G. González, "Introduction," in *Presumed Incompetent: The Intersections of Race and Class for Women in Academia*, eds. Gabriella Gutiérrez y Muhs, Yolanda Flores Niemann, Carmen G. González, and Angela P. Harris (Boulder, CO: The University Press of Colorado, 2012), 3.

31. Lazos, 175.

32. Grace Chang, "Where's the Violence? The Promise and Perils of Teaching Women of Color Studies," in *Presumed Incompetent: The Intersections of Race and Class for Women in Academia*, eds. Gabriella Gutiérrez y Muhs, Yolanda Flores Niemann, Carmen G. González, and Angela P. Harris (Boulder, CO: The University Press of Colorado, 2012), 200.

33. "Quick Facts," *St. Catherine University*, accessed August 31, 2015, https://www2.stkate.edu/about/quick-facts?_ga=1.11193268.1223708657.1432305252.

34. United States Census Bureau, "White Population Alone, Percent – July 2008," accessed August 31, 2015. http://www.census.gov/compendia/statab/2010/ranks/rank05.html.

the first time they had heard of ideas such as white privilege, despite having taken "The Reflective Woman" class their first year) made the course difficult to teach, because we so often had to fill in the gaps in their knowledge. What are we to do with students who don't believe in privilege, or who think that the answer to racism is colorblindness? What are we to do when they matriculate in our MLIS Programs? What kind of practitioners will they be? In the coming years, it is possible that incoming MLIS students will be increasingly polarized in terms of their politics and their ideas about race and justice.[35] That is something we should be concerned about, and is why the ALISE Diversity Statement is important for LIS educators. It provides a framework for why we should have the explicit goal of encouraging people to know, think, and act differently.

The students who enrolled in my original graduate social justice course had already taken "Introduction to Library and Information Science," where they had learned the core values in the library profession.[36] However, I realized I had taken my undergraduate students on a cognitive leap when introducing them to concepts that were familiar to LIS students, but less obvious to students who had previously not even known that LIS was a discipline. I found myself explaining to undergraduate students why a collection needed to be broad and inclusive, why libraries needed to serve all members of their communities, and why diversity and access were important. I could not expect these values— and commitments to these values—to be readily and easily understood by my undergraduate students, because they had no previous exposure. Were I to teach the

35. Just this past semester (fall, 2015), I had one white student in my Introduction to Library and Information Science class say that they had been raised not to "see race," with the implication being that our discussions on racism, unlearning, etc., were moot. In response, I asked the student (and the other students) to do research on what it means to be colorblind, and during the next class we followed up. The student reported that they do not completely agree with what they read about how colorblindness is actually racist, but needs to think about it more.

36. American Library Association, "Core Values of Librarianship," accessed January 4, 2015, http://www.ala.org/advocacy/intfreedom/statementspols/corevalues.

class again, I would introduce these values briefly and explain that they are not limited to the library profession; for example, diversity, access, social responsibility, and other core values are and should be values for society in general.

Rewards

That said, this course resulted in three identifiable rewards. First, it was clear from the students' final presentation that they had, indeed, learned. Throughout the semester, most of my students engaged with the texts on a surface level and it wasn't until the final project—a presentation at the Justice Symposium, which is similar to a poster session—that they began to articulate a more critical engagement with the texts. I think several factors were at work. First, students were reacting to the attendees' enthusiasm—just as my students had not really thought of race, racism, and children's literature, many of the attendees who came to our table were intrigued that we could interrogate how race is depicted in children's literature. Second, students were required to demonstrate in front of their peers and other professors that they were truly learning in class, so more was at stake. And finally, students were able to engage with the texts on a deeper level, because they chose the texts themselves and, fortunately, had selected texts that invited critical engagement. By this time in the semester, they were more on board with what we had been learning all semester.

A second reward was that I saw much evidence of outside interest in my course topic. So, although my students' engagement with the texts was on a relatively superficial level for most of the semester, the Justice Symposium presentations were enough to spark interest in other students. Therefore, although overall I am disappointed in how this first class went (due to both my own failings as well as the level of student resistance), I think it served an important purpose to plant seeds both in the minds of my students as well as in the minds of Symposium attendees. Many asked if the class would be taught again. I hope this wider exposure to dismantling racism through children's literature will encourage more people to think critically about the role that children's books play in socializing young people. This class may help students become more critical consumers of information, specifically in children's books. I also hope it leads to an increased interest in LIS as a possible career, once students have seen the role that LIS professionals play in connecting these books with young people.

Finally, one of the rewards was apparent in the demonstration of institutional support I received from the core co-directors when the one student openly challenged me during class about whether or not *Dear Miss Breed* dismantled racism. Having the support of tenured white women who are highly respected professors on my campus is tremendously helpful for an untenured non-white woman. Knowing that the co-directors of the core supported me and my class gives me hope that those of us doing racial justice work in the academy have committed allies, however "unlikely"[37] we think they may be.

Conclusion

Library and Information Science scholars teach and research topics that impact many different aspects of life. Specifically, children's literature can be taught at any level of education in many different disciplines and can be used to teach an unlimited number of topics. Teaching about racism in a children's literature course is probably one of the most important purposes and potential uses. Children's literature can shape young people's ideas about the world around them, yet children's literature has long engaged in the practices of whitewashing,[38] misrepresenting,[39]

37. Karen L. Dace, *Unlikely Allies in the Academy: Women of Color and White Women in Conversation* (New York: Routledge, 2012).

38. Nancy Larrick, "The All-White World of Children's Books," *The Saturday Review* (September 11, 1965).

39. Debbie Reese, "About," *American Indians in Children's Literature* (blog), October 19, 2014, http://americanindiansinchildrensliterature.blogspot.com/p/about.html.

and silencing the voices of nonwhite and underrepresented peoples.[40] Therefore, teaching about racism in children's literature, racism in the production of children's literature, how radical children's literature can perform anti-racist work, and how all this is related to the world around us, is important and necessary work. It is especially significant in an environment of #BlackLivesMatter protests, student protests regarding racism on university campuses,[41] and the president-elect saying that they might have supported the incarceration of Japanese Americans during World War II.[42] LIS educators who have researched these topics and are continually engaged in the children's literature community are well poised to teach anti-racist children's literature courses to both graduate and undergraduate students.

Although teaching "Dismantling Racism: Social Justice and Children's Literature" was one of the most challenging experiences of my teaching career, upon reflection, I strongly believe in the importance of the class and its potential to change how young people think, what they know, and how they act. I know my course has a place in this world, as evidenced by movements such as We Need Diverse Books (WNDB) and blogs such as *Reading While White*.[43] The WNDB movement erupted in May 2014, just five months after my class ended, and its goal to "raise our voices into a roar that can't be ignored"[44] is certainly being met, with coverage

40. Zetta Elliott, "Something like an Open Letter to the Children's Publishing Industry," *Fledgling: Zetta Elliott's Blog* (blog), September 5, 2009, https://zettaelliott.wordpress.com/2009/09/05/something-like-an-open-letter-to-the-children%E2%80%99s-publishing-industry/.

41. Alia Wong and Adrienne Green, "Campus Politics: A Cheat Sheet," *The Atlantic* (December 8, 2015), accessed January 1, 2016. http://www.theatlantic.com/education/archive/2015/12/campus-protest-roundup/417570/.

42. Michael Sherer, "Exclusive: Donald Trump Says He Might Have Supported Japanese Internment," *Time* (December 8, 2015), accessed January 1, 2016. http://time.com/4140050/donald-trump-muslims-japanese-internment/.

43. *Reading While White* (blog), accessed December 5, 2015, http://readingwhilewhite.blogspot.com/.

44. "We Need Diverse Books Campaign," We Need Diverse Books tumblr, accessed December 5, 2015, http://weneeddiversebooks.tumblr.com/post/83943947418/we-need-diverse-books-campaign.

in major news outlets and WNDB panels at nearly every youth literature-related conference. Googling "We need diverse books" and looking at the images of people of all ages and backgrounds explaining why they need diverse books[45] is a testament to the importance of classes such as mine. Similarly, many children's literature scholars, authors, illustrators, and other stakeholders consider *Reading While White* to be essential reading. While there are many white allies who do powerful work in various areas, it is important to have white allies who write about whiteness in children's literature frequently, consistently, and unapologetically on a public blog. When I teach this class again, I will assign *Reading While White* as required reading and make sure that my students learn both the history of anti-racism activism in children's literature, as well as what is happening today with WNDB and other initiatives.

I hope teaching non-LIS students to think critically about dismantling racism in children's literature will make them smarter and more engaged consumers of children's literature. I hope they will go into bookstores and libraries looking for and demanding children's literature that is more diverse in its perspectives and authorship. This will inevitably come back to us in LIS as, despite some effort, we continue to churn out a generation of LIS professionals who remain white, female, and middle-class, and whose experiences and perspectives are most privileged in literature. I hope they see LIS as a credible and important field, and therefore also view their libraries as places of diverse ideas and community building. Finally, because I believe this class is badly needed, I hope that when I teach it again (scheduled for spring 2017), I will teach it better. Hopefully, this next time I can teach it more effectively and include all the newer resources that have pushed our discussions even further since I last taught this course, so my students will leave knowing, thinking, and acting better.

---

45. For example, middle grade author Mike Jung (Geeks, Girls, and Secret Identities and Unidentified Suburban Object) shared "#WeNeedDiverseBooks because my daughter was 3 when she first said she hates having brown eyes & hair." See: http://deducingbbcsherlock.tumblr.com/post/84674498519/we-need-diverse-books.

Bibliography

American Library Association. "Core Values of Librarianship." Accessed January 4, 2015. http://www.ala.org/advocacy/intfreedom/statementspols/corevalues.

Bemelmans, Ludwig. *Madeline and the Gypsies*. New York: Puffin Books, 2000.

Chancellor, Renate, Clara M. Chu, Nicole A. Cooke, Delicia T. Greene, and Shari Lee. "ALISE Diversity Statement Proposal." *Association for Library and Information Science Education*. Accessed August 31, 2015. http://www.alise.org/assets/documents/alise-diversitystatement-proposal4members.pdf.

Chang, Grace. "Where's the Violence? The Promise and Perils of Teaching Women of Color Studies." In *Presumed Incompetent: The Intersections of Race and Class for Women in Academia*, edited by Gabriella Gutiérrez y Muhs, Yolanda Flores Niemann, Carmen G. González, and Angela P. Harris, 198-218. Boulder, CO: The University Press of Colorado, 2012.

Chow, Keith. "These Actresses are Not Asian or Pacific Islanders." *The Nerds of Color*, June 3, 2015. Accessed December 5, 2015. http://thenerdsofcolor.org/2015/06/03/these-actresses-are-not-asian-or-pacific-islanders/.

Chu, Clara. "ALISE Diversity Statement." Association for Library and Information Science Education. Accessed August 31, 2015. http://www.alise.org/assets/documents/alise-diversitystatement-board_approved4member_vote.pdf.

Dace, Karen L. *Unlikely Allies in the Academy: Women of Color and White Women in Conversation*. New York: Routledge, 2012.

Davis, Danya and Melissa Steyn. "Teaching for Social Justice: Reframing Some Pedagogical Assumptions." *Perspectives in Education* 30, no 4 (2012).

Elliott, Zetta. "Something like an Open Letter to the Children's Publishing Industry." Fledgling: Zetta Elliott's Blog (blog). September 5, 2009. https://zettaelliott.wordpress.com/2009/09/05/something-like-an-open-letter-to-the-children%E2%80%99s-publishing-industry/.

"GSJ Topics and Faculty." *St. Catherine University*. No date.

Hanley, Marla Martin, Nancy A. Heitzig, Sharon Doherty, Robert Grunst, and Russell B. Connors Jr., eds. *The Global Search for Justice Reader.* 4th ed. St. Paul, MN: St. Catherine University, 2009.

Harris, Angela P., and Carmen G. González. "Introduction." In *Presumed Incompetent: The Intersections of Race and Class for Women in Academia*, edited by Gabriella Gutiérrez y Muhs, Yolanda Flores Niemann, Carmen G. González, and Angela P. Harris, 1-14. Boulder, CO: The University Press of Colorado, 2012.

Gutiérrez y Muhs, Gabriella, Yolanda Flores Niemann, Carmen G. González, and Angela P. Harris, eds. *Intersections of Race and Class for Women in Academia.* Boulder, CO: The University Press of Colorado, 2012.

Hoose, Phillip M. *Claudette Colvin: Twice Toward Justice.* New York: Farrar, Straus, Giroux, 2009.

Larrick, Nancy. "The All-White World of Children's Books." *The Saturday Review* (September 11, 1965).

"Liberal Arts Core Curriculum of the St. Catherine University College for Women." *St. Catherine University*. No date.

Lazos, Sylvia R. "Are Student Teaching Evaluations Holding Back Women and Minorities? The Perils of 'Doing' Gender and Race in the Classroom." In *Presumed Incompetent: The Intersections of Race and Class for Women in Academia*, edited by Gabriella Gutiérrez y Muhs, Yolanda Flores Niemann, Carmen G. González, and Angela P. Harris, 164-185. Boulder, CO: The University Press of Colorado, 2012.

Martínez-Roldán, Carmen M. "The Representation of Latinos and the Use of Spanish: A Critical Content Analysis of *Skippyjon Jones*." *Journal of Children's Literature* 39, no. 1, (2013): 5-14.

Naidoo, Jamie Campbell, and Sarah Park Dahlen, eds. *Diversity in Youth Literature: Opening Doors through Reading.* Chicago: ALA Editions, 2012.

Oppenheim, Joanne. *Dear Miss Breed: True Stories of the Japanese American Incarceration During World War II and a Librarian Who Made a Difference.* New York: Scholastic, 2006.

"Quick Facts." *St. Catherine University.* Accessed August 31, 2015. https://www2.stkate.edu/about/quick-facts?_ga=1.11193268.1223708657.1432305252.

Reading While White (blog). Accessed December 5, 2015. http://readingwhilewhite.blogspot.com/.

Reese, Debbie. *American Indians in Children's Literature* (blog). Accessed December 5, 2015. http://americanindiansinchildrensliterature.blogspot.com/.

"St. Catherine University Mission and Vision." *St. Catherine University.* Accessed August 31, 2015. https://www2.stkate.edu/about.

Sherer, Michael. "Exclusive: Donald Trump Says He Might Have Supported Japanese Internment." *Time* (December 8, 2015). Accessed January 1, 2016. http://time.com/4140050/donald-trump-muslims-japanese-internment/.

Slapin, Beverly. "Skippyjon Jones: Transforming a Racist Stereotype into an Industry," *De Colores: The Raza Experience in Books for Children* (blog). April 6, 2013. http://decoloresreviews.blogspot.com/2013/04/skippyjon-jones-and-big-bones.html.

Sturm, Brian W., and Meghan Gaherty. "The Door Has Never Opened for Us: The Roma in Recent Children's Fiction for Grades 4-6." In *Diversity in Youth Literature: Opening Doors Through Reading,* edited by Jamie Campbell Naidoo and Sarah Park Dahlen, 1-5-118. Chicago: ALA Editions, 2012.

Takaki, Ronald. *A Different Mirror for Young People: A History of Multicultural America*. New York: Triangle Square, 2012.

United States Census Bureau. "White Population Alone, Percent – July 2008." Accessed August 31, 2015. http://www.census.gov/compendia/statab/2010/ranhbgks/rank05.html.

"We Need Diverse Books Campaign." We Need Diverse Books (tumblr). Accessed December 5, 2015. http://weneeddiversebooks.tumblr.com/post/83943947418/we-need-diverse-books-campaign.

Wong, Alia, and Adrienne Green. "Campus Politics: A Cheat Sheet," *The Atlantic* (December 8, 2015). Accessed January 1, 2016. http://www.theatlantic.com/education/archive/2015/12/campus-protest-roundup/417570/.

Yang, Gene Luen. "A Mistake in The Shadow Hero." *Diversity in YA* (tumblr). http://diversityinya.tumblr.com/post/104604090974/a-mistake-in-the-shadow-hero.

Chapter 7

Teaching about Race in Cyberspace: Reflections on the "Virtual Privilege Walk" Exercise

Kafi D. Kumasi

Introduction

Research suggests that it takes considerably more time to prepare to teach a class online that it does to prepare to teach one in a traditional face-to-face (f2f) format.[1] Similarly, teaching online courses that have a multicultural focus can be more challenging than teaching other subjects in a fully online format. Unlike most subject areas, multicultural courses are highly dependent on authentic interactions between students and require students to bring their personal backgrounds and cultural experiences into the course activities. In that way, multicultural courses are typically designed to help students engage in "courageous conversations"[2]

1. Joseph Cavanaugh, "Teaching Online: A Time Comparison," *Online Journal of Distance Learning Administration* 8, no. 1 (2005), http://www.westga.edu/~distance/ojdla/spring81/cavanaugh81.htm. Cavanaugh outlines some of the rigors of translating a course from a campus-based format to an online environment.

2. Glenn E. Singleton, *Courageous Conversations about Race: A Field Guide for Achieving Equity in Schools* (Thousand Oaks, CA: Corwin Press, 2014). This text is a seminal work in helping educators develop strategies for teaching about difficult issues of race and powers in contemporary and diverse classrooms.

about all types of human difference and societal inequities that exist along different axes of power and privilege. However, many students choose to take online classes not only out of convenience, but also out of a desire to be relatively anonymous in terms of their physical identity and presumed ability to talk more "freely."[3] For example, Merry Merryfield[4] observed several "paradoxes" between the behaviors in online vs. campus-based versions of a multicultural class. In the online version, she described the teachers as "more open, frank, expansive, curious, even confessional in their willingness to share and discuss prickly issues such as white privilege, racism, educational inequities, injustice, and xenophobia than teachers have been in the campus version of the course." The desire for and presumption of anonymity presents a challenge for teaching online classes where issues of identity are central to the subject matter.

In this chapter, I describe some of the instructional design challenges I faced in translating an exercise called "The Privilege Walk" into a fully online classroom environment. The online version of this exercise (hereafter referred to as "The Virtual Privilege Walk" or VPW) is based on a better known Privilege Walk exercise. The classic Privilege Walk exercise has been adopted in many higher education classrooms, particularly in courses on diversity, multiculturalism, or other forms of power differentiation.[5] The context in which the VPW exercise was developed and specifics about how the activity works will be discussed later in the chapter. I designed the VPW exercise for a three-credit elective course, "Multicultural Information Services and Resources." This course is part of a thirty-six hour Masters of Library and Information Science (MLIS) degree program at a university located in the Midwest United States.

---

3. Glenn Gordon Smith, David Ferguson, and Mieke Caris, "Online vs. Face-to-Face," *THE Journal (Technological Horizons in Education)* 28, no. 9 (2001): 18.

4. Merry M. Merryfield, "The Paradoxes of Teaching a Multicultural Education Course Online," *Journal of Teacher Education* 52, no. 4 (2001): 283.

5. Kelly Sassi and Ebony Elizabeth Thomas, "Walking the Talk: Examining Privilege and Race in a Ninth-Grade Classroom," *English Journal* (2008): 25-31.

By sharing my instructional design decisions and evaluating students' reflections on this exercise, this work may help other LIS educators become more intentional about the decisions they make when choosing to embed multicultural learning activities into their online classrooms.

Multicultural Education as a Social Justice Typology

Teaching a course focused on multicultural issues is in many ways connected to a larger social justice agenda. Both are concerned with changing social reality in ways that make life more equitable for people who have been marginalized or oppressed. The following definition of multicultural education, articulated by scholars James and Cherry Banks, provides a clear basis for this comparison. In Donna Ford's *Handbook of Research on Multicultural Education,* Banks and Banks's chapter describes multicultural education as, "A field of study designed to increase educational equity for all students that incorporates, for this purpose, content, concepts, principles, theories, and paradigms from history, the social and behavioral sciences, and particularly from ethnic and women's studies."[6]

The keywords within this description that coincide with the basic thrust of social justice ideals and language are "to increase... equity." Inherent in this phrase is a change-oriented goal that seeks to rebalance existing power asymmetries that benefit only a select few. This same transformative focal point is present in each of the five major social justice typologies described by Mehra, Rioux, and Albright: "justice as fairness," "utilitarianism," "justice as desert," "egalitarianism/equity," and "distributive justice."[7] The VPW exercise aligns most closely with the aims of the *justice as fairness* typology, which according to these authors embodies:

---

6. Donna Y. Ford, "The Handbook of Research on Multicultural Education" *Journal of Negro Education* 65, no. 4 (1996): xii.

7. Bharat Mehra, Kevin S. Rioux, and Kendra S. Albright, "Social Justice in Library and Information Science," in *Encyclopedia of Library and Information Sciences,* 3rd ed., ed. Marcia Bates and Mary Niles Maack (Boca Raton, FL: CRC Press, 2009), 4820-4836.

> The idea that societies must safeguard the rights of citizens based on rational and unbiased notions of fairness. It was put forth by the American political philosopher John Rawls, who asserts that fairness is based on principles of justice that: 1) ensure extensive and equal liberty; and 2) promote societal benefits to be arranged in such a way that the least [sic] disadvantaged persons obtain the greatest benefits possible. [8]

To some extent, the VPW exercise helps lay the foundation for anti-discrimination by helping students see the privileges they enjoyed while growing up. Doing so can be seen as a necessary precursor for those who enjoy the most privilege to take affirmative actions to help level the playing field for disadvantaged groups.

Contextualizing the "Virtual Privilege Walk" Exercise

While some students may assume that classes with the word "multicultural" in the title will automatically mean learning about "other" (aka non-white) cultures, I approach teaching such classes from a critical standpoint that centralizes issues of power and white privilege. This approach stems from my belief that understanding how whiteness functions in American society is a key component to developing multicultural competence. As a faculty member of color, one of the ways I help my students, who are often from majority white backgrounds, contextualize the concept of privilege is by explaining that "white privilege is my history being taught as elective and yours being taught as the core curriculum." This statement often helps students understand that multicultural education itself emerged as a response to the overwhelming whiteness of mainstream American curricula.[9] The precursor to multicultural education were Ethnic Studies programs, which began in the 1960s when blacks, Latinos, and other communities of color mounted activist campaigns on college campuses.[10] The demand then was for

8. Ibid.

9. Diane Ravitch, "Multiculturalism: E Pluribus Plures," *The American Scholar* 59, no. 3 (1990): 337–354.

10. Christine I. Bennett, *Comprehensive Multicultural Education: Theory and Practice* (Boston: Allyn and Bacon, 1986).

more faculty of color to be hired and for the curriculum to reflect the history and culture of students of color on campus. To continue honoring this struggle toward a more inclusive curriculum, multicultural classes should not be taught as mere celebrations of minority cultures. They should also attend to the white power structure that created the need for multicultural education itself.[11]

Yet, some students still have difficulty understanding the concept of privilege. This difficulty can be particularly acute for whites who, as Peggy McIntosh argues, "are carefully taught not to recognize white privilege, as males are taught not to recognize male privilege...I have come to see white privilege as an invisible package of unearned assets."[12] Within McIntosh's now famous article entitled, "Unpacking the Knapsack of White Privilege," she offers a series of statements directed to white people that describe the various conditions under which whites often enjoy unearned advantages. There are twenty-six statements about privilege featured in the 1990 article. The first three read as follows:

> 1. I can, if I wish, arrange to be in the company of people of my race most of the time.
> 2. If I should need to move, I can be pretty sure of renting or purchasing housing in an area which I can afford and in which I would want to live.
> 3. I can be pretty sure that my neighbors in such a location will be neutral or pleasant to me.[13]

This article is known for helping whites in particular to confront the privileges they benefit from on a regular basis. As a person of color, McIntosh's article was also compelling for me in that it made the effects of macro-level racism easier to detect on a micro-level. It becomes more difficult for white students to argue that racism does not exist in the post-Civil Rights era after they read McIntosh's article. Part of the reason for the belief in a post-racial America has to do with a desire to

---

11. Sonia Nieto, *Affirming Diversity: The Sociopolitical Context of Multicultural Education* (White Plains, NY: Longman, 1992).

12. Peggy McIntosh, "Unpacking the Knapsack of White Privilege," *Independent School* 49, no. 2 (1990): 31-36.

13. Ibid., 32.

see America as a fundamentally just society.[14] This kind of belief system is bolstered, for some, by evidence of a growing black middle class and the election of the nation's first black President, Barack Obama. Yet, Atwi Akom[15] asserts that this sort of thinking is illusory and perpetuates a myth that he describes as "Ameritocracy," which combines the words "American" and "meritocracy." Contrary to this myth of Ameritocracy, Akom argues that "full acceptance into this society is restricted on the basis of racial identity and other forms of social difference."[16]

The "Privilege Walk" Exercise

Undoubtedly, McIntosh's 1990 article on white privilege influenced what later became known as the "Privilege Walk" (PW) exercise. While various facilitators may have revised the PW exercise, its basic instructions[17] remain fairly standard. The participants are instructed to line up in a straight line as a list of statements related to privilege or obstacles are read. Each statement is followed by the instruction to take a step backward or forward. For instance, "If you are a white male take one step forward." Or, "If there have been times in your life when you skipped a meal because there was no food in the house take one step backward." Once all statements have been read, the students are spread out in the room based on levels of privilege. The person in the front is declared the "winner" and the participants have a chance to debrief the activity as a group.

---

14. Garrett Albert Duncan, "Critical Race Theory and Method: Rendering Race in Urban Ethnographic Research," *Qualitative Inquiry* 8, no. 1 (2002): 85-104.

15. Antwi A. Akom, "Ameritocracy and Infra-Racial Racism: Racializing Social and Cultural Reproduction Theory in the Twenty-First Century," *Race Ethnicity and Education* 11, no. 3 (2008): 205-230.

16. Ibid., 205.

17. See for example State University of New York at Albany, School of Social Welfare, "Module 5: Privilege Walk Activity," (Albany, NY: SUNY, 2009), http://www.albany.edu/ssw/efc/pdf/Module%205_1_Privilege%20Walk%20Activity.pdf.

Overall, the "Privilege Walk" exercise is intended to create a visual depiction of the distance between those who have more privilege and those who have less privilege. In theory, the visible gap places the onus on those with more privilege to take responsibility and help disrupt the status quo of oppression in their personal realms of influence. At the same time, the facilitator should take care with the participants to debrief from the activity by asking questions such as:

- What is your "gut reaction" to where you find yourself at the end of this list of privileges?
- Are you surprised at where you are? How does it feel to be in front? In the middle? In back? Did you come to any new realizations? If so, which one had the most impact?

This exercise can work well within a group whose goal is to centralize privilege and help those born with certain advantages to begin unpacking the guilt of privilege while also taking responsibility for dismantling it.

Guiding Questions

Teaching is a practice that requires routine reflection on one's classroom practices and its impact on student learning. Day writes that to practice teaching effectively means "engaging routinely in conscious, systematic collection and evaluation of information about these areas and the relationship between them which affect and result from practice."[18] To that end, the following questions represent an attempt to hold my teaching practices up to scrutiny and to make visible how students perceive their own learning within this Virtual Privilege Walk exercise:

- What pedagogical considerations should educators make when designing a fully online, spatially dependent class activity such as the Virtual Privilege Walk (VPW)?

---

18. Christopher Day, "Researching Teaching through Reflective Practice," in *Researching Teaching: Methodologies and Practices for Understanding Pedagogy*, ed. John Loughran (Abingdon, UK: Routledge, 1999), 216.

- What do the reflective responses of students who participated in the VPW exercise reveal about the complexities of teaching online classes with a multicultural focus?

Instructor's and Students' Reflections

This section discusses the design and delivery of the VPW exercise from both the instructor and the students' viewpoints. As the instructor, my reflections center on the pedagogical considerations, or teaching and learning strategies that I employed in creating this exercise. Such considerations might be relevant to other LIS educators who wish to refine or replicate this activity in their own online classroom. The students' reflections focus more on the conceptual aspects of teaching about issues of diversity and race in cyberspace. Their perspectives are drawn from two classroom activities in which they were asked to reflect on their experiences in the VPW exercise.

Pedagogical Considerations

The success of the VPW activity was dependent upon several teaching and learning strategies that I employed. It should be noted that I did not make these pedagogical decisions alone. I collaborated with our former technology Graduate Student Assistant (GSA), Kevin Barton, who consulted with me on the conceptual design and technical aspects of facilitating the VPW activity. Based on our collaborative discussions, Kevin designed the virtual room where the activity took place. He also provided technical assistance to the students in the class before, during, and after the VPW activity.

Consideration 1: Choosing the online platform.

Perhaps the most influential (and difficult) decision I had to make was deciding where in "cyberspace" to conduct the exercise. With a myriad of choices in today's Internet-based tools for discussion and collaboration, the possibilities seemed endless. I took approximately two weeks to try out different Internet-based tools before the class began. Both Kevin and our former e-Learning lecturer, David Foote, provided me with suggestions for online tools to consider. Many of the tools required registering for two different accounts using two different email addresses so that I could see how the site functioned from both the administrator (instructor) and the user (student) view. Some of the major features I was initially looking for in these Internet tools were: 1) multiple video pods for students to see each other simultaneously during the activity, 2) audio capabilities for students and the instructor, 3) a whiteboard space to allow students to participate in the activity using their own mouse, 4) a chat feature for students to ask questions in case the audio capabilities were not working, and 5) a file space for uploading documents related to the activity.

Ultimately, I decided to use the Adobe Connect platform. This decision was driven by a number of factors, but mainly because the School of Library and Information Science (SLIS) where I teach provides free access to this software for faculty and students. Having such access was a benefit in that students would not need to create any additional profiles or user credentials and that they would have likely used the program to watch instructor-created content (e.g. lectures) or attend virtual meetings hosted by the school.

Consideration 2: Creating a sense of physical space.

As its name suggests, the "Privilege Walk" exercise is highly dependent on physical movement. As mentioned previously, the purpose of the exercise is to help the participants physically see how their unearned privileges position them in relation to the other participants. This is done by asking them to step forward or backwards in response to a set of questions that are asked by the facilitator. With that in mind, special considerations had to be made to ensure that the element of physical space was somehow embedded into this online classroom exercise in order to achieve the intended learning outcomes.

To that end, one of the first actions I had to kake was to obtain permission from the students to host a special synchronous or live session in this otherwise asynchronous class. I polled the students for their availability and granted extra credit for student participation. Whereas the course mainly took place asynchronously over Blackboard, our university's Learning Management System, this special live session took place via Adobe Connect.

In terms of envisioning the online space, I drew a grid on a piece of paper to convey to Kevin my sense of what the virtual room would need to look like in order to make the parameters of the space visible to everyone. The grid design would function similarly to a chessboard, where students could move their virtual selves around the room using their computer's mouse. Students were free to move their icons forward or backwards in a way that mimics taking a step forward or backwards in a physical space.

Kevin replicated the sketch grid within the whiteboard space of Adobe Connect (see **Figure 1**). The whiteboard option allows participants to make synchronous movements that the entire class can see. Kevin created a brief tutorial to show students how to use the whiteboard menu options to move themselves about in the virtual classroom. Essentially, they were to click an arrow menu option to activate movement and then drag their self-icon to a desired location. Having the freedom to move themselves about was one of the reasons that the grid design was useful. It provided a structure for movement that helped to minimize confusion about how students were intending to respond to the set of questions (see **Appendix A**) that were asked throughout the activity.

Consideration 3: Issues of visibility and silence

Online classrooms often generate a sense of presumed anonymity among students. Many students elect to take online classes precisely because they do not have to attend a physical classroom and deal with issues of visibility. This is one of the reasons I did not use the video camera feature within Adobe Connect. Furthermore, Adobe Connect only allowed for two cameras at the licensing level our unit had purchased. This was not necessarily a limitation of the tool because having video camera pods would distract from the whiteboard space where the main activity for the VPW exercise took place. Ultimately, I chose to eliminate the use of video cameras for this activity as a way to simplify matters and keep the focus of the activity on the questions and responses concerning privilege.

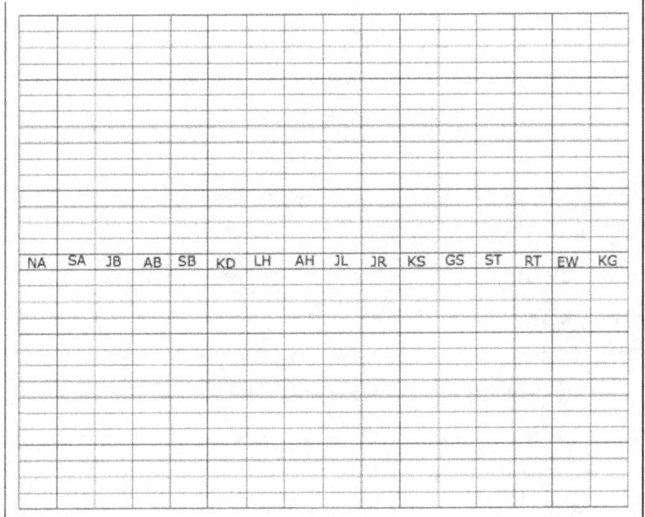

Figure 1.

A related issue that instructors should keep in mind when designing multicultural activities in online spaces is that of dealing with silences from students during the learning activity. Research suggests that silence can be used as a form of resistance in classrooms, particularly for students of color in mainstream white school settings.[19] Educators can leverage silence within a classroom if they are intentional about addressing issues of silence in their lesson planning. For example, there may be times in the exercise when students experience feelings of awkwardness, confusion, embarrassment, or shame related to the silence. One way to deal with these sorts of feelings is to design instructional moments to stop and reflect on what is happening and to candidly ask students how they are feeling in that moment.

Students' Reflections

Immediately following the VPW exercise, students were encouraged to reflect on their experience in an open-ended discussion board on

19. Dorinda J. Carter, "Why the Black Kids Sit Together at the Stairs: The Role of Identity-Affirming Counter-Spaces in a Predominantly White High School." *Journal of Negro Education* 76, no. 4 (2007): 542–54.

Blackboard, our university's learning management system. In addition, I created a survey that students could complete anonymously to share their candid thoughts about various aspects of the exercise. There were a number of themes that emerged across these two sites of reflection that have been teased out below for discussion.

The Aura of Positivity

One of the recurring themes within the students' reflections was the idea that the online nature of this exercise actually helped create a sense of honesty and anti-bias among the participants. In particular, when I asked students to "Please comment on how participating in this activity 'virtually,' or in an online space affected your experience. Were there any benefits or drawbacks to this online setting, in your opinion?"

For example, one student was forthright in her opinion that the online experience provided a "safe environment for honesty." This same student went on to say, "I was not intimidated to move or respond to the questions. It allowed me to put myself out there. No drawbacks that I can identify." Another student commented that the anonymous nature of the activity during which students saw "just initials, not a face" was beneficial because "it makes us avoid stereotypes and grouping certain people together without really knowing them." This idea of the positive benefit of not seeing the other student participants was echoed a number of times by other students with comments such as "I think it was also easier to be honest because we were not all in the same place looking at each other" and "in person I might have felt more uncomfortable being truthful."

There was a single outlier response, which spoke to the drawbacks of online teaching and learning. One student stated, "I think I missed the visual feedback of being with others physically —seeing their faces, body language, hearing their tone of voice. I might have felt more of a bond with classmates if we were doing this in person. That's just one of those things you learn to live without when you take online classes, though." Perhaps most students who take online classes are those who have already reconciled the trade-offs that go along with it. As a result, they may not readily acknowledge the trade-offs or negative consequences to online learning and instead only highlight the positive benefits.

Sameness Versus Difference

A conflicting idea emerged within the students' responses, which centered on notions of sameness versus difference. While there seemed to be a consensus that some people enjoy more privileges than others, there was also a tendency to overlook that difference in the name of "equal access"—a common library mantra. For example, one student commented that, "Going forward, I hope I can take my experience with me into the library field. We don't just hope to serve the privileged but to give the same exemplary service to all." It is not clear from this response whether the student believes that "exemplary service" should or even could be the same for ALL library patrons. Yet, the student acknowledges that not everyone enjoys privilege and therefore providing specialized or targeted outreach to underprivileged and historically marginalized groups is important in his context. This is one of the challenges in teaching about multicultural populations where the normative benchmark for what ALL means tends to be framed within the backdrop of an affluent, white, male, heterosexual, Anglo Saxon Protestant experience.

This dual message reflects the paradox of teaching about multicultural issues regardless of the learning format. There is a basic conundrum of how to be inclusive without either minimizing one group's experience with oppression over another group's experience, or creating a binary between white and non-whites that can reinforce a hierarchy of white supremacy and further objectify and pathologize non-whites.

Broadening the Dimensions of Oppression

A final theme that emerged from the students' responses was the idea that there were some aspects of privilege that the exercise did not recognize. The main dimensions of oppression that were raised in the exercise were race, class, and gender. Yet, a few students commented that issues of obesity and sexual orientation were perhaps areas that should be incorporated into the exercise going forward. For example, one student wrote:

> Someone else mentioned sexual orientation at some point, and I think it would be really interesting to have the Privilege Walk updated since it was written a generation [sic] ago and addressed slightly different (fewer) factors. Including factors like sexual orientation (which might read something like "I can walk down the street holding the hand of the partner of my choice and not be afraid that we will encounter violence because of our genders").

Another student who wanted to include weight as a dimension of privilege/oppression echoed this comment. The student wrote:

> I think that there should be other factors included other than race/ethnicity, religion, sex, etc. I think that how you look and your weight are huge factors in how you're treated. At my very heaviest, I know that I was not chosen for a job because of my size, and a friend who worked there later confirmed it after I'd dropped the first 50 lbs.

I was challenged to provide some shape and coherence to this line of thinking that was gaining traction. This is one of the more difficult realities about teaching multicultural education courses. Students come to the classroom with very different ideas about the meaning and purpose of multicultural education. For that reason I continually open the class with an activity which requires students to choose from one of three definitions of multicultural literature found in the Cai text.[20]

1. Include as many cultures as possible, with no distinctions between dominant and dominated.
2. Focus on people of color, or those who have been most excluded or marginalized.
3. All people are multicultural; there should be no distinction.

Although these definitions refer specifically to multicultural literature, the concept can be applied more generally to education and library services or any sector. Many students come to the class with a sense that

---

20. Mingshui Cai, *Multicultural Literature for Children and Young Adults: Reflections on Critical Issues: Reflections on Critical Issues* (Santa Barbara, CA: ABC-CLIO, 2002).

the first definition is most appropriate. Inevitably, I am challenged to acknowledge that there are other, less accepted forms of disadvantage (e.g. weight) that typically get overlooked in conversations about diversity and culture. Yet I inform students that it is important to avoid the laundry list approach to diversity discourse where everyone's pain or oppression is placed on an even field (e.g. short people, heavy people, vegetarians, etc.). I assert that advantage and disadvantage is more nuanced and systemic.

To help students unpack diversity while also attending to its related power dynamics, I begin the class with an assignment called the "Cultural Mosaic" essay. This assignment is designed to help students understand the layers (or tiles to use the mosaic metaphor) of their own cultural identity as a precursor for developing a broader sense of cultural competence. I refer students to an article by Chao and Moon titled "The Cultural Mosaic: A Metatheory for Understanding the Complexity of Culture." The article breaks culture into three underlying dimensions: demographic, geographic, and associative.[21]

While the Chao and Moon article is useful in helping students grasp the complexity of the concept of culture, it does not address the inherent power dynamics associated with the term, in my opinion. Therefore, I infuse various readings and activities that insert a critical race perspective, which recognizes the permanence of race and racism in the fabric of U.S. society.[22] I also share my own cultural mosaic essay with students at the start of class. Within the essay, I model the nuanced interplay of diversity and power by discussing the ways in which race and racism dominate my own cultural mosaic. For example, in the intro I wrote:

> The primary tiles of my cultural mosaic, or the main identities I claim and occupy on a daily basis are: African American, female, Christian,

21. Georgia T. Chao and Henry Moon, "The Cultural Mosaic: A Metatheory for Understanding the Complexity of Culture," *Journal of Applied Psychology* 90, no. 6 (2005): 1128-40.

22. Adrienne D. Dixson and Celia K. Rousseau, *Critical Race Theory in Education: All God's Children Got a Song* (London: Taylor & Francis, 2006). This text is relevant in its treatment of how educational scholars are applying Critical Race Theory frameworks in their practices some decades after CRT broke into the realm of education research.

> Hip Hop generation/bi-centennial baby, mother, daughter, sister, friend, native Detroiter, college professor, and former school librarian. I'd have to say that the primary hue that would weave through the cracks of my mosaic would be black. I would choose this color because: 1) my blackness is an identity that has been chosen for me by the larger society and, unlike other facets of my identity, I cannot mask or hide this facet of my identity to the world— nor would I choose to. And 2) because being black for me means being part of a legacy of people who have survived racism, genocide, and all kinds of human atrocities to still become some of the worlds greatest thinkers, artists, musicians, athletes, and politicians.

My cultural mosaic reflects my attempt to model the interplay between diversity discourses and critical race perspectives, which often reside as independent spheres of thought.

Another way I insert critical perspectives into the discourse on multiculturalism and diversity is by dissecting political cartoons that are increasingly available on the Internet. In particular, there is one cartoon[23] I use to help students recognize the differences between equality and equity. The cartoon I use shows two side-by-side images of three people standing on podiums being recognized for some unknown achievement. The image on the left has the word "equality" written underneath while the one on the right says "equity." The three podiums on the left side are the same height for each person. However, due to the height differences of the three winners (one tall, one medium, one short), it appears that the shortest person is still somehow less than the others. Meanwhile, the photo on the right has the same three individuals standing on a podium. However, this time the three people appear to be on equal footing. In looking closer, the tall person is not standing on a podium and is still as tall as the others. The medium height person stands on the same size podium as on the left-side image to achieve equal footing. Most strikingly, the shortest person now stands on top of two stacked podiums to achieve equal footing with the other winners. In this way, all three individuals on the "equity" sided photo appear to be the same height, but they got there by different means. In juxtaposing the two

---

23. This political cartoon image can be easily accessed via an Internet search using the words "equity," "equality" and "cartoon".

photos, the message is clear. Equality is insufficient as a social justice goal, whereas equity is a more corrective approach that actually helps level the playing field. Equity helps the person with the least advantage while not taking away anything from those with unearned privilege or advantage. One can believe in equality but also recognize that certain people need additional assistance to get on an equal footing with others due to their circumstances of birth.

Concluding Thoughts

Upon reflection, the VPW exercise accomplished the student learning outcomes I initially established for students, regardless of the online delivery format. I intended for students to discover their unearned privileges and to see how they were positioned in relation to their classmates to invoke a sense of "critical cultural consciousness."[24] In reading the students' comments about their learning, the exercise certainly provided the right environment for this awareness to occur. For example, one student observed:

> I think that this privilege walk was very important because in order to know how to prevent discrimination one needs to understand their position in society, and how that can help or hinder their advocacy. I no longer want to be embarrassed about the privileges I have had, I would like to channel those feelings into constructive action. I am lucky, and I would like to help others not have to depend on luck.

Knowing how race, power, and privilege intersect, and where we each fall on the spectrum of privilege and domination is a part of being a "culturally competent professional."[25] More often that not, however,

24. Geneva Gay and Kipchoge Kirkland, "Developing Cultural Critical Consciousness and Self-Reflection in Preservice Teacher Education," *Theory into Practice* 42, no. 3 (2003): 181-187.

25. Kafi Kumasi and Renee Franklin Hill, "Are We There Yet? Results of a Gap Analysis to Measure LIS students' Prior Knowledge and Actual Learning of Cultural Competence Concepts," *Journal of Education for Library and Information Science* 52, no. 4 (2011): 251-264. This article represents my scholarship

future library and information science students are earning their MLIS degrees online or in non-traditional classroom spaces where multicultural learning activities may be more difficult to replicate.[26] This chapter demonstrates that students can reap the benefit of multicultural learning activities while also having the convenience of online learning. Given the realities of online learning in today's higher education institutions, instructors should not shy away from these critical learning opportunities simply because of the learning modality. It may take deliberate action on the part of energetic faculty, but meaningful learning outcomes can come from teaching about issues of diversity, equity, and race—even in cyberspace!

Bibliography

Akom, Antwi A. "Ameritocracy and Infra-Racial Racism: Racializing Social and Cultural Reproduction Theory in the Twenty-First Century," *Race Ethnicity and Education* 11, no. 3 (2008): 205-230.

Bennett, Christine I. *Comprehensive Multicultural Education: Theory and Practice.* Boston: Allyn and Bacon, 1986.

Cai, Mingshui. *Multicultural Literature for Children and Young Adults: Reflections on Critical Issues: Reflections on Critical Issues.* Santa Barbara, CA: ABC-CLIO, 2002.

Carter, Dorinda J. "Why the Black Kids Sit Together at the Stairs: The Role of Identity-Affirming Counter-Spaces in a Predominantly White High School." *Journal of Negro Education* 76, no. 4 (2007): 542–54.

---

related to the development of cultural competence among future library and information science professionals.

26. See Maria Haigh, "Divided by a Common Degree Program? Profiling Online and Face-to-Face Information Science Students," *Education for Information* 25, no. 2 (2007): 93-110 for a discussion on the issues and trends in online education within Library and Information Science.

Cavanaugh, Joseph. "Teaching Online: A Time Comparison." Online *Journal of Distance Learning Administration* 8, no. 1 (2005). http://www.westga.edu/~distance/ojdla/spring81/cavanaugh81.htm.

Chao, Georgia T., and Henry Moon. "The Cultural Mosaic: A Metatheory for Understanding the Complexity of Culture." *Journal of Applied Psychology* 90, no. 6 (2005): 1128-40.

Day, Christopher. "Researching Teaching through Reflective Practice." In *Researching Teaching: Methodologies and Practices for Understanding Pedagogy,* edited by John Loughran, 215-232. Abingdon, UK: Routledge, 1999.

Dixson, Adrienne D., and Celia K. Rousseau. *Critical Race Theory in Education: All God's Children Got a Song.* London: Taylor & Francis, 2006.

Duncan, Garrett Albert. "Critical Race Theory and Method: Rendering Race in Urban Ethnographic Research." *Qualitative Inquiry* 8, no. 1 (2002): 85-104.

Ford, Donna Y. "The Handbook of Research on Multicultural Education." *Journal of Negro Education* 65, no. 4 (1996): 472.

Gay, Geneva, and Kipchoge Kirkland. "Developing cultural critical consciousness and self-reflection in preservice teacher education." *Theory into Practice* 42, no. 3 (2003): 181-187.

Haigh, Maria. "Divided by a Common Degree Program? Profiling Online and Face-to-Face Information Science Students." *Education for Information* 25, no. 2 (2007): 93-110.

Kumasi, Kafi, and Renee Franklin Hill. "Are We There Yet? Results of a Gap Analysis to Measure LIS Students' Prior Knowledge and Actual Learning of Cultural Competence Concepts." *Journal of Education for Library and Information Science* 52, no. 4 (2011): 251-264.

McIntosh, Peggy. "Unpacking the Knapsack of White Privilege." *Independent School* 49, no. 2 (1990): 31-36.

Mehra, Bharat, Kevin S. Rioux, and Kendra S. Albright. "Social justice in library and information science." In Encyclopedia of Library and Information Sciences, 3rd ed., edited by Marcia Bates and Mary Niles Maack, 4820-4836. Boca Raton, FL: CRC Press, 2009.

Merryfield, Merry M. "The paradoxes of teaching a multicultural education course online." *Journal of Teacher Education* 52, no. 4 (2001): 283-299.

Nieto, Sonia. *Affirming Diversity: The Sociopolitical Context of Multicultural Education.* White Plains, NY: Longman, 1992.

Ravitch, Diane. "Multiculturalism: E Pluribus Plures." The American Scholar 59.3 (1990): 337–354.

Sassi, Kelly, and Ebony Elizabeth Thomas. "Walking the Talk: Examining Privilege and Race in a Ninth-Grade Classroom." *English Journal* (2008): 25-31.

Singleton, Glenn E. *Courageous Conversations about Race: A Field Guide for Achieving Equity in Schools.* Thousand Oaks, CA: Corwin Press, 2014.

State University of New York at Albany, School of Social Welfare. "Module 5: Privilege Walk Activity." Albany, NY: SUNY, 2009. http://www.albany.edu/ssw/efc/pdf/Module%205_1_Privilege%20Walk%20Activity.pdf.

Smith, Glenn Gordon, David Ferguson, and Mieke Caris. "Online vs. Face-to-Face." *THE Journal (Technological Horizons in Education)* 28, no. 9 (2001): 18-26.

Appendix A: Virtual Privilege Walk Questions

- If you are right-handed, please move one-step forward.
- If you are a female under 5-feet tall, please move one-step forward.
- If you are a white male take one step forward.
- If there have been times in your life when you skipped a meal because there was no food in the house take one step backward.
- If you have visible or invisible disabilities take one step backward.
- If you attended (grade) school with people you felt were like yourself take one step forward.
- If you grew up in an urban setting take one step backward.
- If your family had health insurance take one step forward.
- If your work holidays coincide with religious holidays that you celebrate take one step forward.
- If you feel good about how your identified culture is portrayed by the media take one step forward.
- If you have been the victim of physical violence based on your race, gender, ethnicity, age or sexual orientation take one step backward.
- If you have ever felt passed over for an employment position based on your race, gender, ethnicity, or sexual orientation take one step backward.
- If you were born in the United States take one step forward.
- If English is your first language take one step forward.
- If you have been divorced or impacted by divorce take one step backward.
- If you came from a supportive family environment take one step forward.
- If you have completed high school take one step forward.
- If you were able to complete college take one step forward.
- If you are a citizen of the United States take one step forward.
- If you took out loans for your education take one step backward.
- If you attended private school take one step forward.

- If you have ever felt unsafe walking alone at night take one step backward.
- Please take one-step forward: If you studied the culture of your ancestors in elementary school.

SECTION THREE: TEACHING SOCIAL JUSTICE OUTSIDE THE CLASSROOM

Chapter 8

Social Justice in Study Abroad: Intentions and Outcomes

Jenny Bossaller

This paper discusses the intentions and outcomes of three Study Abroad classes offered through the School of Information Science & Learning Technologies (SISLT), the iSchool at the University of Missouri. The courses were taught in the United Kingdom, Ireland, and South Africa and were developed with the intentions of broadening students' understanding of social justice issues in libraries and archives, and of exploring the responsibilities of libraries and archives with regard to national heritage and political viewpoints. Students visited sites and discussed historically dominant/majority and oppressed/minority cultures. They were required to read about the history and politics in the cities they visited, to learn about ethnic or cultural conflicts, and to stay abreast of current social issues. Visits to archives and to national, public, and academic libraries, as well as attendance at cultural events and workshops gave them broad exposure to different information institutions and theories of information in various contexts. Experiential education and social responsibility as core values of librarianship provide the framework for this paper.

Introduction

According to the Institute of International Education, thirteen percent of U.S. graduate students study abroad.[1] Twenty-two percent of those are in the social sciences, and fifty-nine percent of them study short-term, meaning they study for eight weeks or less, usually over the summer. Studying abroad might not be entirely about *study*, though. Many classes offer students the opportunity to see a new country and learn about new cultures and their history in the relative safety of an academic program. Schools are increasingly touting study abroad programs as a way to increase students' employability, claiming that international experience gives students an edge over other applicants. Immersive language experiences are one excellent way to internationalize the student population, but language is certainly not the only reason to study abroad. Tillman explains that the pressures of a globalized workforce and employers' demands for internationally-prepared students are placing pressure on universities to increase international opportunities for students.[2] Bremer agrees, explaining that international education must be included as a core objective in higher education in order to prepare students to be a part of the global, twenty-first century workforce.[3] Universities need to carefully consider exactly what students will get out of international study, though. Service and on-the-job experiences such as internships are more valuable than cultural tourism in relation to the "global workforce," but an argument can certainly be made that travel and first-hand learning about a culture can be quite educational.

Are schools of library and/or information science globalizing their programs? Many do offer study abroad opportunities. A cursory web search of the study abroad landscape in 2015 in schools of information

1. Institute of International Education, http://www.iie.org/.

2. Martin Tillman, "Employer Perspectives on International Education," in *The SAGE Handbook of International Higher Education*, ed. Darla K. Deardorff, Hans de Wit, John Heyl, and Tony Adams (Thousand Oaks, CA: Sage, 2012), 191-206.

3. Darlene Bremer, "Wanted: Global Workers," *International Educator* 15, no. 3 (May/June 2006): 40-45.

science found many such programs; the following were selected to demonstrate the wide variety of subject matters offered:

- Florida State University runs Study Abroad in London, focusing on "theory, concepts and techniques" of Web 2.0 applications.[4]
- University of Southern Mississippi offers students the chance to "explore some of the world's most famous libraries, archives, and special collections around London and Edinburgh."[5]
- Pratt Institute has two Study Abroad programs: a cultural studies (libraries, museums, and archives) program in Florence and a digital humanities program conducted through King's College in London.[6]
- University of Kentucky's Study Abroad in Northern Ireland gives students the opportunity to "examine the organization and delivery of information services…including rural and urban public libraries, school libraries, corporate and industry information centers, and archives."[7]
- University of North Carolina at Chapel Hill offers the Prague Summer Seminar, giving students the opportunity to "experience firsthand how the democratization of the Czech Republic, formerly a communist state, has affected the accessibility of information, in both print and electronic forms."[8]

---

4. Florida State University, "London Program – Summer 2015," http://slis.fsu.edu/London.

5. University of Southern Mississippi, (2015), "Library Science and Information Studies in Historical and Contemporary Britain," http://www.usm.edu/british-studies/library-science-and-information-studies-historical-and-contemporary-britain.

6. Pratt Institute, "International Programs," (2015), https://www.pratt.edu/academics/information-and-library-sciences/international-programs/

7. University of Kentucky, Library and Information Science, "Study Abroad in Northern Ireland," (2015), http://ci.uky.edu/lis/content/study-abroad-northern-ireland.

8. University of North Carolina, School of Information and Library Science, "Prague Summer Seminar," (2015), http://sils.unc.edu/programs/international/prague.

Library and Information Science (LIS) is a broad field, which is reflected in the above study abroad programs. Some of the programs focus on libraries or librarianship, and others cover the tools or platforms that librarians use or make. International venues might not be necessary to learn about, for instance, web 2.0 applications, but taking the class abroad might help students explore a familiar subject in a new way or in a new context. Taking a class abroad gives students a chance to truly immerse themselves in the subject. Study abroad experiences can offer much more than simply studying a subject, though; they offer both planned scholarship and unplanned cultural and social learning experiences.

One of the key draws of study abroad is its experiential nature. There have been a variety of studies by educational researchers claiming that because study abroad (like service learning and other immersive learning environments) is experiential education, it has the power to be transformative. This means that it has the potential to change the way a person thinks about problems or the ways that other people live in the world. The immersive experience and new surroundings can make people more open to new ideas and even increase empathy. Perry, Stoner and Tarrant referred to the study abroad environment as "atypical, different, or disorienting," which allows the student to "bring into question…typical or preprogrammed reactions" to information.[9]

Most studies about the transformative effects of study abroad have concentrated on long-term (semester) programs, but many students are simply not able to leave their life behind for a semester. Short-term study abroad programs can be just as engaging, providing transformative experiences for working adults and people with families (as long as they are not expecting it to be a vacation). Jones, et al., found that short-term study abroad programs are as valuable as longer programs in their potential to open students' eyes to new experiences in an immersive environment: "Prompted by getting out of the bubble, crossing

9. Lane Perry, Lee Stoner, and Michael Tarrant, "More Than a Vacation: Short-Term Study Abroad as a Critically Reflective, Transformative Learning Experience," *Creative Education* 3, no. 05 (2012): 680.

boundaries, and personalizing experiences, students gained new or larger understandings about themselves as well as the issues and cultures that were a focus of their immersion experiences."[10] They found that the programs were very effective at helping students learn about cultures that they had previously only read about. Similarly, Levy found that students need to get lost in the new culture (sometimes literally); letting them explore without the professor requires that they learn to take risks and rely on each other. Levy writes, "As students become immersed in a new culture they open up at least three major areas for learning: the host culture itself, new perspective on their own culture, and self-learning."[11] These learning experiences are outside of the motivation for universities to engage in international internships; the motivations and results are spoken of in terms relating to the humanities and personal value systems rather than the neoliberal reasoning expressed in many newer justifications for study abroad programs (i.e., preparing a global workforce).

Can Study Abroad Help Instill Values?

Lindsey, drawing from Bargal's description of a model for the development of values in the human-centered professions, examines how study abroad could affect the personal and professional values of social work students.[12] The core values of social work loosely correlate with values expressed in public services librarianship. Both professions focus on services to people; social justice means equal access and equitable

---

10. Susan Jones et al., "The Meaning Students Make as Participants in Short-Term Immersion Programs," *Journal of College Student Development* 53, no. 2 (2012): 209.

11. Diane Levy, "The Shock of the Strange, the Shock of the Familiar: Learning from Study Abroad," *Journal of the National Collegiate Honors Council* 1, no. 1 (Spring/Summer 2000): 75-83.

12. Elizabeth W. Lindsey, "Study Abroad and Values Development in Social Work Students," *Journal of Social Work Education* 41, no. 2 (2005): 229-249; David Bargal, "Social Values in Social Work: A Developmental Model," *Journal of Sociology and Social Welfare* 8 (1981): 45-61.

service for all. Both professions have codes of ethics that emphasize values. Some of the correlated values are shown in **Table 1**.

Librarianship	Social Work
Service: Provide the highest level of service to all users	Service: help people in need
Confidentiality/Privacy: necessary for intellectual freedom and fundamental to librarianship	Privacy and confidentiality: should protect the confidentiality of clients, ensure confidentiality in electronic transfer of records
Social Responsibility: solving the critical problems of society through informing and educating	Challenge social injustice: promote sensitivity to and knowledge about oppression and cultural and ethnic diversity
Provide accurate, unbiased, and courteous responses to all requests	Behave in a trustworthy manner (integrity)
Strive for excellence by maintaining and enhancing knowledge and skills	Practice within their areas of competence and develop and enhance their professional expertise

Table 1. Core Values in Librarianship and Social Work
(Sources: American Library Association, Code of Ethics; Lindsey, Study Abroad and Values Development in Social Work Students; National Association of Social Workers, Code of Ethics.)

Lindsey did find that the students who studied abroad gained a greater appreciation for the values of their profession, especially regarding social justice. They became more self-aware, learned to overcome challenges, and developed sympathy towards international and multicultural issues.

They also "reported becoming more receptive to new perspectives and ways of thinking."[13]

SISLT Study Abroad Programs

SISLT has (to date) run three study abroad programs: 2011, to the United Kingdom; 2012, to the United Kingdom and Ireland; and 2014, to Cape Town, South Africa. Inspiration for the 2011 and 2012 trips came from research presented by Muddiman, et. al., in the report "Open to All? The Public Library and Social Exclusion."[14] The report focused on the role of public libraries in tackling social exclusion, which is the theory that some people remain on the outskirts of society because of systemic inequalities. They might be stigmatized because of race or socioeconomic background, or because of personal characteristics such as age or disability. The theory has been adopted in mostly European political contexts as a means to discover how public policy, organizations, and places can be reimagined in order to better reach excluded populations and narrow divisions between groups. The students in 2011 and 2012 were able to attend a workshop by one of the authors of the study (John Vincent), in which students learned about how libraries in the U.K. are serving populations such as new arrivals and immigrants, LGBTQ patrons, youth in trouble, and children in foster care. Vincent also served as a very helpful local scout and connector, identifying libraries to visit that had been particularly active in reducing social exclusion.

Some of the other social-justice highlights of the 2011 trip were participating in a local conference at the Barking Learning Center (a library in London's East End) where the students learned about the financial crisis and how it was affecting England's libraries, and visiting the Leeds Library and learning about how they were helping parents of children with autism and at-risk youth in their multimedia production studio.

13. Lindsey, "Study Abroad and Values Development," 6.

14. Dave Muddiman et al., "Open to All? The Public Library and Social Exclusion," (2000), http://eprints.rclis.org/6283/.

Selected social-justice highlights of the 2012 trip were visiting the Free Derry museum and touring Derry/Londonderry, the site of Bloody Sunday; visiting the Glasgow Women's Library; and participating in a workshop with the teen librarian and teens at the York Public Library, who had created an after-hours practice space for budding musicians.

The 2014 trip to South Africa was developed as part of a burgeoning partnership between the University of the Western Cape and the University of Missouri that centers on website development for the Mayibuye Archives, the collected papers from the Robben Island Museum (RIM) and the Mayibuye Center, which holds the collected papers, artwork, and photographs of the worldwide Apartheid Resistance movement. Students also visited many other libraries, museums, and archives, as well as a school library and a library in a township.

Unplanned Events

It takes many months of hard work on the part of the faculty member to prepare for a study abroad trip. However, one cannot plan for everything or be prepared for all possible events. Part of the fun of travel is the sense of uncertainty and the knowledge that not everything can be controlled. There is also always some inherent danger in travel. Students might get sick, get hurt, stay out too late, get robbed, or miss buses (all of which happened). Professors leading study abroad trips do take precautions to avoid dangerous situations. Speaking from personal experience, one of the precautions emphasized by our International Study Abroad Office is to avoid public protests, as even a peaceful protest can quickly turn violent. On the 2011 and 2014 trips we had to avoid riots and protests. Fortunately, none of our students were drawn into any violent events. However, the events did provide an unplanned way to view the place where we were visiting in a different light and ultimately (and fortuitously) spark conversations about the mission of libraries. The 2011 riots and the 2014 marches provided ways to look at serious national and international politics of identity and belonging. Their significance was perhaps made even more poignant for us because we were not watching them on TV; we were all slightly on edge because the events took us out of our comfort zone.

During the 2011 trip, we saw rioting break out across the U.K.; in fact, it followed us from London to Leeds (and we made our local news). The riots began on August 6 in North London and spread that week[15] throughout London and north towards Leeds and Manchester. We felt that it was somewhat ironic that the students had spent August 5 spread around the London suburbs in a class activity that required them to explore and take pictures of places that represented London's diversity. The amazing diversity that they saw was a recurrent theme in how the riots were portrayed in the news (and also how they were analyzed by academics later on). We gathered around the TV at night to monitor what was going on, noting how the riots were being discussed, how the media portrayed the rioters, and how the social issues dovetailed with our readings on social justice and information. Since then, the riots have been used to explain problems with social policy, consumer culture, and a failing economy in the lives of minorities living in England.[16] The rioters made extensive use of social media and digital communication; this was another topic on the news and one that has been studied extensively in the context of many social movements and protests.[17]

The 2014 trip coincided with a sharp rise in the Middle East conflict, which was met with worldwide Palestinian solidarity marches. The Study Abroad in Cape Town was built around cultural heritage and archives. Our primary (and culminating) activity was creating a finding aid for a collection in the Mayibuye Archives, located in the library of the University of the Western Cape (UWC). The Mayibuye Archives is formed from the collections of the Robben Island Museum and anti-apartheid

---

15. BBC News, "England Riots: Maps and Timeline," August 15, 2011, http://www.bbc.com/news/uk-14436499.

16. Karim Murji and Sarah Neal. "Riot: Race and Politics in the 2011 Disorders," *Sociological Research Online* 16, no. 4 (2011): 24, 5 http://www.socresonline.org.uk/16/4/24.html.

17. Stephanie Alice Baker, "The Mediated Crowd: New Social Media and New Forms of Rioting," *Sociological Research Online* 16, no. 4 (Nov. 30, 2011), http://www.socresonline.org.uk/16/4/21.html. DOI: 10.5153/sro.2553.

materials from around the world. The collection that we worked with was a vertical file— meaning it was something of a mishmash of materials from many different donors. In order to adequately describe the material, the students had to learn a lot about the country's history and culture. Their work was prefaced with many tours, readings, and discussions.

Most people know about the history of apartheid in South Africa (also called the Rainbow Nation), but fewer people in the U.S. know about its incredible diversity in culture and language. There is a large Muslim population, and a smaller Jewish one, in Cape Town. On one day, we had scheduled tours of District Six (where many of Cape Town's Coloured population lived until the forced removals in the 1970s) and the colorful Bo-Kaap district, led by a local chef who also cooked an amazing meal for us at her home. We were late to our second tour because protest marches, spurred by the acceleration of destruction of Palestinian homes, bisected the city and cut us off from our destination. Similar marches were happening around the world that week. Interestingly, we had also just visited the Jewish museum of Cape Town and earlier in the week, had attended a screening of "Village Under the Forest," a film by Mark Kaplan and Heidi Gruenbaum,[18] which focused on the roots of the modern Middle East (Israel/Palestine) conflict. The undercurrent of the film was the development of the filmmaker's own understanding, as a Jewish woman, of the Palestinian point of view.

The interesting result of experiencing the Israeli-Palestinian conflict as we did was that it provided grounds for discussing social justice on a much wider scale. Linking apartheid to the Middle-East conflict was not intentional, nor was it actually even voiced, but both events contributed to the way that we understood the destructive nature of ethnic and cultural divisions and the effects of settler colonialism. The intention of the class was to focus on apartheid, but the unintended consequence of global events led to conversations about preconceptions, prejudice, and media. Events that might not have been more than a blip on the students'

---

18. Mark J. Kaplan and Heidi Grunebaum, "The Village Under the Forest," http://www.villageunderforest.com/.

newsfeed were up-close and personal. Their beliefs were challenged, and we were sometimes put in uncomfortable situations. For instance, one of our drivers became loud (and somewhat frightening) when we were discussing the film and the events, assuming that because we were American we were also pro-Israel. In truth, were trying to process what we were seeing and learning.

The conversations were surprisingly similar to conversations students had in 2012 following the trip to Derry/Londonderry in Northern Ireland. The intention of that side-trip was to find out about the Irish Troubles, but some of us found out how little we knew about the point of view of members of the IRA. As a group, we became more sympathetic to the IRA's cause after visiting the Museum of Free Derry and taking a tour of Derry with the sister of a slain IRA member. This interaction gave us the means to talk about the media's role in forming our views, which led to discussions about the collections of libraries and cultural institutions.

Did the Classes Make a Difference?

I put a lot of effort into crafting trips that would be meaningful and relevant, but in the end I didn't really know what kind of a difference they had made. I thought that the students had a good time and learned a lot, but I wanted to know if the classes actually had any lasting effects on their practice. Had the trips changed their views of the world? Did they experience any transformations? Did their experiences help them develop values or re-form their ideas of equality of access? Each trip was also part of an academic program with specific goals grounded in practice; it was hoped that the trips would help them gather ideas that they might be able to apply "on the job." Most of the interview participants who had gone on the 2011 and 2012 trips had graduated and were either professionals or Ph.D. students. Had anything happened during their study that influenced them later?

Research was conducted through individual interviews. Recruitment for the interviews took place via Facebook and email. All students who had gone on a study abroad trip were invited to participate in the research. We had created a Facebook groups for the trips, and many participants were still members of those groups. Ten out of twenty four participants responded to the request for interviews. Two of the students sent a link to the journal that they kept while they were on the trip, which I used for background information and to help my own recollections (though no quotes from the journals are included in this paper). Not all students responded; for instance, the students who had recently gone to South Africa had just finished writing an article about their experiences[19] and they were most likely tired of reflecting on the trip. They were also not yet employed, so the questions were less relevant for them.

The ultimate goal of the classes had been to make a difference in the students' perspectives on the possibilities of social justice in librarianship, in hopes of eventually improving their practice of librarianship. The two main research questions were:

1. Did the students experience any kind of transformation during the trip that led to a greater awareness of social justice issues?
2. Did the students learn about anything that they have been able to apply to their practice of librarianship?

Other questions sought to find out about students' intentions when they registered for the classes, as intentionality could affect outcomes. Did they students sign up for the classes to learn about the subject matter or did they sign up for other reasons?

Limitations

There were some limitations to this study, as might be expected with an exploratory, qualitative study. Only ten participants responded to the

19. Jenny S. Bossaller et al., "Learning about Social Justice through Experiential Learning Abroad," *Reference & User Services Quarterly* 54, no. 3 (2015): 6-11.

request for interviews. Some responded to the questions via email. This gave them more time to carefully consider how they responded to the questions, but their answers were less spontaneous. In-person interviews provided more opportunities for clarification and expansion in answers.

Furthermore, the three trips were quite different, as a result of both design and happenstance (see "undercurrents" section above). The trips occurred in different locations, and the reading lists were developed to enhance their understanding of the places we were visiting. Therefore, no cross-comparisons can be made regarding the content of the courses. This research sought to discover common factors in the types of activities that influenced their values and understanding of cultural differences.

Findings

The participants' responses to the interview questions are presented according to the interview question order. The Discussion Section draws together themes. The participants were numbered 1- 10; only direct quotes are given a participant number below.

1. When you signed up for the class, how interested were you in the social justice aspects of the course?

Two participants were very interested social justice, in terms of information access in the international context. One explained: "I was very interested, and for two reasons. One, because I was generally interested in social justice issues—specifically in how information technologies impact these issues. Two, because I knew very little about librarianship and informational issues in the UK and I thought the trip would be a good way to learn more about this" (7).

Five participants were somewhat interested in social justice issues at the outset. One explained, "That wasn't the reason I signed up for the course. I thought I might work as an international librarian one day or get a Ph.D., so I took it" (6). Another, likewise, said, "I don't know if I was that interested in the social justice aspects of the course…I made the decision to go fairly impulsively. I had studied abroad as an undergrad, and it was a good experience" (4).

Three were not really interested in the social justice aspects of the course at all. They were more interested in the opportunity to study abroad, or they wanted to travel to the location. One participant explained, "I knew that I would learn a lot about social justice, but that was not the predominant reason why I chose to go…I was more drawn to it for the sake of being able to work in archives on the other side of the world" (5).

2. Can you recall what you learned about social justice while we were abroad?

There were essentially two types of responses to this question. Some participants recalled many specific serendipitous experiences that happened to them that changed their understanding of the world, especially relating to the unplanned events. Others focused on the readings and events that were planned as part of the course. Five quotes, selected below, represent how serendipity and planned events both contributed to their understanding of social justice.

The unplanned events mentioned by the students related to learning about a different point of view. Two participants mentioned how little they knew about the Irish Troubles from the point of view of the Irish: "We visited a museum dedicated to retelling the story of the Troubles and I noticed how much I didn't know about the events. I was disgusted by the lack of information that was shared in the United States about this issue" (10).

Another said, "I learned that there are many more views that you have to take on any issue. The things that I thought were very black and white, like the IRA, were not. Northern Ireland was the most influential for me. Information is very powerful. It causes wars" (4).

One participant who went to South Africa discussed the inequalities that she saw:

> I was exposed to real poverty for the first time in my life. Before the trip I didn't have a good understanding of the extreme discrepancies that can exist between the distributions of wealth in a nation. There were people

> living in shacks on top of trash heaps in a township just a few mils away from extremely wealthy mansion-ridden South African wine country. (5)

While the United States certainly has deep poverty, the student had not really experienced it, or perhaps because she was in a foreign land the experience was different, and was thus very poignant.

There were many planned activities that influenced the participants, as well. Three specifically mentioned John Vincent's half-day workshop, which concentrated on elements of social exclusion: "I learned that while social justice seems to have a fairly standardized definition, many other concepts do not, such as 'integration'" (8). The second said, "I remember learning about social exclusion, how the needs of minority groups aren't always taken into consideration by libraries and other institutions" (2). A third echoed:

> [His] presentation was a critique of the political ideology called the Big Society, which seeks to place more control and power in local government instead of in a centralized government. After describing the ideology…he argued that its assumptions are false and hurt social justice issues…I still think about it today, although I didn't agree with everything he said. (7)

One participant discussed the prison program at the Edinburgh public library; another talked about Leeds Library's autism program: "Who would have even conceived that it was a public library role? That was going out of their way" (1). Another participant discussed the social justice implications of the One Stop Shop in East London, where librarians had created a government information and services center.

3. Do you think that there was anything that occurred during the trip—anything that you read or experienced—that changed your perspective of social justice in any way?

There was some overlap with the participants' answers to the previous question, but some built on their answer or were spurred to remember another event or library that they visited. One said:

> I fell in love with the Glasgow Women's Library and appreciated that the librarians were very warm and welcoming…[especially] the attention that was given to the refugee populations and women and children. I have always had a strong interest in working with international populations and sharing and teaching to help "outsiders" feel more comfortable in their surroundings. (10)

Another reflected on an exchange between a young barrister and our group at a bar:

> I learned that a lot of people don't understand the concept...based on their life experiences. [For instance, one night we went out together and met a young barrister who] didn't see the need for libraries and their services. He read everything on his Kindle and couldn't imagine people who couldn't afford or learn how to use an e-reader…after talking for some time, he finally seemed to get it. There was rioting in London while we were there and he referenced the library as a source of information and education for people…it was interesting to watch him connect the dots. (8)

A third student described a very personal experience regarding cultural sensitivity:

> Walking through the Muslim district late in the evening during Ramadan…there was a peacefulness in the air and it was kind of beautiful. That might be a small thing and unrelated to course programming, but it fits as part of the overall experience, I think. Per the intent of the instructors—social justice comes, at least somewhat for some people, by simply being more aware of other cultures. (7)

4. Have you taken anything from that trip and applied it to your life—either on the job or off the job?

Eight students described various ways that they had taken something that they learned from the trip and applied it to their own lives, with varying degrees of success or frustration. One participant said that it had helped her decide what kind of library she wanted to work in—it would be one that placed importance on helping all individuals in the community. Another said:

> I started taking my teen librarianship out of the library…to the Youth Academy, which is like a prison for troubled teens…we've done book groups and craft programs there. I'm in a really poor school district and trying to do some crowd-funded projects. They don't have money for computers, so I've gotten some funded for the building. Part of the social justice aspect is making people aware. Civil rights programs don't happen if people aren't aware of the problems. (1)

Another explained that the trip gave her the ideas and understanding "to make a difference":

> For the last 2 years I have worked in an urban public library and deal on a daily basis with a wide variety of social justice issues—homelessness, mental illness, digital divide, joblessness, etc. These challenges, and they can be very challenging, certainly wear you down, but I do feel the trip, the class, and my life experiences have given me the patience and understanding to go to work and try to make a difference. (9)

Finally, one student brought up the fact that one of her colleagues, who had gone on the trip with us, was inspired by the One Stop Shop in East London and had founded a similar program for government information in her local library. She felt that was an important initiative for providing equitable services in a town that is known for being very unfriendly for people without a car. She said that she had calculated how much time it took for people to get from one place to another for government services, which provided justification for pulling them together under one roof.

Not all students had positive experiences relating to what they learned on the trip, and they felt frustrated. One said:

> From time to time I am simply reminded of the trip. Every experience of my life does contribute to who I am now—both on and off the job… right now I am a new professional in a public library. There are policies and procedures that I would like to change, but I feel I am too new to rock the boat just yet…I think that the community I live in needs to think about its homeless population…I also think our services are lacking for the refugee population and international visitors in general. (10)

Another brought home great ideas but was unable to successfully implement them:

> I've tried, but just not successfully. For instance, the autism program that we learned about in Leeds—nothing ever came of it. I try to go the extra mile in helping patrons who don't fit the white, straight, middle-class demographic when I'm working at the library to show them that the library is for them, too. (2)

Three students continued working on their Ph.D. following the trip. One found the connections that she made with librarians in the U.K., as well as the terminology that she learned there, to be very helpful with her research. Finally, one student did not have anything specific to say about how it had affected his work, but expressed that the trip "did help open up my world view."(7).

5. Is there anything else that you want to talk about regarding libraries and social justice, or the trip?

This question was asked in order to give the participants a chance to discuss anything else that they might have on their minds. Two emphasized that the trip was a great way to get to know other students and feel reinvigorated in their studies:

> I wanted to go see England. Our classes are mostly online, so we don't have that sense of community. The classwork itself was secondary to the experience of going over there. Walking around the community and seeing how the library impacts the community is important. It's harder to do that in the US—in the tight-knit urban settings, you get a better sense of it. (3)

Being there and experiencing travel was very important to that student. Another explained: "It really reinvigorated my interest in becoming a librarian at a time when classes were starting to wear me down" (2).

Two mentioned how the trip had expanded their conceptions of being a librarian. One said:

> There was an article we read…about the library's role evolving to take the place of the town square or the local pub…working in a public library, I have noticed that in some ways it has—like the children's play area—caregivers do meet and share stories. But I think the library could do more to facilitate interactions between patrons. (10)

Another mentioned the economic development project that we saw in South Africa:

> Seeing a library operating in a township changed my perspective regarding the power that libraries can have in helping to change their community. For example, the public library had a course that taught people in the community practical, marketable skills—they were learning to sew, create mosaics, etc., that they could sell at markets for an income. (5)

Another was slightly worried about the expanded role—what did it mean to be a librarian, anyway?

> I'm really curious about the idea of social workers as librarians, having social workers embedded in the library. We saw that in Leeds—the Autism Counts program, and also a dual degree in social work and librarianship. Are people going to be spread too thin? Would it give you a high degree of burnout? Or is it really great? (3)

Finally, one participant said that the civil unrest that we saw in England had changed the way that she thought about policing:

> I thought about the civil unrest that occurred there recently because of the Ferguson events…the looters there were using Blackberries to organize their events on a frequency that wasn't available or known to the authorities, but there are a lot of cameras in the U.K. and they caught them. (3)

Policing, identity, racial tensions, and communication were common factors in Ferguson and London; the experience of being in London during the riots gave her a different perspective on the events that happened here.

Discussion

Lindsey's study found that students who had participated in study abroad developed six types of values, which align to the findings in this study:

1. Opening the mind to new ways of thinking
2. Awareness and insight into one's own values and beliefs
3. Social awareness and challenges to societal values and beliefs
4. Appreciation of difference
5. Cultural sensitivity
6. Anti-discriminatory practice[20]

Correlations between the two studies demonstrate that the programs helped the students develop values for a human-centered, equality-based professional practice.

Social justice was a main theme of all three classes. Not everyone will discuss social justice using the same language. It is based on a person's preconceptions of injustice. For example, students from the Midwestern United States are quite familiar with injustices related to black/white race relations. Learning about prejudice against the Roma in the U.K. extended their conception of prejudice, and the effects of prejudice. There were similarities, though, when we discussed library programs for people with disabilities or the elderly. Coursework and readings covered inclusive library collections and services, and this was a topic of discussion in public library visits. National libraries and archives tended to reframe our conversations in terms of discussing what was presented, how culture was presented, and what that means in terms of expressions of value. The idea of "community" came up repeatedly. Walking the streets, seeing the neighborhoods, seeing how people get around and where they shop helped the students better understand many different kinds of communities.

---

20. Lindsey, "Study Abroad and Values Development."

During both trips to the U.K., librarians were focused on funding problems due to the austerity measures implemented by the government. Those discussions helped students understand different funding models for libraries and social services (especially those in the U.K.). At the same time, they gained a deeper understanding of the voluntary funding of libraries in the United States, and the strengths and weaknesses of the way our libraries are funded. For instance, we learned that in Britain, the Public Libraries Act of 1850 requires funding for books, but all other services are for-fee. This brought up discussions of charging for movies, for use of rooms, and other services. Some of the questions raised were: Should poor people only have access to books? Was it better to require funding for public libraries rather than having it tied to tax levies? Who benefits the most from different funding models?

There was a strong academic component to all of the classes; students spent time recording their observations and connecting them to their readings so they could demonstrate what they had learned. However, personal transformation is not as easily documented, and long-term effects could not be recorded until later. The following discussion will try to discern whether the classes had transformational effects on the students, and will also summarize any long-term effects of the courses on their career.

Transformation through Experiential Education: New Ways of Thinking

All experiential learning seeks to be transformative in some sense. The students who participated in these trips did report that they had transformative experiences. Several reported that they had learned to critique their own beliefs, or that some of their pre-trip beliefs about types of people were wrong or limited in scope. Several participants mentioned that their experiences helped them uncover false thinking about discrimination. Discovering one's prejudices and challenging the way that one thinks can be transformational.

Participants also reported being able to see the world, or their place in the world, in a new light. While most students had seen immigrants in their own country and they had witnessed poverty, seeing new immigrants and extreme poverty abroad helped them gain a new perspective on the issue, or to see people in their own country experiencing poverty in a new way. They described uncovering a new way of thinking about their own lives as a result. Several mentioned that they were able to see current events in a new way; for instance, one said that the social unrest in Ferguson, Missouri reminded her of the social unrest that happened during the London riots. These connections helped them develop a greater sense of empathy, because they were able to see the situation through another lens, as part of a greater social problem rather than simply a local one.

What Else Did They Learn?

Several students mentioned that they learned how powerful information was in people's lives. They gained a greater appreciation for what librarians do as they saw different models of librarianship. They saw librarians being very inclusive in planning services for their community and even expanding boundaries of what libraries are. Some of the libraries in London are branded as *Idea Stores*. Several students were disturbed by the commercialization of the library, but they loved the space—it was more of a community center than a traditional library, housing spaces such as a ballet studio, exercise rooms, massage services, and study areas as well as a library. Information was at the center, but it was a place that promoted community and health. Likewise, several students mentioned the Glasgow Women's Library, which sought (among other things) to give immigrants an informational home. It was a traditional library in one sense, but it provided education and language-learning in a setting that was intended to be safe for all women, including those who had experienced violence or social exclusion because of their gender or refugee status.

Many public libraries today have become places that invite their patrons to create, not only consume. The Leeds Public Library had sewing machines and a recording studio so that people in their community could develop these skills. In 2014, the students visited a public library that was doing the same thing: they let people from the community come in and use the space to teach art and sewing classes so that the women from the township could sell their crafts in the market. We do read about libraries doing this in the U.S., but perhaps because they saw them in a different environment and spent time talking to the people who were working on the project, participants were very receptive to noticing these low-tech makerspaces for community development.

Conclusions and Suggestions for Future Studies

This paper described interviews with ten participants from one school of information science who had attended study abroad programs focusing on social justice. This is obviously a small subset of students who are enrolled in one LIS program. They were a self-selected group who were motivated to study abroad. For the majority of the students, the social justice foundations of the course were of secondary importance to traveling abroad. Students did report that the course had long-term effects on them; some discussed identifying more strongly with oppressed people and others said that they saw the importance of inclusive library services. Furthermore, their experiences expanded their idea of what it meant to be an inclusive institution. Trips to different libraries gave them ideas for programming. They learned new terminology. Two said that it was valuable because of the camaraderie that they experienced, especially because most of their classes had previously been online.

These findings point towards important questions that future studies should address.

Not all students can study abroad; it is not practical. When so many programs are moving online, how can they foster the sense of connection that occurs during study abroad programs? Visiting libraries and talking to librarians, or experiential education, was very important to the students in this study. How can LIS programs replicate the experience of visiting different libraries in an online environment? Is it possible?

Simply learning skills is not sufficient. Should there be a set of best practices in LIS programs for fostering a sense of social justice and inclusiveness? Is there a platform that could be developed to help students work with librarians to share ideas and best practices?

There are certainly other questions that others might draw from this study. We are living in a time that is marked by changes in library services due to technologies and the purposes of the library as space. Distance learning is becoming a norm in LIS education. Demographic shifts (as always) are changing communities. Library educators, though, still have a fundamental set of values that have not changed. This challenges practitioners to maintain equitable services and equal access and remain engaged with their communities. This article explored one method in LIS education instituted to foster a greater sense of what equitable services might look like, and to inspire future practitioners and scholars.

Bibliography

American Library Association. "Code of Ethics of the American Library Association." Accessed January 22, 2008. http://www.ala.org/advocacy/proethics/codeofethics/codeethics.

BBC News. "England Riots: Maps and Timeline." August 15, 2011. http://www.bbc.com/news/uk-14436499.

Baker, Stephanie Alice. "The Mediated Crowd: New Social Media and New Forms of Rioting." *Sociological Research Online* 16, no. 4 (Nov. 30, 2011). http://www.socresonline.org.uk/16/4/21.html. doi: 10.5153/sro.2553.

Bargal, David. "Social Values in Social Work: A Developmental Model." *Journal of Sociology and Social Welfare* 8 (1981): 45-61.

Bossaller, Jenny S., Jillian Frasher, Sarah Norris, and Claire Presley Marks. "Learning about Social Justice through Experiential Learning Abroad." *Reference & User Services Quarterly* 54, no. 3 (2015): 6-11.

Bremer, Darlene. "Wanted: Global Workers." *International Educator* 15, no. 3 (2006): 40-45.

Grunebaum, Heidi. "Landscape, Complicity and Partitioned Zones at South Africa Forest and Lubya in Israel-Palestine." *Anthropology Southern Africa* 37, no. 3-4 (2014): 213-221.

Jones, Susan R., Heather T. Rowan-Kenyon, S. Mei-Yen Ireland, Elizabeth Niehaus, and Kristan Cilente Skendall. "The Meaning Students Make as Participants in Short-Term Immersion Programs." *Journal of College Student Development* 53, no. 2 (2012): 201-220.

Levy, Diane. "The Shock of the Strange, the Shock of the Familiar: Learning from Study Abroad." *Journal of the National Collegiate Honors Council* 1, no. 1 (Spring/Summer 2000): 75-83. http://digitalcommons.unl.edu/cgi/viewcontent.cgi?article=1192&context=nchcjournal.

Lindsey, Elizabeth W. "Study Abroad and Values Development in Social Work Students." *Journal of Social Work Education* 41, no. 2 (2005): 229-249.

Muddiman, Dave, Shiraz Durrani, Martin Dutch, Rebecca Linley, John Pateman, and John Vincent. "Open to All? The Public Library and Social Exclusion." (2000). http://eprints.rclis.org/6283/.

Murji, Karim, and Sarah Neal. "Riot: Race and Politics in the 2011 Disorders." *Sociological Research Online* 16, no. 4 (2011): 24. http://www.socresonline.org.uk/16/4/24.html.

National Association of Social Workers. "Code of Ethics." 1996. http://www.socialworkers.org/pubs/code/code.asp.

Perry, Lane, Lee Stoner, and Michael Tarrant. "More than a Vacation: Short-Term Study Abroad as a Critically Reflective, Transformative Learning Experience." *Creative Education* 3, no. 5 (2012): 679-683.

Tillman, Martin. "Employer Perspectives on International Education." *The SAGE Handbook of International Higher Education*, edited by Darla K. Deardorff, Hans de Wit, John Heyl, Tony Adams, 191-206. Thousand Oaks, CA: SAGE, 2012.

Chapter 9

Library Leadership-In-Training as Embedded Change Agents to Further Social Justice in Rural Communities: Teaching of Library Management Subjects in the ITRL and ITRL2

Bharat Mehra and Vandana Singh

Introduction

This chapter discusses the integration of social justice agendas in the teaching of library management subjects in courses that formed part of two externally-funded grant projects entitled "Rural Library Professionals as Change Agents in the 21st Century: Integrating Information Technology Competencies in the Southern and Central Appalachian Region" [Information Technology Rural Librarian Master's Scholarship Program Part I (ITRL) and Part II (ITRL2)], funded by the Institute of Museum and Library Services' Laura Bush 21st Century Librarian Program to the School of Information Sciences (SIS) at the University of Tennessee (UT).[1] The purpose of both was to recruit and train rural

1. Rural Library Professionals as Change Agents in the 21st Century: Integrating Information Technology Competencies in the Southern and Central Appalachian Region (ITRL) ($567,660). Institute of Museum and Library Services, *Laura Bush 21st Century Librarian Program*, October 2009-September 2012 (PI: B. Mehra; Co-PI: K. Black, V. Singh). No-cost one-year extension approved till end of September 2013. URL: http://www.sis.utk.edu/rural-librarianship. Rural Library Professionals as Change Agents in the 21st

library paraprofessionals working in the Southern and Central Appalachian (SCA) region to complete their master's degrees part-time in the synchronous distance education program at UT SIS.[2] Sixteen ITRL students completed their graduate education from June 2010-August 2012, combining work experience in regional libraries with a curriculum that focused on information technology (IT) and rural librarianship, while eleven ITRL2 students completed a similarly structured program from June 2013-August 2015.

The ITRL and ITRL2 extend past efforts in library and information science (LIS) education to train future library leadership as embedded change agents to work in traditionally underserved and/or under-represented areas (e.g., rural SCA regions) and develop IT and management

---

Century: Integrating Information Technology Competencies in the Southern and Central Appalachian Region (Part II) (ITRL2) ($478,258). Institute of Museum and Library Services, *Laura Bush 21st Century Librarian Program*, October 2012-September 2015 (PI: B. Mehra, Co-PI: V. Singh). No-cost one-year extension approved till end of September 2016. URL: http://www.sis.utk.edu/13-scholarships-available-itrl2.

2. The U. S. Bureau of the Census defines "rural" as areas with fewer than 2,500 people and open territory (Economic Research Service, "Measuring Rurality: What is Rural?" [Washington, DC: U. S. Department of Agriculture, 2007], last modified December 30, 2013, http://www.ers.usda.gov/Briefing/Rurality/WhatIsRural/). Richard Rathge defined the related concept of "nonmetropolitan" counties to describe the spread of housing developments outside the boundaries of metro areas that have no cities with as many as 50,000 residents ("Rural Demography," in *Encyclopedia of Rural America: The Land and the People*, ed. Gary A. Goreham [Santa Barbara, CA: ABC-CLIO, 1997], 627), in addition to being non-urbanized (Office of Management and Budget, "Part III Alternative Approaches to Defining Metropolitan and Nonmetropolitan Areas," *Federal Register* 63, 1998). The word "rural" in this chapter is used with regard to both meanings. The Appalachian Regional Commission (ARC) ("The New Appalachian Subregions and Their Development Strategies," *Appalachia: A Journal of the Appalachian Regional Commission* 8, (1974): 11-27), created as a United States federal-state partnership, identifies Central Appalachia to include: West Virginia's nine southernmost counties, eastern Kentucky, Virginia's southwestern tip, and the northwestern portion of Tennessee's Appalachian area (William S. Bush, "Bridging the Gap between Culture and Mathematics: The Appalachian Perspective," Occasional Paper [Athens, OH: Ohio University, Appalachian Collaborative Center for Learning, Assessment, and Instruction in Mathematics, 2003]), while southern Appalachia includes: most of Appalachian Virginia and Tennessee as well as the western Carolinas and the northern parts of Georgia, Alabama, and Mississippi.

competencies to further social justice and bring a life-anchoring perspective, both to their regional work environments and the surrounding communities. The metaphor of the collaborating "embedded librarians" has usually referred to the work of an academic librarian "embedding oneself at as many venues as possible" to "ensure that library staff, collections, and services are more fully integrated into all aspects of campus life," where embedding requires a direct and purposeful "integration of one group with another to the extent that the group seeking to integrate is experiencing and observing, as nearly as possible, the daily life of the primary group."[3] In the ITRL and ITRL2, the librarians-in-training are already embedded in the SCA regions, since they are living in these communities. In a departure from past LIS efforts to "help" people on the margins of society, they are "helping people help themselves" in a way that reflects a more progressive approach based on equality, social equity, respect, and community empowerment.[4] They also further asset mobilization in social justice by empowering members belonging to the communities where changes are being proposed to transform their own situations and circumstances.

Relevant Social Justice Constructs

With its deep historical roots, social justice as a concept and mode of practice critically informs, mobilizes, and promotes potential changes in those status quo conditions that perpetuate imbalances in distribution of power, resources, status or prestige, and/or other forms of perceived and/or real marginalization.[5] An important element of social justice that

---

3. Barbara Dewey, "The Embedded Librarian: Strategic Campus Collaborations," *Resource Sharing and Information Networks* 17, no. 1/2 (2004): 5-17.

4. Bharat Mehra, Kendra S. Albright, and Kevin Rioux, "A Practical Framework for Social Justice Research in the Information Professions," Short Paper at *Proceedings of the 69th Annual Meeting of the American Society for Information Science & Technology 2006: Information Realities: Shaping the Digital Future For All*, Austin, TX, November 3-8, 2006.

5. Bharat Mehra, Kevin Rioux, and Kendra S. Albright, "Social Justice in Library and Information Science," *Encyclopaedia of Library and Information Sciences*, (2009): 4820-4836.

makes it especially relevant in the contemporary context is the current attention to actions that might bring about progressive changes that are based on fairness, equality, equity, and/or justice;[6] additionally, the adoption and application of social justice in the twenty-first century calls for the delivery of tangible results and outcomes that can make a meaningful difference in everyday lives and experiences.[7] Jaeger, Taylor, and Gorham propose greater connections between human rights, social justice, and actions that libraries advocate, while mapping interrelationships between digital literacy, digital inclusion, and public policy.[8] Mehra and Rioux recognize a need for a more proactive library leadership that promotes critical social action and community-wide progressive changes.[9]

A positive step in social justice action is to acknowledge and take ownership of the reasons for various forms of gaps and disparities (including those which are information-related) that exist in different settings and contexts (e.g., economic, educational, health, social conditions, social status, etc.).[10] In the past, politicians, policy-makers, religious leaders, news media, managers, administrators, and others in positions of power have either failed to recognize (or overlooked) the actual disenfranchising realities that "cultures of difference" experienced,[11] and/or developed rhetoric, concepts, and buzzwords that merely served as a "lip

---

6. Bharat Mehra and Kevin Rioux, *Progressive Community Action: Critical Theory and Social Justice in Library and Information Science* (Sacramento, CA: Library Juice Press, 2016).

7. Bharat Mehra, "Introduction," *Library Trends: Social Justice in Library and Information Science & Services* 64, no. 2 (2015): 179-197.

8. Paul T. Jaeger, Natalie Greene Taylor, and Ursula Gorham, *Libraries, Human Rights, and Social Justice: Enabling Access and Promoting Inclusion* (Lanham, MD: Rowman & Littlefield, 2015).

9. Mehra and Rioux, *Progressive Community Action*, 2016.

10. Cheryl Holcomb-McCoy, *School Counseling to Close the Achievement Gap: A Social Justice Framework for Success* (Thousand Oaks, CA: Corwin, 2007).

11. Bharat Mehra, Cecelia Merkel, and Ann Peterson Bishop, "Internet for Empowerment of Minority and Marginalized Communities," *New Media & Society* 6, no. 5 (2004): 781-802; Tim Wise, *Colorblind: The Rise of Post-Racial Politics and the Retreat from Racial Equity* (San Francisco: City Lights Publishers, 2010).

service" without making a real difference to change those conditions;[12] even library professionals have been sometimes included in this group.[13]

Another relevant action-oriented strategy in social justice is to adopt methods and approaches that recognize the value, skills, knowledge, experiences, and other assets that multiple stakeholders (including the traditionally defined underserved) bring to specific contextual interactions.[14] In recent years, developing and facilitating collaborations and partnerships that build upon the unique capacities and capabilities of various individuals, groups, and communities in ways that empower them to bring about changes in their own conditions, has become a key methodological stance in social justice initiatives.[15] Such efforts allow "the granting of power—delegation of authority"[16] from a management perspective towards a decentralization of decision-making.[17] Further, from a psychological point of view, empowerment relates to an individual's ability for self-determination and power to cope with events, situations, and/or people.[18] Asset mobilization in community building taps into local assets and the strengths of individuals, the power of local associations and relationships, and the supportive functions of local

---

12. Pat Arneson, *Communicative Engagement and Social Liberation: Justice Will Be Made* (Madison, NJ: Fairleigh Dickinson University Press, 2013); Mehra, Bharat, Hope A. Olson, and Suzana Ahmad, "Integrating Diversity Across the LIS Curriculum: An Exploratory Study of Instructors' Perceptions and Practices Online," *IFLA Journal* 37, no. 1 (2011): 39-51.

13. John Pateman and John Vincent, *Public Libraries and Social Justice*, New ed. (Surrey, UK: Ashgate, 2010), 2.

14. James P. Baily, *Rethinking Poverty: Income, Assets, and the Catholic Social Justice Tradition* (Notre Dame, IN: University of Notre Dame Press, 2010).

15. Albert Bandura, *Social Foundations of Thought and Action: A Social-Cognitive View* (Englewood Cliffs, NJ: Prentice Hall, 1986).

16. W. Burke, "Leadership As Empowering Others," *Executive Power* (1986), 51.

17. J. A. Conger and R. N. Kanungo, "The Empowerment Process: Integrating Theory and Practice," *Academy of Management Review Journal* 13, no. 3 (1988): 471-482.

18. David C. McClelland, *Power: The Inner Experience* (New York: Irvington Press, 1975).

institutions as the essential strategy towards sustainable community development and community empowerment.[19]

In the past two decades, we have begun to see slow shifts in the LIS professions[20] towards embracing the social justice construct in a fuller manner that informs a praxis-based approach and achieves community-relevant outcomes in library service design, action research, service-learning, and other areas.[21] This lethargic pace is surprising considering that the LIS professions (especially librarianship) have historically had service-based (and user-centered) ethics, with emphasis on intellectual freedom, individual liberty, civic responsibility, policies of inclusiveness, and community information services.[22] Limitations in past LIS efforts to develop more equitable and asset-based relationships with underserved communities might have been a result of the cultural inheritance of a very specific socio-religious identification with the term "service" and its association with a missionary zeal to help people who were considered information-deficient, needy, helpless, incapable of improving their own lot, and "in need" of the LIS professional to help them improve their marginalized conditions.[23] Such misperceptions

---

19. John Kretzmann and John L. McKnight, *Building Communities from the Inside Out: A Path Toward Finding and Mobilizing a Community's Assets* (Chicago: ACTA Publications, 1993); Paul Schmitz, *Everyone Leads: Building Leadership from the Community Up* (San Francisco: Jossey-Bass Wiley, 2011).

20. Johannes J. Britz, "Making the Global Information Society Good: A Social Justice Perspective on the Ethical Dimensions of the Global Information Society," *Journal of the American Society for Information Science & Technology* 59, no. 7 (2008): 1171-1183; Randall Jimerson, "Archives for All: Professional Responsibility and Social Justice," American Archivist 70, no. 2 (2007): 252-281.

21. Bharat Mehra, "Guest Editor's Introduction," *Qualitative and Quantitative Methods in Libraries Journal* (2014a): 1-3.

22. Joan. C. Durrance, Karen E. Fisher, and Marian Bouch Hinton, *How Libraries and Librarians Help: A Guide to Identifying User-Centered Outcomes* (Chicago: ALA Editions, 2004).

23. Peter Day, "Sustainable Community Technology: The Symbiosis Between Community Technology And Community Research," *Journal of Community Informatics* 1, no. 2 (2005): 4-13; Bharat Mehra and Ramesh Srinivasan, "The Library-Community Convergence Framework for Community Action: Libraries as Catalysts of Social Change," *Libri: International Journal of Libraries and Information Services* 57, no. 3 (2007): 123-139.

reflect an inherent and underlying power imbalance that shaped the service-based practices and reeked of the LIS professions' internalized arrogance, condescending attitude, and superiority complex in its relation to external communities. The result was that LIS professionals have played a limited role in an inadequate capacity as social justice agents against the hegemonic forces of political constraint[24] and have succumbed to the pressures of the majority and mainstream conservative voices, curtailed as they were within an internally and externally restrictive socio-cultural context.[25] Common arguments that have served as barriers for the LIS professions truly taking a progressive position have included an adoption of a passive role and neutral stance[26] to promote social justice agendas. The lack of advocacy positions has been attributed to perceived threats, both to their financial existence and their professional security, in the forms of reduced tax-support for public libraries, slashes in funding for information researchers, and so on.

Social Justice and LIS Teaching

Within the constraints of limited professional conceptualization, values, practices, and expectations, LIS education (and educators) too has been sluggish in adopting social justice into its teaching and learning experiences. Kevin Rioux calls for LIS educators, researchers, and practitioners to consider social justice metatheory as part of their endeavor to "expand current curricula, theories, and practices," since "it offers new, robust ways of articulating the long-held altruistic stances of LIS to new generations of professionals, while reminding current researchers and

24. R. David Lankes, *The Atlas of New Librarianship* (Cambridge, MA: The MIT Press, 2011).

25. Kevin Rioux, Kendra Albright, and Bharat Mehra, "Conceptualizing Social Justice in the Information Sciences," Panel Abstract at the P*roceedings of the 70th Annual Meeting of the American Society for Information Science & Technology 2007: Joining Research and Practice: Social Computing and Information Science*, Milwaukee, WI, October 18-25, 2007.

26. Alison M. Lewis, "Introduction," in *Questioning Library Neutrality: Essays from Progressive Librarian*, ed. by Alison M. Lewis (Duluth, MN: Library Juice Press, 2008), 1-4.

practitioners of the field's roots."[27] Conspicuous by its absence over the years, the almost entire lack of social justice in LIS research and pedagogy has recently drawn some attention in educational circles. For example, the first author was the coordinating co-chair with Kendra S. Albright (and President Clara M. Chu) of the 2015 Association for Library and Information Science Education (ALISE) Annual Conference, that was themed "Mirrors and Windows: Reflections on Social Justice and Re-Imagining LIS Education" in Chicago, Illinois, January 27-30, 2015. Such gatherings may lead to ongoing discourse and dialogue concerning the possibilities of social justice shaping new directions in LIS teaching, research, and service activities, which are traditionally considered the three cornerstones of higher education in the United States.

The history of service-learning in LIS[28] is a reminder of efforts that involve students in social justice and community-based projects, whether in required, elective, or practicum courses, or via other strategies,[29] to achieve mutually agreed-upon goals and objectives that enhance student learning and help further community agendas.[30] In the twenty-first century, LIS programs and other academic settings in the United States are

27. Kevin Rioux, "Metatheory in Library and Information Science: A Nascent Social Justice Approach," *Journal of Education for Library and Information Science* 51, no. 1 (2010): 14.

28. N. J. Becker, "Service Learning In The Curriculum," *Journal of Education for Library and Information Science* 41, no. 4 (2000): 285-293.

29. Mary Alice Ball, "Practicums And Service Learning In LIS Education," *Journal of Education for Library Science* 49, no. 1 (2008): 70-82; Bharat Mehra, "A Road Map for Integrating Socially Relevant Research Projects into a Required Library and Information Science Course: From a Service Model to Community Engagement," in *Service Learning: Linking Library Education and Practice*, ed. Loriene Roy, Kelly Jensen, and Alex Hershey, 142-152 (Chicago: ALA Editions, 2009); Bharat Mehra and Robert J. Sandusky, "LIS Students as Community Partners in Elective Courses: Applying Community-Based Action Research to Meet the Needs of Underserved Populations," in *Service Learning: Linking Library Education and Practice*, ed. Loriene Roy, Kelly Jensen, and Alex Hershey, 153-168 (Chicago: ALA Editions, 2009).

30. Catherine Bloomquist, "Reflecting On Reflection As A Critical Component In Service Learning," *Journal of Education for Library and Information Science* 56, no. 2 (2015).

adopting the concept of community (or civic) engagement to re-define traditional notions of outreach and service that were earlier applied as add-ons to their teaching, instruction, and research agendas.[31] According to the Higher Education Network for Community Engagement:

> Increasingly, higher education institutions are intentionally connecting academic work to public purposes through extensive partnerships that involve faculty and students in active collaboration with communities. This idea of "community engagement" is renewing the civic mission of higher education and transforming academic culture in ways that are both exciting and challenging.[32]

Community engagement represents a positive and progressive approach to furthering social justice by building equitable partnerships between centers of higher learning and agencies external to the academic institutions.[33]

In the context of current community engagement models in LIS teaching, the following is a brief description of select noteworthy past, present, and future trends regarding intersections of social justice in the LIS curriculum. These are not mutually exclusive patterns. They are based on the authors' observances and experiences in participating in such efforts to further social justice in LIS education.

---

31. Benjamin R. Harris, "Communities As Necessity In Information Literacy Development: Challenging The Standards," *Journal of Academic Librarianship* 34, no. 3 (2008): 248-255; John S. Riddle, "Where's the Library in Service Learning? Models for Engaged Library Instruction." *Journal of Academic Librarianship* 29, no. 2 (2003): 71-81; Tracy M. Soska and Alice K. Johnson Butterfield. *University-Community Partnerships: Universities in Civic Engagement* (Binghamton, NY: Haworth Social Work Practice Press, 2004).

32. "Higher Education Network for Community Engagement," HENCE, last modified 2009, http://henceonline.org/, para. 1.

33. Bharat Mehra and William C. Robinson, "The Community Engagement Model in Library and Information Science Education: A Case Study of a Collection Development and Management Course," *Journal of Education for Library and Information Science* 50, no. 1 (2009): 15-38.

Courses on Social Justice-Related Topics and Subjects

Social justice as a topic has historically received select coverage in LIS courses with content on related concerns such as the digital divide, underserved populations and their use of information and communication technologies (ICT), specific minority communities (e.g., based on race/ethnicity, sexual orientation, etc.), qualitative methods (e.g., action research), and community informatics (or community information systems). This trend might have been one of the early strategies to integrate social justice content into LIS via use of social justice-related terminologies and subject matter, though a direct and explicit reference to using the term "social justice" was often missing. Theoretical, philosophical, and historical materials on related topics were covered and some LIS courses also had students involved in community-building and community development projects, even though the term "social justice" was not conspicuously used in a significant and consistent manner. This introduced an interdisciplinary connection to LIS, since many such courses were cross-listed with social work, sociology, women's studies, psychology, and other areas. Current courses on diversity and intercultural communication in LIS reflect a similar trend to integrate social justice-related vocabularies and to expand its scope of representation and relevance in twenty-first century contexts.

Specialized Social Justice Courses

Another mode of practice in LIS education has been the teaching of specialized courses that focus specifically on social justice and include content related to other issues and concerns, while keeping the topic of social justice in the foreground. The first author taught a course in 2004 entitled "Social Justice in the Information Professions" at the Graduate School of Library and Information Science at the University of Illinois at Urbana-Champaign (previously taught by Ann P. Bishop), which is an example of such a course. It is still in the UIUC GSLIS catalog, and is now taught by Nicole A. Cooke.[34] There are two graduate courses, entitled "Information and Human Rights" and "Inclusion, Literacy, and the Public Good," in the College of Information Studies at the University of Maryland, which have been taught by Paul T. Jaeger, Natalie Greene Taylor, and Ursula Gorham for many years, which integrate social justice and/or community information services, explicitly or implicitly. They respectively address "the social justice issues raised by information, and the ways in which information professionals can support the implementation" of human rights, and "explore the ways in which information professionals are educators and social service professionals who specialize in information, emphasizing the use of the Internet to teach and provide innovative services to community members."[35] These are but a couple of examples; there are others in many LIS programs that are now providing students with exposure to social justice-related principles and topics and their interactions with information-related subjects and concerns.

Social Justice Integrated throughout the Curriculum

One recent approach used in LIS education has been to integrate social justice content in the planning, conceptualization, and implementation of all types of courses that involve information-related work in its varied aspects, including information creation, organization, management, and dissemination processes. This allows for conceptual frameworks in LIS—such as human information behavior, information seeking and use, and social informatics— to combine with interdisciplinary approaches such as critical theory, feminist and cross-cultural studies, postcolonial literature, race and gender research, and the use of ICTs. Through this,

---

34. Nicole A. Cooke, Miriam E. Sweeney, and Safiya U. Noble, "Social Justice as Topic and Tool: An Attempt to Transform a LIS Curriculum and Culture," *Library Quarterly* 86, no. 1 (2016): 107-124.

35. Paul T. Jaeger, Natalie Greene Taylor, and Ursula Gorham, *Libraries, Human Rights, and Social Justice: Enabling Access and Promoting Inclusion* (Lanham, MD: Rowman & Littlefield, 2015), ix.

LIS graduates can be better prepared to empower disenfranchised communities to bring about changes in their sociocultural, sociopolitical, and socioeconomic circumstances (i.e., to achieve social justice) via their information-related work. The underlying notion is that every topic in information science (including information systems design, ICTs, social computing, information organization and representation, and information access and retrieval) has a conceptual and operational potential to integrate social justice based on the ability, willingness, and creativity of the instructor. The purpose of such efforts is to re-conceptualize the LIS professions and services in an expanded capacity in order to study and apply social justice while partnering with people on the margins of society. This has involved collaboration at different levels of engagement with various minorities, including international and cross-cultural communities that have been affected by diaspora, sexual and gender minorities, rural populations, low-income families, homebound and isolated people, and others, in order to represent their perspectives while shaping LIS and other community-based information services. This has increased the relevance and visibility of information-related work in its more varied functionalities and coverage than ever before.

Social Justice Specializations and Programs of Study

One of the new trends in efforts to integrate social justice into the LIS curriculum is emerging in a few LIS schools that are not focusing on one course per se, but are providing students with opportunities to fulfill their degree requirements by selecting from a range of relevant required courses, or to develop a customizable curriculum in a specialization or program of study related to social justice. The Certificate in Community Informatics (http://www.lis.illinois.edu/academics/degrees/specializations/ci) in the Graduate School of Library and Information Science at the University of Illinois at Urbana-Champaign is an example of a program that helps train future library professionals to participate in social justice and community development efforts and to promote progressive changes in society in various information-related roles and capacities.

The ITRL and ITRL2 are individual, one-time, externally funded programs that train library leaders to become change agents embedded within their local communities. This is accomplished by recognizing and extending their skills and competencies in order to potentially develop viable and sustainable solutions for critical problems in the rural SCA areas. They have contributed to the development of a public (rural) library pathway as an advising tool for faculty in the UT SIS to guide future library leaders who are interested in working on social justice advocacy in diverse public/rural environments. This also led to the "Rural Libraries Professional Program" being recognized by the UT's Office of Community Engagement and Outreach as one of the fifty exemplary partnerships that make a difference to represent authentic, two-way relationships between the campus and community that are based on mutuality and reciprocity.[36]

Library Management and Social Justice

Regarding library management in the twenty-first century, researchers have called for the development of innovative approaches to building skills in graduating librarians,[37] transforming libraries to "become new and exciting places,"[38] and recognizing that the "education of skilled information professionals must evolve to meet the many new challenges that have resulted from the complex, knowledge-based environment in which we live."[39] Unfortunately, some of the earlier library management

---

36. "Making a Difference: Rural Libraries Professional Program," IMPACT: A Weekly Newsletter from the Office of Community Engagement & Outreach, University of Tennessee, last updated 2015, http://engagement.utk.edu/blog/2015/rural-libraries-professional-program/; Nicole Stevens, "Information is Power in Rural Librarianship Program," University of Tennessee, last modified August 20, 2015, http://engagement.utk.edu/blog/2015/information-is-power/.

37. Michael Middleton, "Skills Expectations of Library Graduates," *New Library World* 104, no. 1184/1185 (2003): 42-56.

38. R. Missingham, "Library and Information Science," *Library Management* 27, no. 4/5 (2006): 259.

39. Sue Myburgh, "Education Directions for New Information

literature tends to focus disproportionately only on the development of new, technology-related competencies to:

- develop proficiency in hardware, software, and networking applications to further computer use;[40]
- deal with electronic means of communication and social computing;[41]
- work with digital resource management and electronic delivery systems;[42] or
- manage opportunities and challenges of available and emerging technologies to utilize the tools and applications as strategic and tactical resources.[43]

There is no doubt that technology has to be embraced wholeheartedly by the library world, since "people are looking online to access content when they want it, where they want it," and further, "they want to be able to share information with their social networks and interact with their content through ratings, reviews, and lists, similar to the way that they interact with content on social media websites and applications."[44] This has been compounded by ongoing and continuous "changes in the nature of the information environment brought about by technological developments and the increasing use of the Internet as a major

---

Professionals," *Australian Library Journal* 52, no. 3 (2003): 226.

40. Columbia University, "Online Survey of Academic Librarians: Executive Summary," Electronic Publishing Initiative at Columbia, last modified 2003, http://www.epic.columbia.edu/eval/find05/find05a.html.

41. Richard Biddiescombe, "The Development of Information Professionals' Needs for Internet and IT Skills: Experiences at the University of Birmingham," *Program* 35, no. 2 (2001): 157-166.

42. Karin Wikoff, *Electronic Resources Management in the Academic Library: A Professional Guide* (Santa Barbara, CA: Libraries Unlimited, 2011).

43. M. Khosrow-Pour, "Managing Information Technology in a Global Economy," *2001 IRMA Conference Proceedings* (Hershey, PA: Idea Group Publications, 2001).

44. Elyssa Kroski, *The Future of Libraries: Searching for the Deep End*, Kindle ed. (Seattle,WA: Amazon Digital Services, 2013).

source of information."[45] Though at the same time library management scholars have articulated cautionary warnings and insights regarding the tremendous costs of ignoring the non-technical "soft" skills needed to succeed in the newly emerging workplace: "Today, library administrators must simultaneously manage traditional information services and develop new services made possible by advances in technology."[46] There is a resurgence of the idea to represent the non-technology related "people-centric" skills (in addition to the technology competencies) in more recent library management literature.[47] This chapter recognizes the extensive research published on IT management in libraries and as a result focuses on select non-technology related library management subjects that were significant in the ITRL and ITRL2.

Additionally, a shift in the use of terminology associated with library management and library administration towards library leadership has also been discussed to reflect newer modes of understanding library organizational change in the twenty-first century.[48] This has included a need to integrate the teaching of sustainability into the LIS curriculum as the "development that meets the needs of the present without compromising the ability of future generations to meet their own needs"[49] in a management (or leadership) course. The purpose has been to prepare "graduates to deal with contemporary issues involved

---

45. Mohammed Nasser Al-Suqri and Ali Saif Al-Aufi, *Information Seeking Behavior and Technology Adoption: Theories and Trends* (Hershey, PA: IGI Global, 2015): xv.

46. James Castiglione, "Organizational Learning and Transformational Leadership in the Library Environment," *Library Management* 27, no. 4/5 (2006): 293.

47. Gary W. White, "Business Information Courses In LIS Programs: A Content Analysis," *Journal of Business & Finance Librarianship* 10, no. 2 (2005): 3-15.

48. Donald E. Riggs, "The Crisis and Opportunities in Library Leadership," *Journal of Library Administration* 32, no. 3 (2001): 5-17; Peter Edward Sidorko, "Fostering Innovation in Library Management and Leadership: The University of Hong Kong Libraries Leadership Institute," *Library Management* 28, no. 1/2 (2007): 5-16.

49. World Commission on Environment and Development, *Our Common Future* (Oxford, UK: Oxford University Press, 1987): 43.

in managing information organizations,"[50] while introducing them to its social dimension, which relates to social justice through issues ranging from "how working conditions affect quality life to policies that direct available human services" and library efforts to increase information literacy, amongst other aspects. Library management subjects thus have a significant potential to include social justice-related content in training future library leadership as change agents to make a positive impact in local and regional settings. According to Page and Scott, a change agent "facilitates a 'bedding down' of new practices within organizations," develops skills that they learn and pass on to others based on "changed work practices…and changes in their relationship to colleagues," and an "ability to take understandings arising in one 'world'" to use them to instigate change in another.[51]

The Rural Context of the ITRL and ITRL2

The authors have discussed the rural context of the SCA regions and explored the role of LIS education in the ITRL and ITRL2 programs as grounds to further social justice elsewhere. For example, Mehra, Black, and Lee[52] presented an initial discovery of rural librarians' perspectives about their need for professional library education. Mehra, Black, Singh, and Nolt[53] discussed the types of collaborations that were significant

---

50. Deborah Turner, "Sustainability and Library Management Education," *Journal of Sustainability Education* 7, (December, 2014), retrieved November 27, 2015, http://www.jsedimensions.org/wordpress/wp-content/uploads/2014/12/Turner-JSE-Vol-7-Dec20141.pdf, #The Social Dimension.

51 Margaret Page and Anne Scott, "Change Agency and Women's Learning: New Practices in Community Informatics," *Information, Communication and Society* 4, no. 4 (2001): 530, 548.

52. Bharat Mehra, Kimberly Black, and Shu-Yueh Lee, "Perspectives of East Tennessee's Rural Public Librarians about the Need for Professional Library Education: An Exploratory Study," *Journal of Education for Library and Information Science* 51, no. 3 (2010): 142-157.

53. Bharat Mehra, Kimberly Black, Vandana Singh, and Jenna Nolt, "Collaboration between LIS Education and Rural Libraries in the Southern and Central Appalachia: Improving Librarian Technology Literacy and Management Training," *Journal of Education for Library and Information Science* 52, no. 3

for developing social justice outcomes and results in the ITRL program. Mehra, Black, Singh, and Nolt[54] identified rural librarians' expectations regarding the role of LIS education to make social, cultural, political, economic, management, and technological changes possible and to improve the conditions they experienced in their communities. Mehra, Black, Singh, and Nolt[55] highlighted the use of mixed data collection methods in the ITRL to gather feedback from a range of rural stakeholders to achieve social justice agendas. Mehra, et al.,[56] summarized computer-enabled innovations in the ITRL to promote positive changes in rural environments. Mehra[57] applied social justice lessons learned in the ITRL and ITRL2 in working with rural library paraprofessionals to gain insights from them regarding the provision of services to other underserved populations (e.g., children with special needs). Mehra et al.[58] presented the ITRL and ITRL2 experiences in the language and constructs of social justice (social justice elements and social justice

---

(2011): 238-247.

54. Bharat Mehra, Kimberly Black, Vandana Singh, and Jenna Nolt, "What is the Value of LIS Education? A Qualitative Analysis of the Perspectives of Rural Librarians in Southern and Central Appalachia," *Journal of Education for Library and Information Science* 52, no. 4 (2011): 265-278.

55. Bharat Mehra, Kimberly Black, Vandana Singh, and Jenna Nolt, "Mapping the Education of Rural Librarians' Technology Literacy and Management Training: Use of Mixed Data Collection Methods in the ITRL Program," *Proceedings of the World Library and Information Congress: 77th International Federation of Library Associations and Institutions General Conference and Assembly*, San Juan, PR, August 13-18, 2011.

56. Bharat Mehra et al., "Computer-Enabled Innovations in the Information Technology Rural Librarian Master's Scholarship Program: Bridging Rural Digital Divides in the Southern and Central Appalachia," *Proceedings of the 57th Indian Library Association Annual Conference*, Mangalore, Karnatakaja, February 23-25, 2012.

57. Bharat Mehra, "Perspectives of Rural Librarians about the Information Behaviors of Children with Special Needs in the Southern and Central Appalachian Region: An Exploratory Study to Develop User-Centered Services," in *New Directions in Children and Adolescents' Information Behavior Research*, ed. Dania Bilal and Jamshid Beheshti (Bingley, UK: Emerald, 2014), 157-189.

58. Bharat Mehra et al., "The Social Justice Framework in the Information Technology Rural Librarian Master's Scholarship Program: Bridging the Rural Digital Divides," *Qualitative and Quantitative Methods in Libraries Journal*, Special Issue 2014, (2014): 5-11.

philosophies) to contextualize them in terms of bridging rural digital divides. Mehra and Singh[59] discussed the recruitment and retention strategies in the ITRL and ITRL2 that were significant in terms of reaching out to the rural areas of the SCA region. Using multiple strategies (in person, telephone, online, etc.) was useful for connecting with people located in remote rural areas in order to identify and recruit library paraprofessionals who had the interest, motivation, need, and dedication to pursue a master's degree, while developing IT and rural management products that would be used in their local and regional environments. Retention efforts in the ITRL and ITRL2 programs involved working with each student one-on-one to guide, mentor, advise, and mobilize them to achieve the best outcomes in their rural library and community. Mehra and Singh[60] provided a glimpse of critical reflections on the ITRL and ITRL2 programs to expand social justice outcomes into an international context of rural communities in Pakistan. Further discussion asked LIS professionals to pay critical attention to who is "left out" in the margins of society and what actions could be taken to improve the life circumstances and experiences of the "marginalized" within a particular political, economic, social, cultural, and environmental setting.[61]

Common across the past documentation of the ITRL and ITRL2 experiences has been descriptions of the rural communities and library conditions in the SCA regions that traditionally have had a debilitating impact on the information world of the library professional working in these settings. Some of the challenges included information poverty and

---

59. Bharat Mehra and Vandana Singh, "Recruitment and Retention in the Information Technology Rural Librarian Master's Scholarship Program (Part I and Part II): Implications of Social Justice in the Southern and Central Appalachian Region," *Qualitative and Quantitative Methods in Libraries Journal* (2014): 13-22.

60. Bharat Mehra and Vandana Singh, "A Social Justice Framework to Further Community Engagement in Pakistan's Information Management and Library Professions," *Proceedings of the International Conference on Information Management & Libraries*, Lahore, Pakistan, November 10-13, 2015.

61. Bharat Mehra, "Guest Editorial: What is the Value of Social Justice in Pakistan's Library and Information Science Professions?" *Pakistan Journal of Information Management and Libraries* 15, no. 1 (2014): i-ii.

unemployment, low levels of information literacy and educational attainment, a lack of access and use of information resources and technology, and other unique cultural and environmental factors.[62] The role of LIS education in addressing some of these traditionally experienced issues has also been discussed. What is missing in past research descriptions about the ITRL and ITRL2 is a detailed analysis of the information technology and management courses and a mapping of the course objectives for developing very specific and tangible technology literacy and management products. This gap is addressed in a more recent effort to analyze IT courses in the ITRL and ITRL2 from a community informatics perspective.[63] This chapter focuses on management subjects and their application for developing library leadership as social justice change agents, with an understanding that the IT courses serve as a

---

62. American Library Association, Office for Literacy and Outreach Services, "The Small But Powerful Guide to Winning Big Support for your Rural Library," American Library Association, last modified 2011, http://www.ala.org/offices/olos/toolkits/rural; Appalachian Regional Commission, "Moving Appalachia Forward: Appalachian Regional Commission Strategic Plan 2011-2016," The Commission, last modified November 2010, http://www.arc.gov/images/ newsroom/publications/sp/ARCStrategicPlan 2011-2016.pdf; Genevieve Bardwell et al., "Feasibility of Adolescents to Conduct Community-Based Participatory Research on Obesity and Diabetes in Rural Appalachia," *Clinical and Translational Science* 2, no. 5 (2009): 340-349; Dan A. Black, Mark Mather, and Seth G. Sanders, "Standards of Living in Appalachia, 1960 To 2000," Appalachian Regional Commission, last modified 2007, http://www.arc.gov/images/reports/2007/standardsliving/Standards_Living_Appalachia.pdf; Ronald D. Eller, *Uneven Ground: Appalachia Since 1945* (Lexington, KY: The University Press of Kentucky, 2008); S. Herzenberg, M. Price, and H. Wial, *Displacement in Appalachia and the Non-Appalachian United States, 1993-2003: Findings Based on Five Displaced Workers Surveys* (Washington, DC: Appalachian Regional Commission, 2005); Bharat Mehra, Vandana Singh, and Hannah Parris, "Open Source Software Collaborations in Tennessee's Regional Library System: An Exploratory Study," *Library Review* 59, no. 9 (2010): 690-701; C. Eugene Scruggs, *The View From Brindley Mountain: A Memoir Of The Rural South* (North Charleston, SC: BookSurge Publishing, 2010); Linda Spatig et al., "Like a Mountain: Performing Collaborative Research eith Youth in Rural Appalachia," *Collaborative Anthropologies* 2 (2009): 177-212.

63. Bharat Mehra, Vandana Singh, Natasha Hollenbach, and Robert P. Partee II "Rural Librarians as Change Agents in the 21st Century. Applying Community Informatics in the Southern and Central Appalachian Region to Further ICT Literacy Training" in *Rural and Small Public Libraries: Challenges and Opportunities,* ed. Brian Real (Bingley, UK: Emerald Group, forthcoming).

complementary module which may be integrated into the management course stream.

The Library Leadership-In-Training Cohorts

The twenty-seven students/paraprofessionals in the ITRL and ITRL2 library leadership-in-training cohorts were chosen from fifty-one applicants, coming from seven states and twenty-four cities, representing five academic libraries (college and university libraries), sixteen public libraries (including individual libraries, county libraries, and regional library systems), four school library/county schools, one special library, and one community agency. **Table 1** summarizes this information as well as some demographic information including their sex, race/ethnicity, and work titles.

The ITRL and ITRL2 library leadership-in-training cohorts shared their perspectives and reflections on the impact that their rural community and library had in shaping their educational journey. They also reflected on the kinds of deliverables they believed were needed to help their regions improve their limited conditions. This feedback was provided as part of their application materials and as they began their master's degree in the form of an in-depth narrative of their strategic academic plan. The plan was regularly referred to throughout the duration of their program of study to insure that there was on-going tracking in terms of continuous compatibility, tailoring of deliverables to context, and in situ relevance of the course work they were developing.

The Management Stream in the ITRL and ITRL2

As change agents, the ITRL and ITRL2 library leadership-in-training cohorts applied technology literacy and management competencies to develop services/products in their courses that were directly applicable and tailored to their SCA contexts. The select IT deliverables for rural libraries included: (1) technology infrastructure planning and analysis, (2) web design, development, and usability,

Demographic Category	Category with Number of Students	
Sex	female = 24	male = 3
Race/Ethnicity	White/Caucasian = 27	
Work Geography [State (City/Town)]	Georgia (Dahlonega-1) = 1	
	Kentucky (Barbourville-1, Harlan-1) = 2	
	Maryland (Hancock-1) = 1	
	North Carolina (Marshall-1) = 1	
	Tennessee (Athens-1, Bristol-1, Cleveland-1, East Ridge-1, Harrogate-1, Kingsport-2, Knoxville-3, Lebanon-1, Maryville-1, Mountain City-1, New Market-1, Sevierville-2) = 16	
	Virginia (Big Stone Gap-1, Glade Spring-1, Goshen-1, Lexington-1, Wise-1) = 5	
	West Virginia (Harmon-1) = 1	
Type of Library	community agency = 1	
	community college library = 3	
	county public library = 7	
	county school system = 2	
	elementary school library = 2	
	public library = 9	
	research and education center = 1	
	university library = 2	
Work Title	acquisitions assistant = 1	
	branch manager/program specialist = 5	
	business and program administrator = 1	
	circulation assistant = 1	
	children's library assistant = 1	
	children's room assistant = 1	
	director = 3	
	elementary school teacher/media team member = 1	
	emerging technologies specialist = 1	
	information specialist = 1	
	instructional supervisor for materials and supplies = 1	
	library assistant = 1	
	library media specialist = 1	
	library technical assistant = 1	
	library technologist = 1	
	public services coordinator = 1	
	resource center/education coordinator = 1	
	reference librarian = 1	
	systems business coordinator = 1	
	technology software support specialist = 1	
	youth program specialist = 1	

Table 1: The demographic characteristics of the ITRL and ITRL2 library leadership-in-training cohorts.

(3) database design and implementation, (4) building digital library and web portals, (5) establishing hardware and software networking, and (6) creating Library 2.0 tools. Select management outcomes included: (1) service evaluation in rural libraries, (2) management of a rural library program for adults and children/young adults, (3) reader's advisory, and (4) grant writing and collection development. Through the entire experience, student training was geared towards transforming participating paraprofessional librarians into change agents who learned to introduce new approaches, strategies, practices, and specific deliverables that responded to and addressed the twenty-first century challenges facing their SCA libraries and communities.

ITRL and ITRL2 had structured course requirements in that the students were expected to take the three required courses (providing knowledge of the core functions of the profession, namely, information environments, information representation and organization, and information access and retrieval), six courses focusing on IT, and five courses on rural library management and services.[64] The curricula, however, also integrated an element of flexibility and were individually-tailored based on the: (1) sequence and choice of courses, which could be changed on a limited basis after considering an individual student's interests, skills, specific career path, and prior experiences, as well as the schedule of course offerings during various semesters, (2) analysis of students' experiences in their unique SCA environments, since the course deliverables and tangible products that students individually developed in their course assignments were expected to be useful and applied to the local contexts of their rural libraries and communities, and (3) a requirement for students in the school media track that stipulated a partially altered list of courses based on the state certification requirements.

---

64. Bharat Mehra and Vandana Singh, "Recruitment and Retention in the Information Technology Rural Librarian Master's Scholarship Program (Part I and Part II): Implications of Social Justice in the Southern and Central Appalachian Region," *Qualitative and Quantitative Methods in Libraries Journal* (2014): 13-22.

Discussion of Social Justice Themes

The ITRL and ITRL2 library leadership-in-training cohorts were able to develop tangible products on non-technological management subjects and topics in their management-related courses that were directly relevant and usable in their rural SCA libraries and communities. These were implemented and delivered via technological solutions in these courses, in addition to the products developed by students in their technology courses. The students served as bridges in the sense-making of the rural contexts,[65] owing to their embeddedness as paraprofessionals working in those settings and living in those areas.[66] The following is a select analysis of the characteristics that were significant in nurturing the ITRL and ITRL2 librarian-in-training individuals in the process of transformation to future library leadership that could serve as social justice agents of change in the SCA regions. Specific examples of the select products that students developed in their management-related courses help explicate the connections between program expectations, implementation, and potential social justice outcomes.

Knowers of Experienced Realities at Ground-Zero

In order for the ITRL and ITRL2 library leadership-in-training cohorts to transform into change agents that potentially would be able to generate extended impact in the rural SCA regions, an essential program requirement was for them to be working as paraprofessionals in the areas where the change was desired. The assumption was that, by knowing and experiencing these (workplace and living) realities firsthand, they would be able to identify and transform local conditions in terms of the "whys, whats, and hows." The embeddedness in the SCA rural library was valuable, for example, in the INSC 559 (Grant Development

65. Brenda Dervin, Lois Foreman-Wernet, and Eric Lauterbach, *Sense-Making Methodology Reader: Selected Writings of Brenda Dervin* (New York: Hampton Press, 2003).

66. Michelle M. Kazmer, "Community-Embedded Learning," *Library Quarterly* 75, no. 2 (2005): 190-212.

for Information Professionals) course where the librarians-in-training cohorts applied strategic relationship management to a partnership with a community agency and developed a complete information-related grant proposal to meet the unmet needs in the particular information setting.

Access to Contextual Information to Support Decision-Making

As a result of working at the agencies where the changes were proposed and implemented, the ITRL and ITRL2 library leadership-in-training cohorts were able to gain access to essential information (including the staff, users, and policies) that served as evidence to support the rationale and justify the tangible products they delivered in their courses. For example, access to contextual information about the SCA rural library and patron communities helped the ITRL and ITRL2 librarians-in-training cohorts develop a thorough process-oriented, user-centered assessment and evaluation of a selected library service in the INSC 554 (Public Library Management & Services) course. They also participated in website development efforts to represent their process stages and product.[67] The components in task analysis included: assessment of agency, identification of users, service to evaluate, case-study analysis, development of an evaluation action plan, collection and analysis of data, and user-centered assessment.

Development of Tailored Useful Solutions Relevant to Context

Further, being experiential knowers developing products based on solid evidence contributed to meaningful and relevant solutions that had potential to generate maximum impact in the local and regional rural workplace and surrounding SCA communities. For example, based on individual students' career paths, select students registered for the INSC 560 (Development and Management of Collections) course in which they participated in a collection development project that included completion of various activities in the process by partnering with a

67. See the websites ITRL and ITRL2 librarians-in-training cohorts developed in the INSC 554 (Public Library Management and Services) course at ITRL-554 URL: http://athena.cci.utk.edu/bmehra/IS554/IS554Sp11/IS554ProjectDescription.html; ITRL2-554 URL: http://zeus.cci.utk.edu/INSC554Sp14/.

community agency. They also participated in website development efforts to represent their process stages and product.[68] The components in task analysis included: the parent organization, development rationale, community analysis, policy statement, information agency variables, collection evaluation, and selection and promotion.

Role of Embedded Practitioner-Mentors and Partners[69]

Each ITRL and ITRL2 library leadership-in-training student was assigned a student-or-program identified practitioner-mentor who provided key information to her/his mentee to nurture professional etiquette and professional culturalization skills, introduce them to relevant professional social networks, and help them respond to unique politics and other challenges that they encountered in the workplace. Additionally, the role of the ITRL and ITRL2 partners was significant in shaping the overall trajectory of the two programs, providing information support perspectives to think through select details in operationalization and implementation, and serving in a mentoring capacity to select students working in their regions. For example, Kaurri C. Williams-Cockfield, Director of the Blount County Public Library, a program partner, taught the INSC 590 (Rural Library Management) course where ITRL and ITRL2 librarians-in-training learned management of rural libraries in community context as a business entity. As instructor of the course, Williams-Cockfield focused on external and internal analysis of libraries and their communities for long range planning, and students developed a detailed public relations portfolio with an implementation timeline for

---

68. See similar kinds of collection development projects select ITRL and ITRL2 librarians-in-training cohorts worked in the INSC 560 (Development and Management of Collections) course at URL: http://heramac.cci.utk.edu/INSC560Fa14.

69. The Blount County Public Library in Maryville, Tennessee; Clinch-Powell Regional Library (now the Clinch River Regional Library) in Clinton, Tennessee; Fort Loudoun Regional Library (now the Ocoee River Regional Library) in Athens, Tennessee; Nolichucky Regional Library in Morristown, Tennessee; Sevier County Public Library System in Sevierville, Tennessee; and the Watauga Regional Library (now the Holston River Regional Library) in Johnson City, Tennessee, and their leadership personnel served as project partners.

their library or library system. The course provided direct application of theoretical management techniques in an actual rural library setting of the student's choosing.

Role of Non-Embedded Educators

In addition to serving as instructors of select courses in the ITRL and ITRL2, the role of other educators was to provide advising and help the librarians-in-training cohorts make connections between information-related concepts, theories, frameworks, approaches, and methods and practice-based realities. These educators also helped their advisees make connections between course content and products they could develop that would be relevant and useful in their work environments. Exposure to professional standards and research processes and expectations were also key areas of advising. The educators also helped students cope with, and work around, unforeseen circumstances (e.g., illness, family issues, personal matters) while ensuring that administrative and educational expectations continued to be met.

Role of Online Synchronous and Asynchronous Technologies

The use of cutting-edge synchronous distance technology (e.g., Saba Centra 7.6 and Blackboard Collaborate software) at UT SIS allowed for real-time online interactions between the instructor and the students, and from student to student, in the virtual classroom via voice-over-Internet protocols that made the interactive experience a truly unique offering in this part of the country.[70] Without the real-time synchronous learning technologies it would have been impossible to achieve the same level of engagement in the classroom, and the same value of the course experiences and course products developed. In addition, other online tools (e.g., Blackboard) and e-mail served as asynchronous communication and information-sharing tools. For example, in the INSC 574 (Resources and Services of Adults) course, thanks to guidance delivered via the online synchronous and asynchronous tools, the ITRL

---

70. Rajendra Kumbhar, "Use Of E-Learning In Library And Information Science Education," *DESIDOC Journal of Education in Library and Information Science Education* 29, no. 1 (2009): 37-41.

and ITRL2 librarians-in-training cohorts were able to develop websites[71] to represent one of the following work projects: (1) Reader's Advisory Analysis: Included genre selection, analysis of listserv discussions, subject or genre appeal analysis and current awareness, survey professionals, appeal elements analysis and annotations, and browsing analysis, or (2) Management of Adult Materials and Services: Included "What business are we in?", lifestyle analysis, website analysis, program evaluation, and facility design. In addition, students completed a "Memorable Fiction Analysis" and "Library 2.0 Analysis."

Individual, Library, and Community Empowerment

The entire ITRL and ITRL2 learning process contributed to individual library leadership-in-training students acquiring professional skills and personal abilities to become change agents in their SCA communities. Their rural libraries workplaces were empowered by receiving trained personnel who could serve as role models in making change in the local and regional communities. Along the way, the ITRL and ITRL2 librarians-in-training cohorts developed information-related skills and deliverables that were directly usable and useful in their SCA communities. For example, in the INSC 571 (Resources and Services for Children) course, students conducted a critical survey of books and related materials for children and applied analysis of the development of genres to their library settings. It also included evaluation, selection, and utilization of works for school and public libraries. The course work included picture book analysis, nonfiction and fiction critique, professional blog analysis, genre clinic management, and book talk presentation. In the INSC 572 (Resources and Services for Young Adults) course, students read, viewed, and wrote detailed analyses of materials suitable for adolescents in leisure time and classroom activities; applied criteria for selecting books, magazines, movies, videos, and related materials;

71. See the websites ITRL and ITRL2 librarians-in-training cohorts developed in the INSC 574 (Resources and Services for Adults) course at ITRL-574 URL: http://zeus.cci.utk.edu/IS574Sp12/; ITRL2-574 URL: http://heramac.cci.utk.edu/INSC574Sp15/.

and developed materials and resources for specific research projects. Students conducted work on teen magazine and teen movies analysis, collection development, book talk presentations, genre-specific reading responses, and challenged/banned book analysis. These activities were directly related to their rural SCA settings and contributed to empowerment at individual, library, and community levels.

Actions and Products (Leadership) Towards Future Change

Future efforts will be made to engage with the ITRL and ITRL2 library professionals (now graduates) and document their perspectives about the impact they are making in their libraries and communities as a result of their learning process and educational experiences. Efforts will also be made to document the actions they have taken and the products they have developed after graduating from the two programs. For example, select professionals attended a panel program titled "Insights of Rural Librarians on Making an Impact in their Appalachian Communities," presented during the 2016 Tennessee Library Association Annual Conference. During the panel, the participating rural librarians discussed the challenges, opportunities, outcomes, and impact they are making in their SCA workplaces and rural communities since they graduated in August 2015.

The above discussion provided a brief overview of the kinds of management-related experiences, skills, outcomes, and course products ITRL and ITRL2 librarians-in-training developed to make a positive difference, not only in their own career paths, but also in their rural libraries and SCA communities. Lessons and insights from ITRL and ITRL2 provide meaningful implications for the teaching of social justice in LIS. Social justice efforts in the LIS classroom should: (1) provide librarians-in-training cohorts with opportunities to experience embeddedness in a particular work setting where they might be proposing information-related changes, (2) nurture students to learn how to serve as bridges in the sense-making of particular information-related contexts by collaborating with entities from those settings as equals who know the realities and circumstances that the students are not aware of, (3) evaluate their course work and educational program experience in terms of actual products and deliverables they create that are not agency/system-centric but community-centric in terms of potential outcomes and impacts in the local setting, (4) propose information-related products (e.g., information services, collections, programs, etc.) that empower people and underserved communities while also developing their own skills and competencies to challenge and change imbalanced power dynamics, and (5) adopt information-related practices that do not perpetuate inequities, but rather help people help themselves as change agents while following the principle of "teaching people how to fish" instead of fishing for others.

Conclusion

The concept of embedded change agents for social justice in LIS education needs to be recognized as an important strategy to further actions that potentially promote progressive transformations in future librarians and the libraries and communities of which they are a part. In addition to teaching technology courses, non-technological focused management-related subjects need to continue to receive attention. Moreover, these areas are not isolated, and there needs to be ongoing integration of technology skills and competencies in the delivery of "soft" management subjects and topics. The ITRL and the ITRL2 provided grounds to explore and test some of these issues and assumptions, while nurturing embedded change agents in rural SCA communities to further social justice and potentially promote community-wide transformations in this traditionally underserved geographic setting. Future possibilities are endless, and we have to build on past efforts to continue mobilizing people in these areas to develop progressive leadership. This will create positive advancements via information-related work in the SCA rural libraries and beyond towards prospective growth and economic development.

Acknowledgements

The authors appreciate the recently funded IMLS grants that supported the ITRL and ITRL2 programs reported in this chapter. We also gratefully acknowledge the generous contributions of various rural library stakeholders and collaborators. A special word of thanks to Robert P. Partee II for his attention to details in creating the bibliography.

Bibliography

Al-Suqri, Mohammed Nasser, and Ali Saif Al-Aufi. *Information Seeking Behavior and Technology Adoption: Theories and Trends*. Hershey, PA: IGI Global, 2015.

American Library Association, Office for Literacy and Outreach Services. "The Small but Powerful Guide to Winning Big Support for Your Rural Library." *American Library Association*. Last modified 2011. http://www.ala.org/offices/olos/toolkits/rural.

Appalachian Regional Commission. "The New Appalachian Subregions and Their Development Strategies." *Appalachia: A Journal of the Appalachian Regional Commission* 8 (1974): 11-27.

Appalachian Regional Commission. "Moving Appalachia Forward: Appalachian Regional Commission Strategic Plan 2011-2016." *Appalachian Regional Commission*. Last modified November 2010. http://www.arc.gov/images/ newsroom/publications/sp/ARCStrategicPlan2011-2016.pdf.

Arneson, Pat. *Communicative Engagement and Social Liberation: Justice Will Be Made*. Madison, NJ: Fairleigh Dickinson University Press, 2013.

Bailey, James P. *Rethinking Poverty: Income, Assets, and the Catholic Social Justice Tradition* Notre Dame, IN: University of Notre Dame Press, 2010.

Ball, Mary Alice. "Practicums and Service Learning in LIS Education." *Journal of Education for Library Science* 49, no. 1 (2008): 70-82.

Bandura, Albert. *Social Foundations of Thought and Action: A Social-Cognitive View.* Englewood Cliffs, NJ: Prentice Hall, 1986.

Bardwell, Genevieve, Cathy Morton, Ann Chester, Petr Pancoska, Shama Buch, Alfred Cecchetti, Marcella Vecchio, Stephanie Paulsen, Stephen Groark, and Robert A. Branch. "Feasibility of Adolescents to Conduct Community-Based Participatory Research on Obesity and Diabetes in Rural Appalachia." *Clinical and Translational Science* 2, no. 5 (2009): 340-349.

Becker, N. J. "Service Learning in the Curriculum." *Journal of Education for Library and Information Science* 41, no. 4 (2000): 285-293.

Biddiscombe, Richard. "The Development of Information Professionals' Needs for Internet and IT Skills: Experiences at the University of Birmingham." *Program* 35, no. 2 (2001): 157-166.

Black, Dan A., Mark Mather, and Seth G. Sanders. "Standards of Living in Appalachia, 1960 to 2000." *Appalachian Regional Commission.* Last modified 2007. http://www.arc.gov/images/reports/2007/standardsliving/Standards_ Living_Appalachia.pdf. Accessed on November 8, 2008.

Bloomquist, Catherine. "Reflecting on Reflection as a Critical Component in Service Learning." *Journal of Education for Library and Information Science* 56, no. 2 (2015).

Britz, Johannes J. "Making the Global Information Society Good: A Social Justice Perspective on the Ethical Dimensions of the Global Information Society." *Journal of the American Society for Information Science & Technology* 59, no. 7 (2008): 1171-1183.

Burke, W. "Leadership as Empowering Others." *Executive Power* (1986): 51-77.

Bush, William S. "Bridging the Gap between Culture and Mathematics: The Appalachian Perspective." Occasional Paper. Athens, OH: Ohio University, Appalachian Collaborative Center for Learning, Assessment, and Instruction in Mathematics, 2003.

Castiglione, James. "Organizational Learning and Transformational Leadership in the Library Environment." *Library Management* 27, no. 4/5 (2006): 289-299.

Columbia University. "Online Survey of Academic Librarians: Executive Summary." *Electronic Publishing Initiative at Columbia.* Last modified, 2003, http://www.epic.columbia.edu/eval/find05/find05a.html.

Conger, J. A., and R.N. Kanungo. "The Empowerment Process: Integrating Theory and Practice." *Academy of Management Review Journal* 13, no. 3 (1988): 471-482.

Cooke, Nicole A, Miriam E. Sweeney, and Safiya U. Noble. "Social Justice as Topic and Tool: An Attempt to Transform a LIS Curriculum and Culture." *Library Quarterly* 86, no. 1 (2016): 107-124.

Day, Peter. "Sustainable Community Technology: The Symbiosis between Community Technology and Community Research." *Journal of Community Informatics* 1, no. 2 (2005): 4-13.

Dervin, Brenda, Lois Foreman-Wernet, and Eric Lauterbach. *Sense-Making Methodology Reader: Selected Writings of Brenda Dervin.* New York: Hampton Press, 2003.

Dewey, Barbara. "The Embedded Librarian: Strategic Campus Collaborations." *Resource Sharing and Information Networks* 17, vol. 1/2 (2004): 5-17.

Durrance, Joan C., Karen E. Fisher, and Marian Bouch Hinton. *How Libraries and Librarians Help: A Guide to Identifying User-Centered Outcomes.* Chicago: ALA Editions, 2004.

Economic Research Service. "Measuring Rurality: What is Rural?" Washington, DC: U. S. Department of Agriculture. Last modified December 30, 2013. http://www.ers.usda.gov/Briefing/Rurality/WhatIsRural/.

Harris, Benjamin R. "Communities as Necessity in Information Literacy Development: Challenging the Standards." *Journal of Academic Librarianship* 34, no. 3 (2008): 248-255.

Henderson, Everett. "Service Trends in U.S. Public Libraries, 1997-2007." Research Brief No. 1. Washington, DC: Institute of Museum and Library Services, 2009.

Herzenberg, S., M. Price, and H. Wial. *Displacement in Appalachia and the Non-Appalachian United States, 1993-2003: Findings Based on Five Displaced Workers Surveys*. Washington, DC: Appalachian Regional Commission, 2005. Retrieved November 2, 2008, from http://www.arc.gov/images/reports/2006/displacement/pdf/displacement_arc.pdf

"Higher Education Network for Community Engagement." *HENCE*. Last modified 2009. http://henceonline.org/.

Holcomb-Eller, Ronald D. *Uneven Ground: Appalachia Since 1945*. Lexington, KY: The University Press of Kentucky, 2008.

Holcomb-McCoy, Cheryl. *School Counseling to Close the Achievement Gap: A Social Justice Framework for Success*. Thousand Oaks, CA: Corwin, 2007.

Jaeger, Paul T., Natalie Greene Taylor, and Ursula Gorham. *Libraries, Human Rights, and Social Justice: Enabling Access and Promoting Inclusion*. Lanham: Rowman & Littlefield, 2015.

Jimerson, Randall. "Archives for All: Professional Responsibility and Social Justice." *American Archivist* 70, no. 2 (2007): 252-281.

Kazmer, Michelle M. "Community-Embedded Learning." *Library Quarterly* 75, no. 2 (2005): 190-212.

Khosrow-Pour, M. "Managing Information Technology in a Global Economy." *2001 IRMA Conference Proceedings*. Hershey, PA: Idea Group Publications, 2001.

Kretzmann, John, and John L. McKnight. *Building Communities from the Inside Out: A Path Toward Finding and Mobilizing a Community's Assets*. Chicago: ACTA Publications, 1993.

Kroski, Elyssa. *The Future of Libraries: Searching for the Deep End.* Kindle ed. Seattle: Amazon Digital Services, 2013.

Kumbhar, Rajendra. "Use of E-Learning in Library and Information Science Education." *DESIDOC Journal of Education in Library and Information Science Education* 29, no. 1 (2009): 37-41.

Lankes, R. David. *The Atlas of New Librarianship*, Cambridge, MA: The MIT Press, 2011.

Lewis, Alison M. "Introduction." In *Questioning Library Neutrality: Essays from Progressive Librarian*, edited by Alison M. Lewis, 1-4. Duluth, MN: Library Juice Press, 2008.

"Making a Difference: Rural Libraries Professional Program." *IMPACT: A Weekly Newsletter from the Office of Community Engagement & Outreach*. University of Tennessee. Last updated 2015. http://engagement.utk.edu/blog/2015/rural-libraries-professional-program/.

McClelland, David C. Power: *The Inner Experience*. New York: Irvington Press, 1975.

Mehra, Bharat. "Guest Editorial: What is the Value of Social Justice in Pakistan's Library and Information Science Professions?" *Pakistan Journal of Information Management and Libraries* 15, no. 1 (2014): i-ii.

———. "Guest Editor's Introduction." *Qualitative and Quantitative Methods in Libraries Journal* (2014): 1-3.

———. "Introduction." *Library Trends: Social Justice in Library and Information Science & Services* 64, no. 2 (2015): 179-197.

———. "Perspectives of Rural Librarians about the Information Behaviors of Children with Special Needs in the Southern and Central Appalachian Region: An Exploratory Study to Develop User-Centered Services." In *New Directions in Children and Adolescents' Information Behavior Research*, edited by Dania Bilal and Jamshid Beheshti, 157-189. Bingley, UK: Emerald, 2014.

———. "A Road Map for Integrating Socially Relevant Research Projects into a Required Library and Information Science Course: From a Service Model to Community Engagement." In *Service Learning: Linking Library Education and Practice*, edited by Loriene Roy, Kelly Jensen, and Alex Hershey, 142-152. Chicago: ALA Editions, 2009.

Mehra, Bharat, Kendra S. Albright, and Kevin Rioux. "A Practical Framework for Social Justice Research in the Information Professions." Short Paper at *Proceedings of the 69th Annual Meeting of the American Society for Information Science & Technology 2006: Information Realities: Shaping the Digital Future For All*, Austin, TX, November 3-8, 2006.

Mehra, Bharat, Kimberly Black, and Shu-Yueh Lee. "Perspectives of East Tennessee's Rural Public Librarians about the Need for Professional Library Education: An Exploratory Study." *Journal of Education for Library and Information Science* 51, no. 3 (2010): 142-157.

Mehra, Bharat, Kimberly Black, Vandana Singh, and Jenna Nolt. "Collaboration between LIS Education and Rural Libraries in the Southern and Central Appalachia: Improving Librarian Technology Literacy and Management Training." *Journal of Education for Library and Information Science* 52, no. 3 (2011a): 238-247.

———. "Mapping the Education of Rural Librarians' Technology Literacy and Management Training: Use of Mixed Data Collection Methods in the ITRL Program." *Proceedings of the World Library and Information Congress*. 77th International Federation of Library Associations and Institutions General Conference and Assembly, San Juan, PR, August 13-18, 2011.

———. "What is the Value of LIS Education? A Qualitative Analysis of the Perspectives of Rural Librarians in Southern and Central Appalachia." *Journal of Education for Library and Information Science* 52, no. 4 (2011b): 265-278.

Mehra, Bharat, Kimberly Black, Vandana Singh, Jenna Nolt, Kaurri C. Williams, Susan Simmons, and Nancy Renfro. "Computer-Enabled Innovations in the Information Technology Rural Librarian Master's Scholarship Program: Bridging Rural Digital Divides in the Southern and Central Appalachia." *Proceedings of the 57th Indian Library Association Annual Conference*, Mangalore, Karnataka, February 23-25, 2012.

———. "The Social Justice Framework in the Information Technology Rural Librarian Master's Scholarship Program: Bridging the Rural Digital Divides." *Qualitative and Quantitative Methods in Libraries Journal* Special Issue 2014, (2014): 5-11.

Mehra, Bharat, Cecelia Merkel, and Ann Peterson Bishop. "Internet for Empowerment of Minority and Marginalized Communities." *New Media & Society* 6, no. 5 (2014): 781-802.

Mehra, Bharat, Hope A. Olson, and Suzana Ahmad. "Integrating Diversity Across the LIS Curriculum: An Exploratory Study of Instructors' Perceptions and Practices Online." *International Federation of Library Associations and Institutions (IFLA) Journal* 37, no. 1 (2011): 39-51.

Mehra, Bharat and Kevin Rioux. *Progressive Community Action: Critical Theory and Social Justice in Library and Information Science*. Sacramento, CA: Library Juice Press, 2016.

Mehra, Bharat, Kevin Rioux, and Kendra S. Albright. "Social Justice in Library and Information Science." *Encyclopaedia of Library and Information Sciences* (2009): 4820-4836.

Mehra, Bharat, and William C. Robinson. "The Community Engagement Model in Library and Information Science Education: A Case Study of a Collection Development and Management Course." *Journal of Education for Library and Information Science* 50, no. 1 (2009): 15-38.

Mehra, Bharat, and Robert J. Sandusky. "LIS Students as Community Partners in Elective Courses: Applying Community-Based Action Research to Meet the Needs of Underserved Populations." In *Service Learning: Linking Library Education and Practice*, edited by Loriene Roy, Kelly Jensen, and Alex Hershey, 153-168. Chicago: ALA Editions, 2009.

Mehra, Bharat and Vandana Singh. "Recruitment and Retention in the Information Technology Rural Librarian Master's Scholarship Program (Part I and Part II): Implications of Social Justice in the Southern and Central Appalachian Region." *Qualitative and Quantitative Methods in Libraries Journal (2014): 13-22.*

———. "A Social Justice Framework to Further Community Engagement in Pakistan's Information Management and Library Professions." *Proceedings of the International Conference on Information Management & Libraries*, Lahore, Pakistan, November 10-13, 2015.

Mehra, Bharat, Vandana Singh, Natasha Hollenbach and Robert P. Partee II. "Rural Librarians as Change Agents in the 21st Century: Applying Community Informatics in the Southern and Central Appalachian Region to Further ICT Literacy Training." In *Rural and Small Public Libraries: Challenges and Opportunities,* edited by Brian Real. Advances in Librarianship. Bingley, UK: Emerald, forthcoming. .

Mehra, Bharat, Vandana Singh, and Hannah Parris. "Open Source Software Collaborations In Tennessee's Regional Library System: An Exploratory Study." *Library Review* 59, no. 9 (2010): 690-701.

Mehra, Bharat, and Ramesh Srinivasan. "The Library-Community Convergence Framework for Community Action: Libraries as Catalysts of Social Change." *Libri: International Journal of Libraries and Information Services* 57, no. 3 (2007): 123-139.

Mellon, Constance A., and Diane D. Kester. "Online Library Education Programs: Implications for Rural Students." *Journal of Education for Library and Information Science* 45, no. 3 (2004): 210-220.

Middleton, Michael. "Skills Expectations of Library Graduates." *New Library World* 104, no. 1184/1185 (2003): 42-56.

Missingham, R. "Library and Information Science." *Library Management* 27, no. 4/5 (2006): 257-268.

Myburgh, Sue. "Education Directions for New Information Professionals." *Australian Library Journal* 52, no. 3 (2003): 213-227.

Office of Management and Budget. "Part III Alternative Approaches to Defining Metropolitan and Nonmetropolitan Areas." *Federal Register* 63, (1998).

Page, Margaret, and Anne Scott. "Change Agency and Women's Learning New Practices in Community Informatics." *Information, Communication and Society* 4, no. 4 (2001): 528-559.

Pateman, John, and John Vincent. *Public Libraries and Social Justice.* New edition. Surrey, UK: Ashgate, 2010.

Rathge, Richard W. "Rural Demography." In *Encyclopedia of Rural America: The Land and the People*, edited by Gary A. Goreham, 626–629. Santa Barbara, CA: ABC-CLIO, 1997.

Riddle, John S. "Where's the Library in Service Learning? Models for Engaged Library Instruction." *Journal of Academic Librarianship* 29, no. 2 (2003): 71-81.

Riggs, Donald E. "The Crisis and Opportunities in Library Leadership." *Journal of Library Administration* 32, no. 3 (2001): 5-17.

Rioux, Kevin. "Metatheory in Library and Information Science: A Nascent Social Justice Approach." *Journal of Education for Library and Information Science* 51, no. 1 (2010): 9-17.

Rioux, Kevin, Kendra Albright, and Bharat Mehra. "Conceptualizing Social Justice in the Information Sciences." Panel Abstract at the *Proceedings of the 70th Annual Meeting of the American Society for Information Science & Technology 2007: Joining Research and Practice: Social Computing and Information Science*, edited by Bharat Mehra and Kevin Rioux. Milwaukee, WI, October 18-25, 2007.

Rioux, Kevin, and Bharat Mehra. "Introduction." In *Progressive Community Action: Critical Theory and Social Justice in Library and Information Science*, edited by Bharat Mehra and Kevin Rioux, 1-10. Sacramento, CA: Library Juice Press, 2016.

Schmitz, Paul. *Everyone Leads: Building Leadership from the Community Up.* San Francisco: Jossey-Bass Wiley, 2011.

Schlak, Timothy M. "Social Capital and Leadership in Academic Libraries: The Broader Exchange around 'Buy In.'" *Library Management* 36, no. 6/7 (2015): 394-407.

Scruggs, C. Eugene. *The View from Brindley Mountain: A Memoir Of The Rural South.* North Charleston, SC: Book Surge Publishing, 2010.

Sidorko, Peter Edward. "Fostering Innovation in Library Management and Leadership: The University of Hong Kong Libraries Leadership Institute." *Library Management* 28, no. 1/2 (2007): 5-16.

Soska, Tracy M., and Alice K. Johnson Butterfield. *University-Community Partnerships: Universities in Civic Engagement.* Binghamton, NY: Haworth Social Work Practice Press, 2004.

Spatig, Linda, Shelley Gaines, Ric MacDowell, Betty Sias, Leanne Olson, and Cassi Adkins. "Like a Mountain: Performing Collaborative Research with Youth in Rural Appalachia." *Collaborative Anthropologies* no. 2 (2009): 177-212.

Stevens, Nicole. "Information is Power in Rural Librarianship Program." *University of Tennessee.* Last modified August 20, 2015. http://engagement.utk.edu/blog/2015/information-is-power/.

Turner, Deborah. "Sustainability and Library Management Education." *Journal of Sustainability Education* 7 (2014). Retrieved November 27, 2015 from http://www.jsedimensions.org/wordpress/wp-content/uploads/2014/12/Turner-JSE-Vol-7-Dec20141.pdf.

Wikoff, Karin. *Electronic Resources Management in the Academic Library: A Professional Guide*. Santa Barbara, CA: Libraries Unlimited, 2011.

White, Gary W. "Business Information Courses in LIS Programs: A Content Analysis." *Journal of Business & Finance Librarianship* 10, no. 2 (2005): 3-15.

Wise, Tim. *Colorblind: The Rise of Post-Racial Politics and the Retreat from Racial Equity*. San Francisco: City Lights Publishers, 2010.

World Commission on Environment and Development. *Our Common Future: Report of the World Commission on Environment and Development*. Oxford, UK: Oxford University Press, 1987.

Afterword

A Call to Action

Nicole A. Cooke and Miriam E. Sweeney

> The academy is not paradise. But learning is a place where paradise can be created. The classroom with all its limitations remains a location of possibility. In that field of possibility we have the opportunity to labour for freedom, to demand of ourselves and our comrades, an openness of mind and heart that allows us to face reality even as we collectively imagine ways to move beyond boundaries, to transgress. This is education as the practice of freedom.[1]

The LIS classroom should be a venue where educators and students engage in the practice of freedom. Embracing and embodying social justice is part of achieving this goal. This volume was a natural extension of the ALISE workshop where so many wonderful ideas were exchanged and participants left inspired and with hopes of revitalizing their classrooms (see appendices). It is hoped that the reflections of each chapter contributor will continue to inspire other teachers (in LIS and beyond) to rethink their approach to teaching and harnessing the power of a social justice framework.

But what's next? What comes after inspiration? This volume is meant to help centralize attention and participation in LIS and share ideas, but it certainly isn't all inclusive of all of the powerful teaching and learning

1. bell hooks, *Teaching to Transgress* (Routledge, 1994), 207.

that occurs in classrooms. Looking forward, how can educators continue to share resources, support one another, and garner institutional support to continue this important work? How do we sustain this momentum and effect long-lasting change? The editors and contributors would love to continue the conversation with you, the readers, and strategize about how to make innovative long-term and sustainable change in LIS pedagogy and research. We challenge you to join us in conducting research and writing about these issues; we challenge you to present this work at conferences; we challenge you to *host* conferences, and other professional development opportunities, about social justice; we challenge you to find innovative ways to promote social justice on social media platforms (i.e., Facebook, Twitter, and Pinterest); and finally, we challenge you to be the instructors our students need.

Bibliography

hooks, bell. *Teaching to Transgress*. Routledge, 1994.

Appendix A: ALISE Academy 2015 Resources List

Lesson Planning Resources / General Information about Teaching Social Justice:

Teaching Social Justice in Higher Ed

- Inside Higher Ed
  https://www.insidehighered.com/views/2008/03/03/tritton

Teaching Social Justice

- Race, Class, Gender, Sexuality and Other Social Justice Issues for the Classroom
  http://teachingsocialjustice.com/
- Lesson Plan: Social-Issue Documentaries - A Mini Curriculum
  http://www.pbs.org/pov/behindthelens/lessonplan2.php
- Resource List for Including Social Justice Issues in Curricula
  School of Education, Health and Human Behavior
  http://www.siue.edu/education/diversity/resources.shtml
- Teaching with Zines
  Barnard Zine Library
  https://zines.barnard.edu/teachingwithzines
- Raising Awareness of Class Privilege Among Students
  Diversity & Democracy: Civic Learning for Shared Futures
  http://www.diversityweb.org/DiversityDemocracy/vol11no3/gilbert.cfm

K-12 Resources That Could Be Useful and/or Provide Resources:

- Media Construction of Social Justice - A Digital Media Literacy Curriculum
  Project Look Sharp
  http://www.projectlooksharp.org/?action=justice
- Seattle University's Poverty Education Center Lesson Plans
  https://www.seattleu.edu/poverty-education/resources/lesson-plans/
- Using Photographs to Teach Social Justice
  Teaching Tolerance: A Project of the Southern Poverty Law Center
  http://www.tolerance.org/lesson/using-photographs-teach-social-justice
- Resource List for Including Social Justice Issues in Curricula
  School of Education, Health and Human Behavior
  http://www.siue.edu/education/diversity/resources.shtml
- Diversity Toolkit: Social Justice
  National Education Association (NEA)
  http://www.nea.org/tools/30414.htm
- Teachers for Social Justice (TSJ Chicago)
  Curriculum Resources
  http://www.teachersforjustice.org/search/label/all%20curriculum

Specific Examples:

- Exploring Social Justice Through Music
  http://www.psychologicalscience.org/index.php/publications/observer/2013/april-13/exploring-social-justice-through-music.html
- Social Justice Quilt
  http://www.quiltindex.org/lessonplan.php?kid=3-98-2C

- The Storytelling Project Curriculum - Racial Equity Tools- www.racialequitytools.org/resourcefiles/stp_curriculum.pdf
- The Death of Michael Brown: Teaching About Ferguson- Teaching & Learning with the New York Times http://learning.blogs.nytimes.com/2014/09/03/the-death-of-michael-brown-teaching-about-ferguson/?_r=0

Suggested Readings / Syllabi Material

Accardi, Maria T., Emily Drabinski, and Alana Kumbier, eds. *Critical Library Instruction: Theories & Methods.* Duluth, MN: Library Juice Press, 2010.

Allard, Suzie, Bharat Mehra, and M. Asim Qayyum. "Intercultural Leadership Toolkit for Librarians: Building Awareness to Effectively Serve Diverse Multicultural Populations." *Education Libraries 30*, no. 1 (2007): 5-12.

Ayers, William C., Jean Anne Hunt, and Therese Quinn, eds. *Teaching for Social Justice.* New York: Teachers College Press, 1998.

Bell, Lee A. *Storytelling for Social Justice: Connecting Narrative and the Arts in Antiracist Teaching.* New York: Routledge, 2010.

Bornstein, David, and Susan Davis. *Social Entrepreneurship: What Everyone Needs to Know.* New York: Oxford University Press, 2010.

Brown, Kathleen M. "Leadership for Social Justice and Equity: Weaving a Transformative Framework and Pedagogy." *Educational Administration Quarterly* 40, no. 1 (2004): 77–108.

Burnett, Gary, and Paul T. Jaeger. "Small Worlds, Lifeworlds, and Information: The Ramifications Of The Information Behavior Of Social Groups In Public Policy And The Public Sphere." *Information Research* 13, no. 2 (2008). Retrieved from http://www.information.net/ir/13-2/paper346.html.

Burns, C. Sean. "Social Justice and An Information Democracy with Free and Open Software."*Information, Society, and Justice* 4, no.2 (December 2011): 19-28.

Charbonneau, Deborah H., ed. *Global Information Inequalities: Bridging the Information Gap.* Oxford, UK: Chandos, 2008.

Cooke, Nicole A. Creating Opportunities for Empathy and Cultural Competence in the LIS Curriculum. *SRRT Newsletter* 187 (2014): 1.

Cooke, Nicole A., Miriam E. Sweeney, and Safiya Umoja Noble. "Social Justice as Topic and Tool: An Attempt to Transform an LIS Curriculum and Culture." *The Library Quarterly* 86, no. 1 (2016): 107-124.

Durrani, Shiraz. *Information & Liberation: Writings On The Politics Of Information & Librarianship.* Duluth, MN: Library Juice Press, 2008.

Elturk, Ghada. "Diversity and Cultural Competency." *Colorado Libraries* 29, no. 4 (Winter 2003): 5-7.

Gilliland, Anne. "Neutrality, Social Justice and the Obligations of Archival Education and Educators in the Twenty-First Century." *Archival Science* 11, no. 3-4 (2011): 193–209.

Graham, Patterson T. "Public Librarians and the Civil Rights Movement: Alabama, 1955-1965." *Library Quarterly* (2001): 1-27.

Gregory, Lua and Shana Higgins, eds. *Information Literacy and Social Justice: Radical Professional Praxis.* Duluth, MN: Library Juice Press, 2014.

Hersberger, Julie. "Chatman's Information Poverty." In *Theories of Information Behavior*, edited by Karen E. Fisher, Sanda Erdelez, and Lynne Mckechnie, 75-78. Medford, NJ: Information Today, 2005.

Honma, Todd. "Trippin' Over the Color Line: The Invisibility of Race in Library and Information Studies." *InterActions: UCLA Journal of Education and Information Studies* 1, no. 2 (2005). http://escholarship.org/uc/item/4nj0w1mp.

Kagan, Alfred. "IFLA and Social Responsibility: A Core Value of Librarianship." In *Libraries, National Security, Freedom of Information Laws and Social Responsibilities: IFLA/FAIFE World Report*, edited by Susanne Seidelin and Stuart Hamilton, 33-43. Copenhagen: IFLA/FAIFE, 2005.

Kendall, Frances E. "Talking About Race: What If They Call Me a Racist?" In *Understanding White Privilege: Creating Pathways to Authentic Relationships Across Race*, 138-155. New York: Routledge, 2013.

Lewis, Alison, ed. *Questioning Library Neutrality: Essays From Progressive Librarian.* Duluth, MN: Library Juice Press, 2008.

Lievrouw, Leah A. & Sharon E. Farb. "Information and Equity." *Annual Review of Information Science & Technology* 37 (2003): 499-540.

McIntosh, Peggy. "White Privilege: Unpacking the Invisible Knapsack. In *Race, Class, and Gender in the United States: An Integrated Study*, 165-169. New York: Worth Publishers, 1988. http://www.library.wisc.edu/EDVRC/docs/public/pdfs/LIReadings/InvisibleKnapsack.pdf.

McIntosh, Peggy. "White Privilege and Male Privilege." In *Privilege: A Reader*, 147-160. New York: Westview Press, 2003. http://www.iub.edu/~tchsotl/part2/McIntosh%20White%20Privilege.pdf.

Mehra, Bharat, Kendra S. Albright, and Kevin Rioux. "A Practical Framework for Social Justice Research in the Information Professions." *Proceedings of the American Society for Information Science and Technology* 43, no. 1 (2006): 1-10.

Morrone, Melissa, ed. *Informed Agitation: Library and Information Skills in Social Justice.* Duluth, MN: Library Juice Press, 2014.

Morrone, Melissa, & Friedman, Lia. "Radical Reference: Socially Responsible Librarianship Collaborating with Community." *The Reference Librarian* 50, no. 4 (2009): 371-396.

Noble, Safiya Umoja. "Teaching Trayvon: Race, Media, and the Politics of Spectacle." *Black Scholar* 44, no. 1 (2014): 12–29.

Overall, Patricia M. "Cultural Competence: A Conceptual Framework for Library and Information Science Professionals." *Library Quarterly* 79 (2009): 175-204.

Pateman, John, and John Vincent. *Public Libraries and Social Justice.* Farnham, UK: Ashgate Publishing, 2012.

Pawley, Christine. Unequal Legacies: Race and Multiculturalism in the LIS Curriculum. *Library Quarterly* 76, no. 2 (2006): 149–168.

Peterson, Lorna. "The Definition of Diversity: Two Views. A More Specific Definition." *Journal of Library Administration* 27, no. 1-2 (1999): 17-26.

Pyati, Ajit. "Understanding the Role of Public Libraries in (Inter)-National Development: Lessons from India." *Canadian Journal of Information and Library Science* 33, no. 3/4 (2009): 233-253.

Rioux, Kevin. "Metatheory in Library and Information Science: A Nascent Social Justice Approach." *Journal of Education for Library and Information Science* (2010): 9-17.

Rioux, Kevin. "Teaching Social Justice in an Information Literacy Course: An Action Research Case Study." *Catholic Library World* 83, no. 3 (March 2013): 191-197.

Rioux, Kevin, Bharat Mehra, and Kendra S. Albright. "Conceptualizing Social Justice in the Information Sciences." *Proceedings of the American Society for Information Science and Technology* 44, no. 1 (2007): 1-4.

Samek, Toni. *Librarianship and Human Rights: A Twenty-First Century Guide.* Oxford, UK: Chandos, 2007.

United Nations. *Universal Declaration of Human Rights.* 1945. http://www.un.org/en/documents/udhr/index.shtml#atop.

Shaughnessy, Kathryn. *Course Guide: Global Development and Social Justice.* 2014. http://campusguides.stjohns.edu/content.php?pid=13036&sid=389747.

Venturella, Karen M. ed. *Poor People and Library Services.* Jefferson, NC: McFarland, 1998.

Zeman, Marybeth. *Tales of a Jailhouse Librarian: Challenging the Juvenile Justice System One Book at a Time.* Brooklyn, NY: Vinegar Hill Press, 2014.

Appendix B: ALISE Academy 2015 Session Outcomes

Part three of the ALISE Academy included DIY roundtables where workshop participants discussed a list of questions provided by the moderators. The groups were asked to compile and hand in notes based on their discussions. Each of the questions asked is listed below along with the compiled participant notes. These were distributed amongst the workshop participants as part of a set of post-workshop outcomes.

What are some of the challenges that you face in your institutions/ classrooms in terms of teaching social justice topics?

- Dealing with students, administration, and other faculty
- Students not seeing social justice as being important
- Students taking diversity/social justice courses because they are required, not because they are interested in the topic
- Instructors feeling like they need to "hide" the social justice in the curriculum
- Negative course evaluations related to students' discomfort in engaging with challenging material
- Difficulty in engaging students from wide range of backgrounds, particularly students from relatively conservative or sheltered backgrounds
- Administrative barriers encountered when trying to develop new courses and electives
- ALA not requiring social justice classes for accreditation
- Fatigue, feeling spread too thin, emotionally taxing nature of constantly facing all of these challenges. PARTICULARLY for faculty of color.
- Making social justice relevant to technology courses

What do you find most personally challenging as an instructor when engaging with social justice topics and strategies?

- Fear of "getting it wrong" in terms of making missteps in teaching challenging material
- Excavating personal prejudice/bias/privilege; being reflective of your own identity
- Balancing sharing, self-disclosure, and knowing how personal to get with students
- How to define social justice
- Evaluating student progress when some students may be openly resistant the course materials

What are some strategies for teaching social justice that have worked for you?

- Welcoming dissent and debate
- Underscoring that is ok to be uncomfortable with the class topics
- Use writing exercises that invite reflection and connection among the students' experience and class topics
- Invite guest speakers who can bring different perspectives, voices, experiences
- Not speaking for communities you do not belong to
- Relating social justice to professional practice and institutions
- Teaching the history of the profession within national and regional history, prioritizing social justice context
- Sharing teaching philosophies with colleagues and also students in the classroom
- Have students take turns facilitating discussions as a part of being ethical engaged in class discussions
- Distributing the labor of leading challenging discussions as ethical practice
- Encouraging students to "break the argument", or asking "what could go wrong" as ways to challenge students to try on different perspectives
- Differentiating between "safe spaces" and "brave spaces"

How might we, collectively, help social justice become a priority in LIS education?

- By not being afraid of the term "social justice", or of naming racism, specifically in class discussions
- Focus on institutionalizing social justice (as part of curricula and in other ways)
- Continue to make social justice a priority for ALISE
- Develop/strengthen infrastructure
- Create core social justice courses, rather than always leaving those courses on the margins
- Collaborate broadly, interdisciplinarily, not just inside of LIS
- In individual institutions: work to connect with LIS alum, and get students on board
- Create concrete, long-lasting entrenched relationships with community groups and stakeholder in these conversations
- Get on editorial boards to help shift publishing to be more inclusive of social justice oriented research/topics/epistemologies
- What kinds of topics related to social justice in LIS would you like to see prioritized at future conference workshops?
- Terminology and personal identity (ontology for social justice as identity),
- Longitudinal views on impact and effect of courses on social justice in the profession
- More discussion on distinction and tensions between "liberty vs. justice"
- More theory building
- Case studies of exemplar institutions
- Workshops on teaching social justice focused on: assessing effects of courses; developing syllabi with a social justice emphasis; methodologies; assessing and transforming student attitudes
- Building strategies for collaborating with practitioners

About the Contributors

Jenny S. Bossaller is an assistant professor at the School of Information Science & Learning Technologies (SISLT) at the University of Missouri–Columbia (MU). Her teaching and research interests broadly encompass constraints on information flow, including aspects of information policy and history, and related social and technological phenomena. She has focused especially on the public's access to information and has co-developed a public library leadership program (PuLL) that emphasizes community and professional immersion. She has published articles in venues such as *Library Quarterly*, *IFLA Journal*, *Mediatropes*, *Journal of Library Administration*, *Journal of Documentation*, *Progressive Librarian*, and *Reference and User Services Quarterly* (RUSQ). Jenny is Member at Large of the ALA's Library History Round Table and serves on the editorial board of RUSQ. Prior to her work in academia, she held positions in public and academic library settings, and as a software analyst for the MOBIUS Consortium Office. She has degrees in Archaeology (B.A.), Library Science (M.A.), and Information Science (Ph.D.) from the University of Missouri. She has taught at the University of Southern Mississippi and MU.

John T. F. Burgess is an assistant professor and distance education coordinator at the School of Library and Information Studies at the University of Alabama. Burgess holds a Ph.D. in Communication and Information Science and an MLIS from the University of Alabama, an Advanced Masters in Sacred Theology from Boston University, and a

Masters in Theological Studies from Weston Jesuit School of Theology. He provided virtual reference support for Troy University for a decade. Burgess teaches extensively in the LIS core, and offers a course on information ethics for information professionals. He publishes on information ethics in LIS education and practice, particularly on virtue ethics, cognitive justice, and opposing epistemicide. As distance education coordinator he provides technological support and works to foster a hospitable learning community for MLIS students in several online and hybrid cohorts. Burgess is currently the co-convener of the ALISE Information Ethics Special Interest Group.

Nicole A. Cooke is an assistant professor at the Graduate School of Library and Information Science at the University of Illinois at Urbana-Champaign and a faculty affiliate at the school's Center for Digital Inclusion. She holds an M.Ed. in Adult Education from Penn State, and an MLS and a Ph.D. in Communication, Information and Library Studies from Rutgers University, where she was one of the first 12 ALA Spectrum Doctoral Fellows. She was named a "Mover & Shaker" by Library Journal in 2007 and was the 2016 recipient of the ALA's Equality Award. Her research and teaching interests include human information behavior (particularly in the online context), critical cultural information studies, and diversity and social justice in librarianship (with an emphasis on infusing them into LIS education and pedagogy). Her work has appeared in *JASIST, Library Quarterly, InterActions: UCLA Journal of Education and Information, Polymath: An Interdisciplinary Arts and Sciences Journal, Library and Information Science Research, Information Research,* and *New Review of Academic Librarianship.* Cooke is professionally active in ALA, ALISE, and ASIS&T, and she is currently a co-convener of the ALISE Multicultural, Ethnic, and Humanistic Concerns special interest group.

Sarah Park Dahlen is an assistant professor of Library and Information Science at St. Catherine University in St. Paul, Minnesota. She earned her Ph.D. and M.S. in Library and Information Science from the University of Illinois Graduate School of Library and Information

Science (GSLIS), where she was an IMLS Athena Fellow. She also has an M.A. in Asian American Studies and a B.A in History and Asian American Studies from UCLA. She teaches courses on youth materials and library services, storytelling, and library science. Her research addresses transracially adopted Koreans in children's literature, the information behaviors of adopted Koreans, and diversity in children's literature and library education. Sarah serves on the University of Minnesota Kerlan Friends Board (Children's Literature Research Collection) and the ALSC Children and Libraries advisory committee. In 2015, together with Lee & Low Books, she administered the Diversity Baseline Survey, which surveyed thirty-four publishers and eight review journals regarding diversity within the publishing industry. She co-edited *Diversity in Youth Literature: Opening Doors Through Reading* with Jamie Campbell Naidoo and the Special Issue on Orphanhood and Adoption in Children's Literature of *Children's Literature Association Quarterly* with Lies Wesseling. sarahpark.com @readingspark

Sandra Hughes-Hassell is a professor and coordinator of the School Library Media Program in the School of Information and Library Science at the University of North Carolina at Chapel Hill. In her current research, she focuses on social justice issues in youth library services, diverse youth literature, and the role of school library media specialists in education reform. She has written and presented extensively on culturally relevant pedagogy, critical race theory, and the role of libraries in serving diverse youth. She is co-editor of a forthcoming book from Libraries Unlimited entitled *Libraries, Literacy, and African American Youth: Research & Practice*. She is currently president-elect of the Young Adult Library Services Association, a division of ALA.

Kafi D. Kumasi is an associate professor of library and information science (LIS) at Wayne State University, Detroit, MI, where she teaches in the areas of school library media, urban librarianship, multicultural services and resources and research methods. A Laura Bush 21st century scholar, she holds a Ph.D. from Indiana University, Bloomington and a master's degree in LIS from Wayne State. Her research interests revolve around issues of literacy, equity and diversity, particularly in urban educational environments spanning K12 and graduate school contexts. She has received numerous awards including University of Michigan's National Center for Institutional Diversity (NCID) Exemplary Diversity Scholar Citation and the Association for Library and Information Science's (ALISE) Best Conference Paper Award. Her work has been published in numerous journals including, *Library and Information Science Research, Journal of Education for Library and Information Science, Journal of Research on Libraries and Young Adults, School Libraries Worldwide, School Library Media Research,* and *Urban Library Journal.* Her service commitments are vast, ranging from serving as an editorial board member of *Library Quarterly* and as a mentor for Project Lilead, an IMLS grant-funded project aimed at studying, supporting, and building community among school library supervisors.

Robin F. Kurz is an assistant professor in the School of Library and Information Management (SLIM) at Emporia State University in Emporia, Kansas, having earned her Ph.D. in Library and Information Science in 2012 from the University of South Carolina's School of Library and Information Science (SLIS), where she was a Laura Bush 21st Century Librarian Teaching and Research Fellow. Prior to her doctoral studies, Kurz taught in secondary schools and worked in public and academic libraries. Her research and teaching interests include diversity and inclusion in library collections and services, collections and services for traditionally marginalized youth and communities, critical theory in LIS education, and best practices for public library collection development and management. She teaches with a social justice focus and maintains the blog, *Transforming American Libraries*, writing about "the ways in which library staff, scholars, educators, and students can interrogate current practices to transform American libraries into equitable spaces." She also earned a Master of Library and Information Science (MLIS) from SLIS at the University of South Carolina.

Bharat Mehra is an associate professor in the School of Information Sciences at the University of Tennessee. His research examines diversity and intercultural communication, social justice in library and information science (LIS), critical and cross-cultural studies, and community informatics or the use of information and communication technologies to empower minority and underserved populations to make meaningful changes in their everyday lives. Mehra has applied conceptual frameworks in LIS (e.g., human information behavior, information seeking and use, social informatics, etc.) with interdisciplinary approaches from critical theory, feminist and queer studies, postcolonial literature, and race and gender research, amongst others, to expand the profession's traditional definition, scope, extent, representation, and relevance in the 21st century. He has collaborated with various racial/ethnic groups, international communities, sexual minorities, low-income families, rural librarians, small businesses, and others, to represent their experiences and perspectives in shaping the design and development of community-based information systems and services. Mehra primarily teaches courses on public library management, collection development, resources and services for adults, diversity services in libraries, information organization and representation, and grant development for information professionals.

Kevin Rioux is an associate professor of Library and Information Science at St. John's University, New York, where he teaches courses in public and academic librarianship, collection development, and information use and users. He is also attached to St. John's University's Center for Global Development, where he teaches an information literacy and research methods course for students in a Master's program focusing on global development and social justice. In his teaching and research, Rioux uses social justice metatheory, information behavior frameworks, and integrated human development models to explore issues related to information access and information technologies as tools of social and economic development in both local and international contexts. He has written articles and contributed book chapters on social justice stances in the information professions and in LIS education. Rioux completed his graduate work in LIS at the School of Information, University of Texas at Austin.

Vandana Singh is an associate professor in the School of Information Sciences at the University of Tennessee. Her research interest areas are use of information technology for learning in work places as well in distance education, computer supported cooperative work, human computer interaction, and information systems. Dr. Singh has received multiple research grants from federal agencies, including the National Science Foundation (NSF), the Institute of Museum and Library Services (IMLS), and the United States Geological Society (USGS).

Miriam E. Sweeney is an assistant professor at the School of Library and Information Studies at the University of Alabama. She holds a M.A in Library and Information Science from the University of Iowa, and a Ph.D. in Library and Information Science from the University of Illinois, Urbana-Champaign. Sweeney's research investigates how cultural values around gender and race inform the design, use, and meaning of information and communication technologies and associated practices. Particularly, her research uses critical cultural frameworks to explore digital artifacts and practices. Her current research projects examine emojis, anthropomorphic interfaces, and artificial intelligence at sites where ideologies about race and gender are both reproduced and actively contested by both designers and users. Sweeney's research contributes to her teaching so that she can help equip LIS students with the necessary critical skills from which to approach and evaluate information technologies and practices in their career roles as information professionals. Sweeney's research has appeared in *Library Quarterly*, *Journal of Education for Library & Information Science*, *Proceedings of the American Society for Information Science and Technology*, and *Journal of International Social Studies.*

Katy Jean Vance is head of the library at Yokohama International School in Yokohama, Japan. She has worked as a librarian and English teacher in the United States, Brazil, and Angola. She holds an MSLS from the University of North Carolina at Chapel Hill and a B.A. in English from the University of North Carolina at Greensboro.

Julie Ann Winkelstein is currently a postdoctoral researcher on an IMLS grant through the University of Tennessee, Knoxville (UTK). She also teaches undergraduate and graduate students at UTK, where she received a Ph.D. in Communication and Information in 2012. Her dissertation topic, public libraries serving LGBTQ+ youth who are experiencing homelessness, continues to be a strong research interest. Other research and teaching interests include diversity in children's and young adult literature, library services for those who are unstably housed, public libraries and social inequities, accessibility and public libraries, emerging adults and libraries, and public libraries in community partnerships. All of her research and teaching relates to social justice, as she believes it is the backbone of responsive and responsible library services. Before entering the Ph.D. program, she was a public librarian for twenty years, working as a jail and prison librarian as well as in family literacy and children's and young adult services. She has presented widely, both inside and outside the library world, on the topic of LGBTQ+ youth homelessness, homelessness, and public libraries. She has published articles in *Library Journal, Young Adult Library Services, Multicultural Review*, and several San Francisco Bay Area newspapers.

INDEX

A

B

C

D

CPSIA information can be obtained
at www.ICGtesting.com
Printed in the USA
BVHW091912270319
543880BV00012B/283/P